The book of

THE HAND

an illustrated history of palmistry

FRED GETTINGS

HAMLYN

LONDON · NEW YORK · SYDNEY · TORONTO

NOTE FROM THE AUTHOR

I would like to make it clear that prediction of future
events by examination of the hand is quite possible.
It is, however, an extremely difficult business,
demanding a close analysis of the hand as well as
a period of attunement with the subject. The student
of palmistry is therefore warned to be wary of making
such judgments until he has learned at least to
appreciate the dangers of prediction, not to mention
its attendant difficulties. Palmistry of any worth must
spring from an honest attempt to understand the
mystery of the hand; it cannot spring from a wish
to impress, astonish or control another human being.
There are numerous palmists, of varying degrees of
honesty, practising in this country. Part of the
services they offer is to read 'character and fortune'
by post. This may, in very special cases, be possible,
but it must be noted that these 'palmists' usually
demand that a precise date of birth should be
submitted with each palm print, and their readings
are probably based on astrological calculation rather
than solely on palmistic interpretation.
This practice has nothing to do with real palmistry,
and it is precisely this type of 'hand reading' which
has given palmistry such a bad name. I would like to
dissociate myself from such practice. I am not
prepared to do 'readings by post'. I would, however,
by very grateful to receive clear hand impressions to
augment my collection, particularly if the sender is
prepared to answer a short questionnaire. I cannot
undertake to enter into correspondence concerning
such prints other than to acknowledge their receipt,
and most certainly no 'readings' will be sent by me.
Needless to say, any print received by me will be
treated confidentially. My publisher will be pleased
to forward any prints or correspondence to my home
address.

To Graham
and then for Peil
and Tiffany,
all for having put up with me

The Publishers gratefully acknowledge permission to use copyright
material from the following books: *An Encyclopedia of Psychological
Astrology* by Charles Carter, published by W. Foulsham and Co.;
Finger Prints, Palms and Soles by Cummins and Midlo, published by
Dover Publications Inc.; *The Laws of Scientific Hand Reading* by
Benham, published by Putnam and Co.; *La Main de votre Enfant* by
Mangoldt, published by Delachaux and Niestlé; *The Hands of Children*
by Spier, published by Routledge and Kegan Paul; *The Philosophy of
Analogy and Symbolism* by S. T. Cargill, published by Ryder and Co.

Published by THE HAMLYN PUBLISHING GROUP LIMITED
London · New York · Sydney · Toronto
Hamlyn House, Feltham, Middlesex, England

Copyright © 1965 Paul Hamlyn Ltd.

ISBN 0 600 00433 3

First published 1965
Reprinted 1967, 1968, 1970, 1971
Printed in Czechoslovakia by Svoboda, Prague
51629/5

CONTENTS

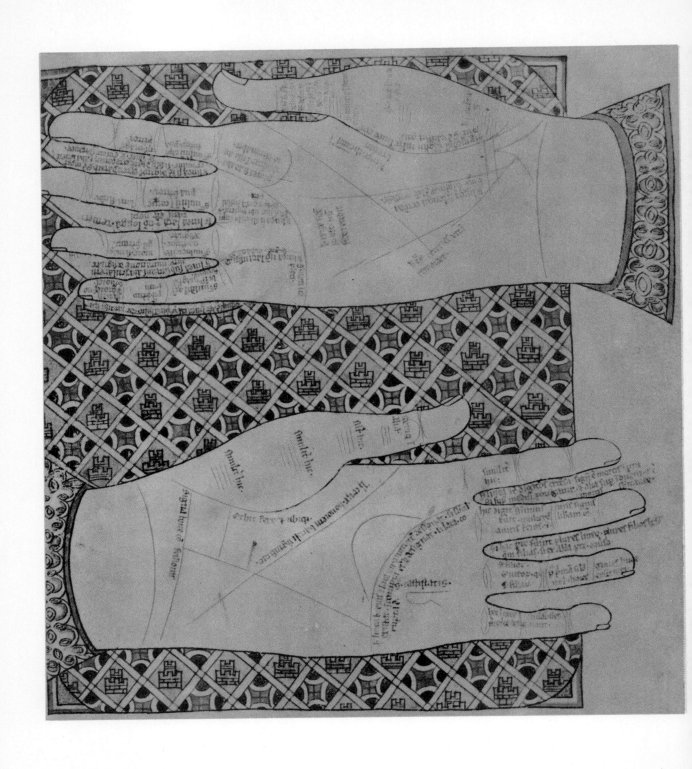

*1   An illuminated page from a 13th century Palmistry in
the Bodleian Library, Oxford*

INTRODUCTION

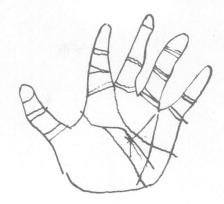

It may be asked how I come to have this knowledge about heavenly things which are far removed beyond human ken. My answer is that the sages have been taught by God that this natural world is only an image and material copy of a heavenly and spiritual pattern; that the very existence of this world is based upon the reality of its heavenly archetype . . . Thus the sage sees heaven reflected in Nature as in a mirror, and he pursues this Art, not for the sake of gold or silver, but for the love of the knowledge which it reveals.

Sendivogius (*1750*)

As Kretschmer says, the Devil must have a pointed nose, whilst the comic must have a fat one. He must not only have a pointed nose, he must have also sharp horns, a tail and cloven hooves, and his face must be distorted with mean eyes, lewd mouth and hollow cheeks, all of which manifest his evil inner being. And, of course, he must be thin: the Devil is too active ever to grow fat.

In such a portrayal of the Devil we have the kernel of truth around which traditional palmistry has been wrapped. In what has been called 'folk psychology' there is no doubt that certain physical characteristics are accompanied by certain temperaments: that, as Blake put it, one may perceive the soul of beauty through the forms of matter.

Palmistry is one of the oldest of the beliefs which sprang from the realisation that the outward body of man is merely 'an image and material copy', a visible sign, of his inner nature. It is also one of the most popular and persistent of such beliefs, and because of this alone, one feels, it must contain within it some element of truth. As Jung wrote of alchemy, an art only half as old as palmistry, 'when an idea is so old and so generally believed, it must be true in some way, by which I mean that it is psychologically true'.

The word palmistry is derived from two Middle English roots, *Paume*, which means 'the palm of the hand', and *estrie*, which is of obscure origin and meaning, but which carries with it the idea of 'study'. The word, in one form or another, was probably used in England before the end of the fourteenth century, but its earliest datable appearance is not until the beginning of the fifteenth century, in John Lydgate's *Assembly of Gods*, of circa 1420. Several documents which use the word *Pawmestry* and its variant spellings have come down to us from the early part of the fifteenth century, and there are certain indications that these documents are in fact copies of older ones, so we must assume the true age of the word to be completely lost.

Palmistry is defined in the Oxford Dictionary as 'divination by inspection of the palm of the hand; the art or practice of telling a person's character and fortune by examination of the lines and configurations of the palm; chiromancy.'

The word chiromancy is older and more cosmopolitan than palmistry. It is used in all early Latin treatises on the art of palmistry and has a slightly different meaning from its English counterpart.

Chiromancy is derived from two Greek roots; χείρ, meaning 'hand', and μαντεία, meaning 'prophecy'. The original connotation of the word has been changed slightly over the centuries, and nowadays it means 'the art of foretelling events by the lines on the hand'. Originally the meaning was less restricted, for it was not confined merely to the lines of the hand, but was related to the hand as a whole. The original Greek meaning corresponds more to our modern word chirosophy, which may be properly defined as 'the art of telling the future, character and psychological disposition of an individual by means of his hand'.

Chirosophy is usually subdivided into chirognomy,

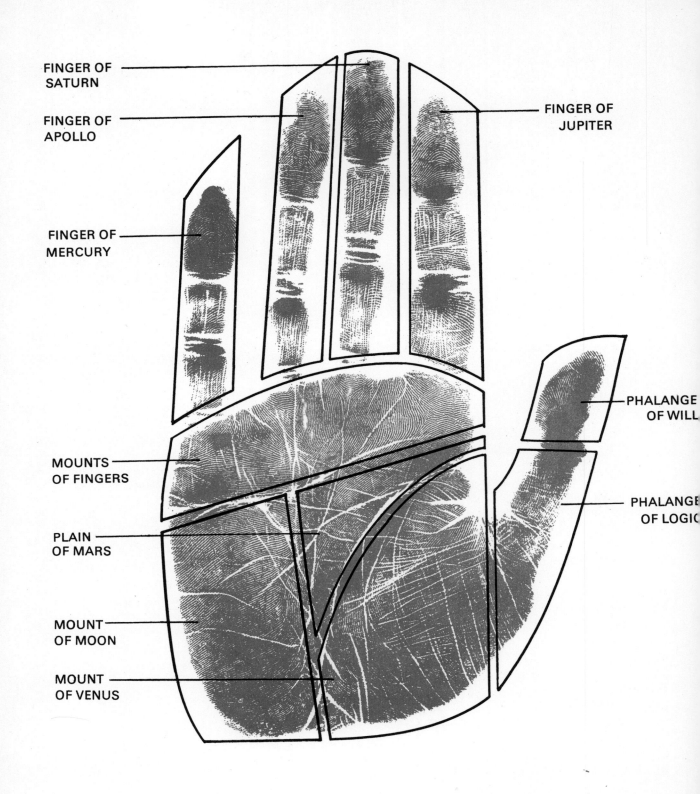

FINGER OF
SATURN

FINGER OF
APOLLO

FINGER OF
MERCURY

FINGER OF
JUPITER

PHALANGE
OF WILL

MOUNTS
OF FINGERS

PHALANGE
OF LOGIC

PLAIN
OF MARS

MOUNT
OF MOON

MOUNT
OF VENUS

2
THE PARTS OF THE HAND

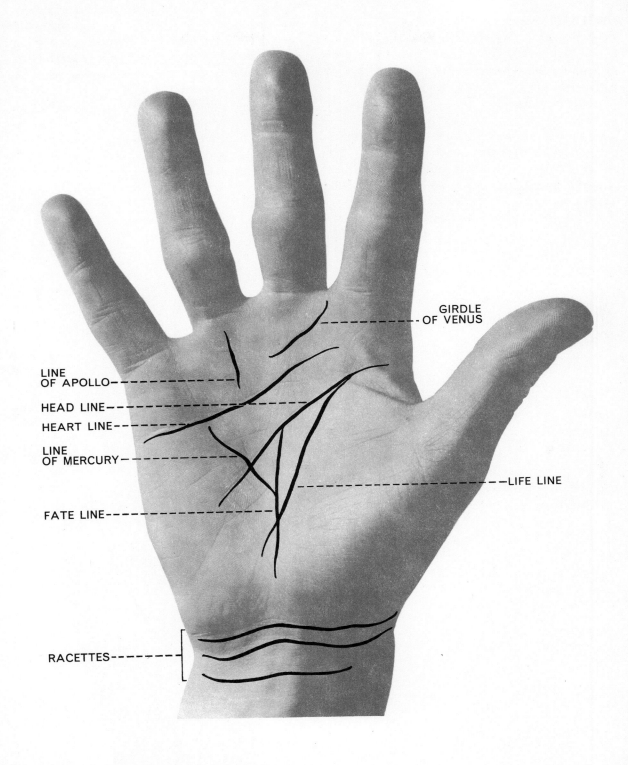

GIRDLE
OF VENUS

LINE
OF APOLLO

HEAD LINE

HEART LINE

LINE
OF MERCURY

LIFE LINE

FATE LINE

RACETTES

3

THE LINES OF THE HAND

a science developed in the last century by the Frenchman D'Arpentigny, and which concerns itself with the study of the general formation of the hand, and chiromancy, which now means the study of the lines of the hand. As the etymology would suggest, chirognomy has tended to be associated with the study of character and psychological dispositions, whilst chiromancy has been associated with the prediction of fortunes, past and future events, and the general course of an individual's life. These associations are unfortunate, for the two are complementary studies, each capable of revealing different aspects of the same truths.

In recent years several palmists have tried to rid the art of its old 'unscientific' connotations, and have invented many new words to take the place of the older ones. They have chosen the word chirology to take the place of the word chirosophy. Unfortunately chirology is older than modern psychology, and was defined in 1644 as 'the art of communicating ideas by signs made with the hands and fingers'.

The traditional nomenclature for the individual parts of the hand, the fingers and the line markings found on the palmar area, has an ancient derivation and was firmly established in the earliest chiromantical writings which have survived from the mediaeval world. Each finger and palmar zone is named after a god of the ancient world in a manner which,

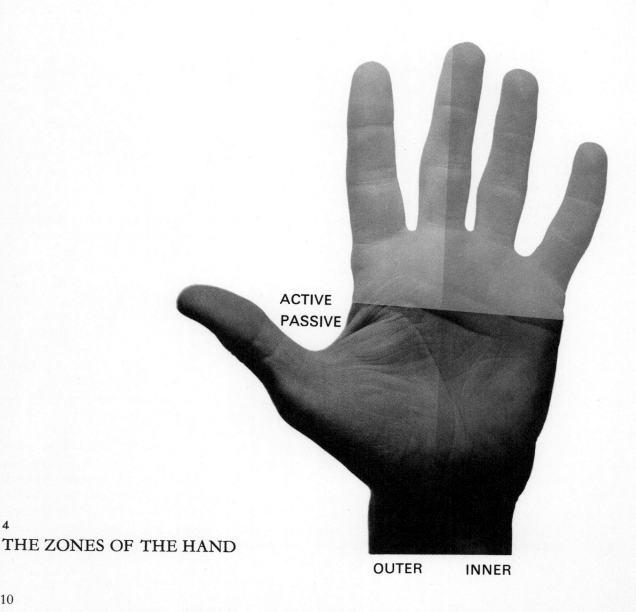

4

THE ZONES OF THE HAND

as the following chapters will reveal, is not entirely haphazard. In fact it has been shown fairly conclusively that the nomenclature was based on astrological theory, and that at one time the hand must have been regarded as a miniature zodiac which exhibited the 'horoscope' of each individual person.

The system of names are tabulated at [2] from a chirognomical point of view, and [3] sets out the system of names from a chiromantic point of view. It is essential that both these name systems be memorised before reading further. The deep significance and possible origin of these names will be dealt with in the individual chapters ascribed to each line or palmar zone. For the moment we shall examine only their general significances.

In its simplest divisions the hand must be regarded as consisting of four areas [4]. Imagine a line dividing the hand down the middle, running through the long middle finger to the exact centre of the base of the palm. With this division one half of the hand will contain the thumb, ball of the thumb, the index finger and the radial half of the middle finger. This half of the hand represents the externalised part of man, that active part of his being which deals with his outward life, his ambitions, strength of will and power of dominance.

The second half of this division includes the little finger, the ring finger, the ulnar half of the middle finger, and the ulnar half of the palm — sometimes called the percussion. This half of the hand represents that part of man which is the opposite of his external life; that is to say, his inner, less active world of emotions and inwardly directed energies.

Another division must be made directly across the hand and just below the 'roots' or 'mounts' of the fingers. With this division one half of the hand includes the fingers and that part of the palm immediately below the fingers. This half of the hand relates to a person's activity and to his specifically human intelligence.

The second and lower half includes the palmar area below the finger roots. This half of the hand relates to the passivity and to those characteristics, such as instinct, which he holds in common with all nonhuman creatures.

When these two chief divisions of the hand, vertically and horizontally, are superimposed, the one on the other, the hand will be found to consist of four main areas. The first quarter which includes the ulnar and uppermost part of the hand contains the little finger, the ring finger and their roots. As the previous analysis would suggest, this part of the hand relates to inwardly directed factors of an active and specifically human nature. In fact the small finger is directly linked with a person's relationships to people who are close to him, parental relationships and sex. The ring finger is directly linked with a person's more distant relationships, with how a person presents himself emotionally. In traditional palmistry the little finger is called Mercury, and the ring finger is called Apollo. Mercury was directly concerned with relationships between Men and Gods. Apollo was the patron of the arts: arts and crafts are the perfect examples of people presenting themselves and their emotions to the world. Both Mercury and Apollo were concerned with communicating: the first dealt with communications of a personal and private nature, the second with communications addressed to the world at large, *via* the media of emotions.

The radial and uppermost quarter of the hand includes the index finger, the top phalange of the thumb, and the radial half of the middle finger. As the previous analysis would suggest, this part of the hand relates to the externally directed factors of an active and specifically human nature. In fact the index finger relates to the manner in which the person presents himself and adapts himself to life; to his ambition and social attitude. The top phalange of the thumb represents a person's strength of will and power of endurance. In traditional palmistry the index finger is called Jupiter, and the thumb is associated both with Venus and with Mars. Jupiter connotes expansiveness, preservation and all those characteristics which might be described as jovial; a happy person, no matter what his situation, may be said to be well adapted to life. The traditional associations of the thumb with Mars and Venus are too complex to be discussed here, but one must bear in mind the aggressiveness of Mars and the solicitude of Venus.

The middle finger, called the finger of Saturn in traditional palmistry, has, so to speak, a foot in both camps. Its radial side is externally directed, representing the half presented openly to the world, whilst the ulnar side is internally directed, representing the half kept more privately. Because Saturn is the meeting ground for two opposing directions it must be regarded as the finger of reconciliation. It is the finger which indicates the degree of balance which the personality has established between the conscious aspect of his life and the subconscious aspects of his life. That the finger was at one time described as the finger of Fate is highly significant, for the passage of man through life might be described as an attempt to reconcile inner demands to outer exigencies. A man's life, his Fate, as one might say, is the sum total of this continuous adaptation between the desire and the possibility. Saturn symbolises this struggle.

The ulnar and lower part of the hand is largely occupied by what is called the hypothenar ridge in medicine, and the mount of Moon or Lunar in palmistry. As the previous analysis would suggest,

5 *A vignette from the title page of Desbarrolles' book on Palmistry*

this part of the hand relates to the internally directed and passive elements in man. In fact the mount of Moon relates to the subconscious of the individual. In traditional palmistry the Moon is the planet of fluctuation, growth, meditation and madness. The word *lunatic* came from the ancient tradition which links a certain type of madness with the lunar cycles.

The radial and lower part of the hand is largely occupied by the root of the thumb, the thenar eminence as it is called in medicine. This part of the hand relates to the internally directed and active elements

in man, to the sensual and creative potentiality, the energy source of the person, so to speak. In traditional palmistry this eminence is called the mount of Venus. Venus was the goddess of beauty and love.

The positions, point of origin, point of insertion, quality and even the presence of the lines of the hand vary a great deal. In the normal hand there are four main lines, and for the moment I shall give the names and general significance of these four only. The others will be dealt with in the section on chiromancy.

The Life line, as it is called in palmistry, encases the mount of Venus, demarcating the ball of the thumb from the rest of the palm. I have never seen a palm without a Life line. The line indicates the quality of energy available to the subject, his energy potential, and in general it records certain types of traumas. The length of the Life line does not, generally speaking, afford any clue as to the length of the person's life.

The Head line of palmistry springs either from or slightly above the origin of the Life line, and usually runs across the palm of the hand to end about half an inch from the Percussion. This line is most variable in its course: it may run in a deep sweep down to the racettes at the base of the hand, or it may run in an upward course towards the finger of Mercury. In general the Head line refers to mental capabilities — it records traumas of the head.

The Heart line of palmistry springs from the ulnar side of the hand and runs in the direction of the root of Jupiter. Its point of origin does not vary very much, but its course, quality and point of insertion vary a great deal. It may sometimes join up with the Head line, or it may run in a wide strong sweep between the fingers of Jupiter and Saturn. In general it relates to the emotional life and intensity of the individual. It affords an indication of the sexual type and records certain emotional experiences.

The line of Saturn, the line of Fate, the line of Destiny, as it is variously called, runs upwards through the centre of the palm towards the roots of Saturn. Its various complexities will be dealt with in due course, but for the moment we must regard it as representing the adaptability of the person. I shall refer to it in future as the line of Saturn.

We have now examined the main areas and lines of the hand briefly, and are in a position to discuss the hand in greater detail.

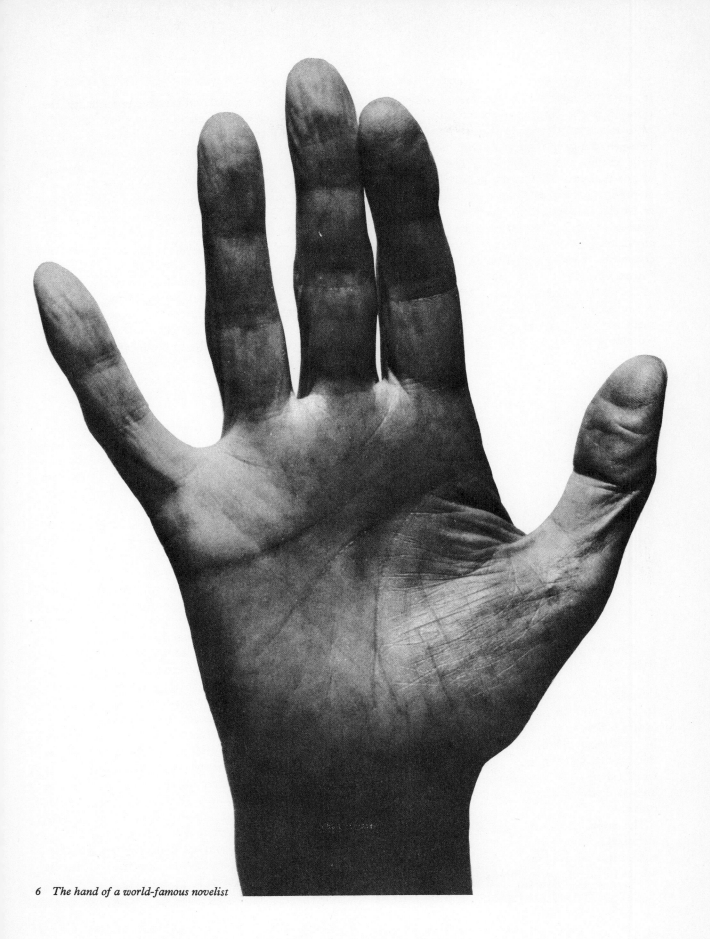

6 *The hand of a world-famous novelist*

7 *A 16th century palmistry consultation. This plate is taken from Cocles' book on chiromancy, and the palmist may well be Cocles himself. It is interesting to speculate on the identity of his client — could it be the ill-fated Bentivoglio?*

METHODS OF STUDY

The historical division of chirosophy into two studies is usually preserved in palmistry books for quite definite practical reasons. Such a division enables a student to assimilate the more easily grasped principles of chirognomy before approaching the more complicated principles of chiromancy. It is, however, as well to remember that the division is not strictly speaking a valid one, for the two studies are so interlinked and interdependent that the art as a whole suffers when they are treated separately. The aim of the student at first should be to examine each available hand from two points of view; that is from the point of view of its general formation, its morphology, and then from the point of linear markings. As his ability to interpret hands improves he will find that the two points of view gradually coalesce and form between them the one integrated study properly called chirosophy.

There is an extensive literature dealing with the purposes served by studying the left and right hands. The traditional viewpoint is to regard the left hand as representing the inherited disposition of the subject, and the right as representing his personal psychological make-up.

Experience has shown me that although there is a great deal of truth in the traditional idea, both hands must be examined in order to draw a clear and satisfactory picture of the subject's life, temperament and propensities. In a right-handed person the left hand may certainly be regarded as relating to the 'inherited background' of the individual, and the right as relating to his own specific individuality. In such a person the left hand [8] is usually more richly marked than the right, and may often contain some atavistic feature which will give a vital clue to an inherited mental or emotional 'problem'. The right hand [9] is usually more 'defined', showing a greater certainty of direction in the employment of life energies. Quite certainly the right hand relates to the energies and propensities which govern his personal life. Both hands must be examined in detail in order to gain the full picture of background, motivation and direction, so essential to palmistic analysis.

The 'central dominance theory' of modern psychology might be said to support the traditional chiromantical viewpoint on the significance of left and right hands. In its simplest form this theory suggests that the dominant half of the brain controls that half of the body, and hence that hand, which is on the opposite side. In other words, if the dominant hemisphere of the cerebrum is on the left, a *naturally* right-handed person will be the result. The theory claims that if this natural control is disturbed in any way, for instance by educating a naturally left-handed child to write with his right hand, then disturbances of various kinds, such as stuttering and difficulties in writing and reading, may result. It would appear, from this theory, that one part of the brain is particularly suited for educational means. Education, taken in its widest sense of meaning, is responsible for the 'personality' of man, for his social mask, his *persona*, as the Greek actors called the face mask which they used to hide their real expressions and their real emotions.

At all events, I have found the practice of taking the *most used* hand in an individual as being the representative of that person's own specific individuality. The other hand I have taken as revealing his inherited tendencies.

In the actual examination of hands it is advisable that some systematic approach be evolved, for this will facilitate both a speedy and accurate 'reading'. Merely to look at a hand with no particular aim in view and with no systematic application of principles is so much waste of time. The best practice is to examine each hand first from a chirognomical point of view, which will lead to a general assessment of the subject's psychological disposition, and then from a chiromantical point of view, which will give a more precise understanding of his individual characteristics, such as his emotional and intellectual calibre and background attitudes. Within these two main practices, the approach of each palmist will differ, but the most practical way to begin to evolve a personal method would be to examine each aspect of the hand in the same order as they are presented in this book. If a systematic approach is adhered to for any length of time it will become a second nature, and one will instinctively assimilate the most essential features of the subject without too close an analysis. What must of necessity begin as an intellectual attempt to grasp the meaning of the hand will eventually turn into an emotional attempt; and in this particular field of study the emotions are infinitely more qualified to make judgments than the comparatively slow and cumbersome mind. The task of the emotions is to make discoveries about the world: the task of the intellect is to co-ordinate these discoveries.

The most difficult part of any preliminary analysis is the mental effort demanded in synthesising all the many facts collated from a hand. It is at this point that the ingenuity and intelligence of the palmist is in most demand, for out of the complexity of data arrived at in the examination of the hand, a picture of the whole of the subject's background and present direction must be constructed piece by piece. Almost any good palmist can arrive at an understanding of the data — there is little difficulty, after practice, in seeing all the complexities of the subject's psychological make-up — but how this is translated and combined depends absolutely on the palmist himself. The hand cannot lie, but the interpretation of its language can lead to lies.

Individual experiment, an open attitude of mind, and a readiness for effort is the only way to good palmistry. It is as well to remember that good palmistry is an art as well as a science, and the emotions can play just as important a role as the intellect. At

intervals throughout a consultation one should try to stop all active thought and analysis, and attempt to 'catch the feeling' of the subject's hand — listen to what the emotions have to say about it. As Georges Muchery, the famous French chiromancer, would have it, 'you must put yourself into the very skin of the individual whom you have just dissected, and in this way make him live again through the presence of your own soul'.

A complete analysis of a hand may take hours, and it is not always possible or even advisable for a subject to spend so much time merely having his hand examined. It is usually more convenient, and certainly more practical, to make some sort of record of the hand to examine at leisure. The common practice is to make a hand print or to take a photograph. Some palmists make plaster casts of hands from wax impressions, and although these are excellent for their purpose, they are both difficult to make and awkward to store.

Print [10] is of the same hand as the photograph at [11]. The striking difference between these two

9 The right hand of the same person; note how the lines are less vacillatory, particularly (in this instance) the lines of Life and Head

8 The left hand of a physicist

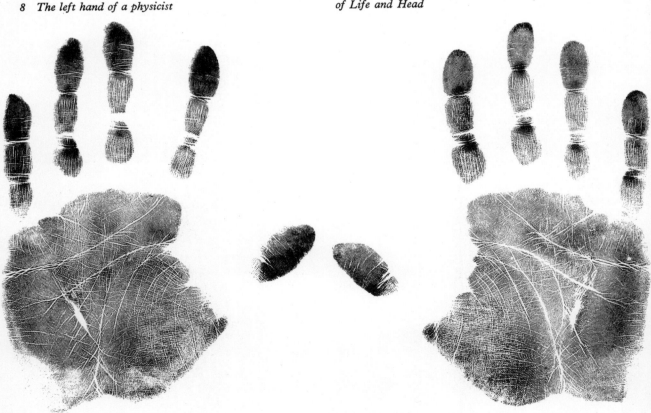

illustrates well the problems involved in making the records so essential to the study of palmistry. Hand prints, even when carefully made, have the disadvantage of revealing little about the shape and formation of the hand as a whole, and are of slight value from a chirognomical standpoint. They do, however, have the distinct advantage of showing clearly all the lines and epidermal ridge formations which cover the surface of the hand, and in this respect they are invaluable from a chiromantical aspect. In practice a series of hand prints will be found more satisfactory than the hand itself, as they show to more advantage several of the minute linear markings which are almost invisible on the naked hand but are invaluable in character reading.

Photographs form an excellent record of the chirognomy of the hand, but they are difficult to take and are usually rather expensive. Even the best of hand photographs does not show the lines to the same advantage as a print. The beginner, unless he happens to be either a photographer or a rich man, is advised to leave photography alone. Professional photography is the only sure way to establish a collection of good hand forms.

From these considerations it will be seen that the best way for a student to begin his collection is from prints, augmented with copious descriptive notes. This is a cheap and practical method, and although it leaves much to be desired, the making of notes helps a great deal to sharpen the observation of hand types. The ideal method of collecting hands, and the one I employ myself, is to combine prints with photography; but such a method is hardly to be expected of a beginner.

One should get into the habit of taking prints of every person one meets socially. There are several ways of making hand prints for record purposes, but the most satisfactory is by means of ink. The materials required are a tube of water-based lino printing ink, a rubber roller about five inches wide, a sheet of glass on which to roll the ink and a rubber pad about a foot square on which the impression can be made. Experience has convinced me of the superiority of lino ink for making prints: it does not dry quickly like ordinary water colour; it is fine enough in quality to catch even the minutiae of the epidermal ridges, and it gives an even impression of even a very greasy hand. The quality of paper used for actually taking the prints should be good.

10 Reproduction of a hand by the print method, which clearly shows lines and ridge formations

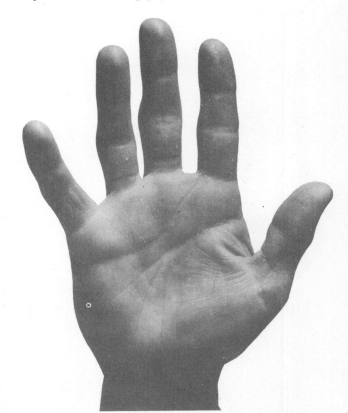

11 A photograph of the same hand clearly showing the chirognomy, but lacking in chiromantical detail

12

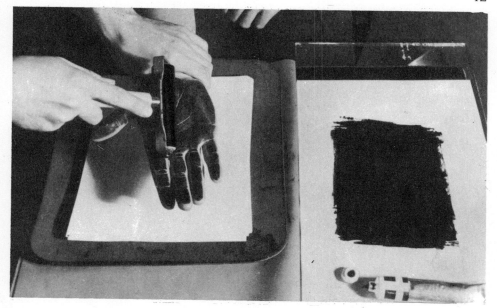

13
14

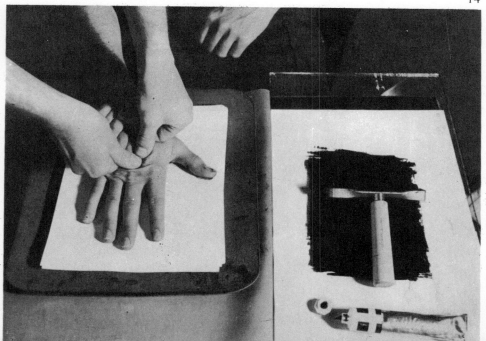

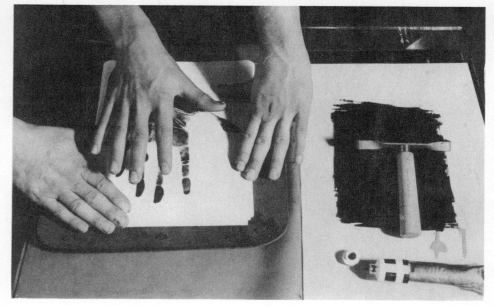

15

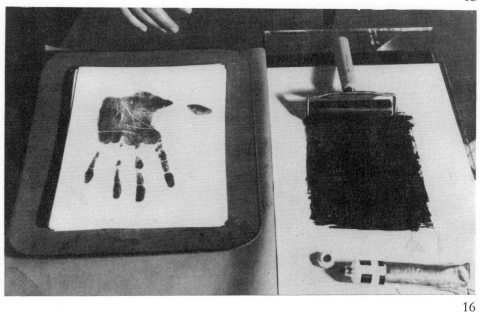

16

HOW TO MAKE A PRINT

*12   The ink is rolled out onto a sheet of glass; note the wad
of paper ready to receive the impression, and the pad of rubber
underneath to help mould the paper to the uneven hard surface*

13   Inking the subject's hand

*14   Making the impression. On a previous attempt, an area
beneath the finger of Saturn had not reproduced, so it is now
being pressed down firmly onto the paper*

*15   To prevent blurring the print as the hand is withdrawn,
the paper should be held down firmly on the mat*

*16   The finished impression is ready for drying; prints are not
always perfect, and in this one a deficient mount of Apollo
has failed to reproduce*

I have found a smooth absorbent paper to be the most practicable, though a high-quality typing paper will suffice. It is advisable to have a selection of papers with different surface textures and coatings, as different hand types require different types of paper for perfection of impression.

When taking prints it is advisable for the subject to be seated, for this reduces flexion of certain muscles which sometimes, especially in a soft hand, mars the impression. The subject's hand should have been washed, and immediately before the impression is made the hand should be rubbed with a dry cloth to remove the grease which is secreted from the tiny glands in the epidermal ridges. The series of photographs [12—16] demonstrate the method I use for taking prints, but each individual must find for himself the method most suited to his own demands.

Immediately after a print has been taken, a note of the subject's name, address, sex, age and life situation should be made, along with a detailed analysis of the chirognomy of the hand, and where necessary with a record of any special physiological and psychological features. Each print must be dried, mounted on a sheet of paper, dated and filed away for future reference.

With a little practice and care, prints of a first-rate quality can be made in this way, and a fine collection of hands will soon be available for reference.

Anyone who takes the trouble to make even a few hundred prints by this method will be bound to observe that different hand types print differently. A very hard hand, for example, is quite difficult to print, particularly if it is also a calloused hand. A medium hand, with an elastic-textured skin, prints beautifully, whereas a soft hand is a very difficult one to record. I have never yet succeeded in printing a perfect impression of a really soft hand.

Often difficulties arise. One has occasionally to take an imprint when no equipment is available, for example. In one instance, I very much wanted a record of a hand whilst travelling in Northumberland, and I was very surprised to find how well a tube of lipstick, smeared on the hand with a piece of newspaper, could print on a fine-ruled exercise book. A recurring difficulty is that encountered in taking imprints of young children, who are usually shy and sometimes frightened. The only hope here is perseverance and downright bribery: I took over twenty prints, each entailing careful washing and re-rolling, before I obtained the very imperfect impression of a year-old baby [17].

Sometimes one meets an interesting person who will not permit one to look at his hand, let alone make a record of it. The reasons are not often divulged, and it is as well not to enquire too deeply. One person of my acquaintance, a brilliant physicist, has steadfastly refused to show his hand for several years. His explanation is that about seven years ago he had his hand read by a remarkable old woman, who told him so much about himself, about his past and future, and all this so accurately, that he has since had no inclination to have his hand examined again. A refusal, however, is usually the exception, and most people are only too happy to lend their hand for observation.

There is probably no one simple reason why any person would want to practise the difficult art of palmistry. Perhaps there is a degree of exhibitionism which is satisfied by being the centre of attraction at a party. Perhaps there is a craving for power and for domination which is satisfied by suggesting, quite wrongly, that there is some strange and inhuman power to palmistry. Perhaps there is a desire to create a sense of mystery — to hide oneself behind a thin and crumbling mask of 'occultism'. Perhaps there is a genuine need to contribute something new

17   The hand of a year-old baby girl

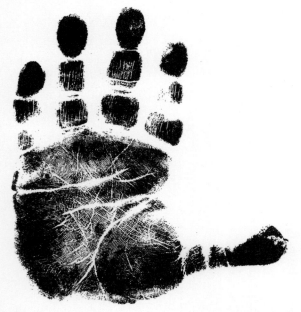

to human learning. The reasons are, inevitably, manifold — and certainly not all of them are sincere or honest. Because of this it is as well to remember that palmistry can be a dangerous thing when used with any purpose not strictly honourable. Only when one has met the psychological state of anxiety which can be created in certain types of people when they have been told by some charlatan or misinformed amateur that they have a break in the Life line which means that they will die at the age of thirty, can one understand the dangerous power and strength behind mere superstition. One must practise palmistry in a state of humility, and always with the basic desire to learn more, rather than merely with the desire to impress. In palmistry, at least, tact, consideration for other people's sense of reality and, in some cases, silence, can be virtues.

The moral side of palmistry apart, there is another consideration which is often overlooked. Palmistry is illegal. Judicial interpretation of the Vagrancy Act of 1824 and the Fraudulent Mediums Act of 1951, has set a precedent which leads to the fact that palmistry, practised for any purpose at all, for money or merely for pleasure, for dishonest motives or for honest motives, is illegal. Any person convicted of practising palmistry (and of course of casting horoscopes) may be sentenced to not more than three months in prison. Apparently, even to advertise oneself as a palmist or astrologer is sufficient proof that one practises, and conviction may follow.

The law is not always acted upon, as is evident from the numerous palmists, astrologers and fortune-tellers who abound in London, not to mention the daily horoscopes which appear in newspapers and journals, which render the proprietors liable to conviction. One cannot help feeling amused at the number of doctors, psychologists and serious statisticians who could be arrested for pursuing their occupations. On the other hand a little serious thought on the dangers behind unskilful and insensitive practice of palmistry will convince one that the law should have power to convict the fraud and charlatan. But reflection leads one to wish for a law to protect the innocent practitioner.

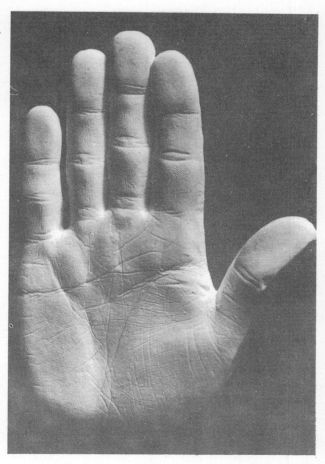

18   A plaster cast. These make very useful records but they are difficult to make and even more difficult to store. The photograph does not do this cast justice, as on the original even the finger patterns are faithfully recorded.

This hand is much more sensitive than would appear, for the pads on the finger-tips have been flattened as they pressed into the warm wax. This is the major disadvantage in making casts, as the flattened areas tend to spread out and give a false idea of their size

19 Right: *Detail from* Portrait of a man in black *by van der Helst (1613—1670) in The National Gallery, London. The proportions of finger to hand, and a distinct lack of vitality in the fingers, indicate a weak 'Fire' form*

Far right: *Detail from* The Brazen Serpent *by 'Studio of Rubens' (Rubens 1577—1640) in The National Gallery, London. The short fingers, and the exaggerated mounts of Venus and Moon, indicate a distinctly lascivious hand form*

Below: *The hands of St. John the Evangelist, from* Virgin and Child with Saints *by Costa (1460—1535) in The National Gallery, London. The extremely long fingers compare interestingly with the short fingers on the Rubens hand. The long spiritual fingers indicate an austere, intellectualised hand*

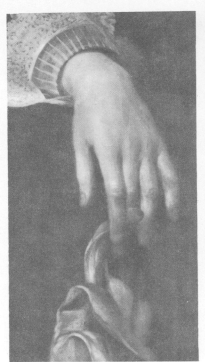

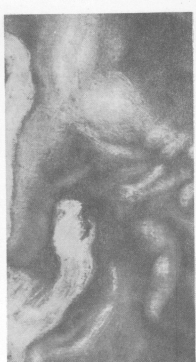

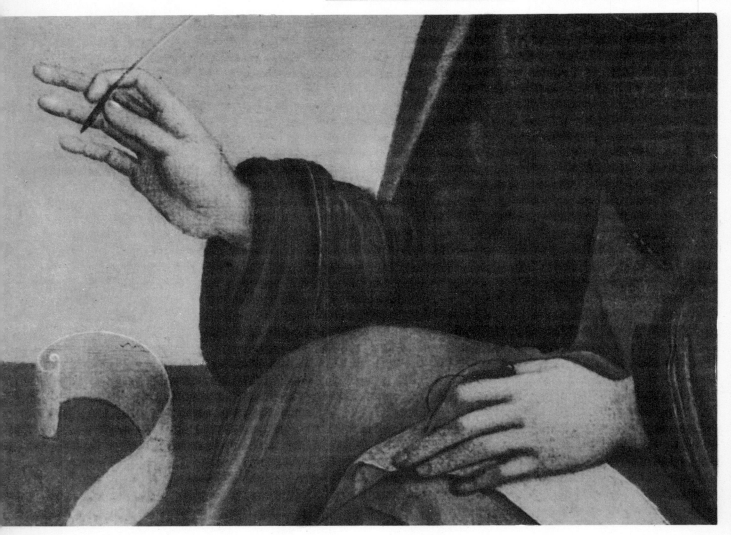

CHIROGNOMY

Anyone who looks for genera and species outside the things of sense is wasting his time.

John of Salisbury (1180)

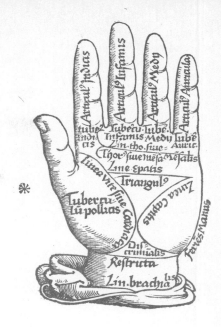

In both medical and palmistic circles it has been recognised for very many years that certain types of hands are invariably accompanied by certain types of mental and emotional disposition. In consequence there have been attempts in both fields of study to classify 'types' of people in terms of their hand characteristics. The system of classification which I use, and which will be presented in these pages, is in its essential form an amalgam of the aspects of all the traditional and modern morphological and chirognomical teachings which my own experience and research has shown to be the most practicable and reliable. It is based in its simplest aspects on an analysis of hand types in terms of the so-called 'Cosmic Theory' which has come down to us from remotest antiquity, and which pervades all the ancient teaching such as alchemy, astrology and early medicine. To this theory I have added a considerable body of teaching derived from modern medical and psychological research.

The resulting theory of hand types is highly complex, and at first difficult to grasp, but it is one which can, and indeed must, be enriched by subsequent research and experience. It is not only highly practicable as an art, which like medicine strives towards being a science: it is also satisfying and stimulating to the mind and emotions, for it is founded on theories which were established long before the modern belief was current that the nature of the world can best be understood by the mind and intellect alone.

The ancient theories of 'analogy', which attempt to relate not merely the hand to man, and the man to his inner world, but also these things to the earth, solar system and cosmos, are not entirely foreign to our understanding, but there has been a tendency either to misunderstand their function or to reject them completely. In fact the integrated theories of *microcosm* and *macrocosm*, which have persisted in one form or another for over two and a half thousand years, constitute a sweeping hypothesis of the inter-relation of things which is based on a sound understanding of the inner and outer natures of the universe and its constituent elements, and which finds no satisfying equivalent in modern science.

Without going into a detailed analysis of these ancient cosmic ideas, it would be as well to describe simply something of the theory behind them, a theory directed towards both our intellectual and our emotional understanding. The theory which encompasses the whole applies equally to each aspect of the teaching.

The theory behind Cosmic Relationships, and thus behind palmistry, is rooted in an instinctive platonism centuries older than Plato. Its mainspring belief is that the material world is merely 'the outward image and copy of a heavenly and spiritual pattern'. The pattern of the whole is reflected lawfully in the pattern of each of its parts: the same laws which act in the universe, act in Man, and again, on a different scale of being, in the world of the atom. No one thing can be meaningful except in relation to its higher and lower functions, and because each is part of the whole, nothing can be without meaning.

Palmistry is one of the arts or sciences which has

& inftabiles.Prȩterea & illud traditū ab Alexādro
Aphrodifȩo , quòd humor ille qui mafculis in co-
mam refoluitur , mulieribus conuertitur in men-
ftruum,vel in lac,fi conceperint.Et quibus barbi-
tium fuccrefcit , has quoque viragines dicimus,
certi quòd coïtus funt appetentiffimi.

De phyfionomia faciei.   CAP.   IX.

20   *An example of the early form of physiognomy, which
was so bound up with early palmistry, and which eventually led to the theory of planetary types (From Indagine's*
Introductiones, *British Museum)*

*Is it not to be thought a great marvel that among so many
men's faces you shall scarcely find two which do not agree
the like? Wherefore no man can give certain conjecture
or judgment of a state of mind. For how is it possible to
examine the spirits of all men? However, if any man be so
curious, he may colour the proportions by which to judge,
for as the uttermost colour in a picture does show the temperament thereof, even so in the face it does argue good or
evil. A hot complexion and swarthy and leaden colour is
never condemnable, for besides a Saturnine disposition
and black choler doth also shew the evil affections of the
mind, as envy, anger, rancour, machinations and infideli-
ties. A white feminine colour, soft and cold, declareth a
cold, soft and tender person.*

X tot hominū faciebus an non mirū vide-
tur tibi,quòd vix duo fibi cōueniūt ? Quo
fit etiā,vt ne hîc tradi certa cōiectura pof-
fit.Quis enim poterit.omniū animos fcrutári ? Si-
quis tamē curiofior fuerit,habeat id colorē & pro-
portionē. Colorē extrema vel temperaméta,vt in
picturis prȩftāt,ita in faciebus vel bonitatē arguūt
vel malitiā. Rubeus nullibi nō fufpectus eft,etiam
ex prouerbio,cōplexionem indicās calidam.Illau-
datus & liuidus , vel plūbeus prȩter Saturnicā in-
clinationē & atrā bilem , etiā peffimas animi affe-
ctiones fignificās:vtputa inuidiā,irā,rancorē, ma-
chinationes,infidias. Albus fœmineus,mollis,fri-
gidus, frigidū quoq; & mollē efficit. Prȩterquam
                                              f 5   vbi

for many centuries been directed at grasping the
significance of the whole by means of its parts.
It argues that if the outward forms of life are merely
copies or reflections of a hidden pattern, then this
pattern may be understood and comprehended by
examination of the outward form.

The outward form of man is his body, his physiognomy, whilst his spiritual pattern is manifest in his
particular physiological tendencies, his disposition,
motivations and complex of attitudes. Each person
has an individual outward form, 'for God has carefully differentiated all his creation from the beginning, and has never given to different things the
same shape and form'. And certainly each person is
an individual inwardly, so far as his own psychology

is concerned. From the very earliest times an equa-
tion has been drawn between these two individuali-
ties, between the outer and the inner. The assumption is that there exists some close relationship
between what a person is internally and how he
appears and manifests himself; an assumption based
on the argument that the outer is merely a reflection
of the inner. The outer reveals the inner, for according to the oldest teaching the very existence of
this outer world is based upon the reality of its
heavenly archetype.

The 'instinctive platonism' relates to everything,
not merely to the hand, for as Paracelsus said, over
four hundred years ago:

There are many kinds of chiromancy, not only the

chiromancy of man's hands, from which it is possible to infer and discover his inclinations and his fate, to ascertain what good or evil will befall him: there are yet other kinds of chiromancy, for example, that of herbs, of tree leaves, of wood, of rocks, of minds, or the chiromancy of landscapes, of their roads and rivers and so on.

But another aspect of the ancient teaching is that Man is a perfect microcosm *in himself*; he is a self-contained entity reflecting in small the workings and laws of the macrocosm, he is made in the image of God. Thus, the argument continues, any attempt to know the meaning of the universe, to grasp the pattern of the heavenly and spiritual worlds, can best be done through an analysis of man, which is a perfect reflection of this pattern. In knowing man, one would know the universe of the stars and the universe of the atoms. The ancient Delphic inscription 'Know thyself' was in fact an injunction to know everything.

Palmistry developed as a subsidiary science in this quest for knowledge of the whole. Even its nomenclature testifies to its common parentage with astrology: and whilst astrology aimed at the individual by means of the whole, palmistry aimed at the whole by means of the individual. Naturally, in the beginning, at that tremulous point in history when man set out to attain cosmic knowledge, palmistry can only have been one of many 'chiromancies'. If every aspect of nature has meaning, in theory it would matter little which aspect was investigated in the attempt to reach into the secrets of the microcosm and macrocosm. However, since man was the perfect miniature of the universe it was only reasonable to seek in him the meaning of the cosmos. Thomas Hyll, one of the earliest English writers on palmistry, put the argument clearly, if quaintly:

Although it be of al creatures, both stones, plantes, herbes, fish, foule, beastes, and Men, whose inward propertyes and difference are knownen by the outward shapes, yet because that of all the rest man is most excellente, therefore it specially belongeth to hym. All these poynts are marked by nature . . . and specially in the face and hands whyche as it should seme, god hath made open and uncoverable because all men myghte at all tymes see and perceyve them. And so that no man should thynke thys incredible (as the grosse heades doe of all thynges whych they cannoth comprehende) I will council them by thynges moe evident, to credit such as be

obscure, yet not obscure of themselves, but hidden from us for lacke of searche.

Of course, the true search of palmistry is now completely lost: it has degenerated into mere fortune-telling and unthinking superstition, but something of its grandeur, something of its real significance is still preserved in its terminology which pictures the hand as the microcosm of man, and man as the microcosm of the Solar system. We can no more go back to the intensity of its true meaning than we, so far removed from Ancient Greece, can understand the *Timaeus*. We have, through our present method of splitting up nature to investigate it, almost forgotten that a whole exists. We have lost sight of the wheeling cosmic system in our minute and specialist investigation of its fragments. In trying so disparately to understand with our intellect, we have lost the sense of wonder which went with ancient knowledge.

But for all our specialisation and for all our lack of wonder, the 'instinctive platonism' which is so deeply rooted in our way of thinking cannot help showing through in our thought. Dimly we are aware that there are certain types of people, and that these types, whom we perceive in the first instance as 'physical' types, with distinctive bodily characteristics, have, besides a physiological resemblance, some sort of psychological resemblance. Rightly or wrongly we believe that certain facial expressions are accompanied by certain psychological moods: our whole basis of relationships with other people, conscious or unconscious, is based on this assumption. All this is the manifestation of our 'instinctive platonism'. However, the variety of types we see around us is so great that we are tempted to explain away resemblances between people in terms of 'pure chance' of heredity. Neither of these two 'explanations' is sufficient.

In the past hundred years certain individuals, sometimes men of science, having perceived that there is a hierarchy of types, have attempted to establish some classification in terms of their physical and psychological resemblances. Lavatar, Gall, Carus, D'Arpentigny, Kretschmer, Sheldon and Jung have all approached the subject in a fresh, exciting and sometimes productive way. Unfortunately none of their findings can be in any way described as superior to the ancient classification of humanity into the seven basic types, each with some admixture of the others. In fact, the indications are, particularly in medical research, that the ancient theory of types was founded on a deep understanding of man's nature. Several attempts have been made to show the relationship between the types suggested by endocrinological theory and the seven types of man which were preserved for us by the Greeks. 'You can find all the new ideas in the old books,' Chesterton said, 'only there you will find them balanced, kept in their place, and sometimes contradicted and overcome by other and better ideas.'

The point to be made is not that the modern classifications are valueless — they are in fact of extreme importance — but that mankind is once more returning to a state of mind in which he can quite openly relate psychological and physiological characteristics. He is tentatively feeling his way towards an understanding of types which was, it appears, second nature to the Ancients.

So far the main difficulty in these attempts to establish a classification of types has revolved around our own ignorance of what the actual psychology of man is. Psychology is the youngest, and the least informed, of all the sciences: in fact it cannot properly be described as a science at all. Only on the most tenuous ground can we try to establish some sort of rule concerning the interdependency which exists between body and soul, when nothing or almost nothing is known of the soul.

Of late years there has been considerable research in relation to hands as a possible means of establishing a classification of physiological and psychological types, but the findings, particularly in the field of medicine, are not very exciting:

The totality-concept of modern biology (writes Jung) *which is based on the evidence of a host of observations and research does not exclude the possibility that hands, whose shape and function are so intimately connected with the psyche, might provide revealing, and therefore interpretable, expression of psychical peculiarity, that is, of the human character.*

Jung's argument is merely a round-about way of admitting that a very ancient art, which was in some respects employed by the father of medicine, might well be based on truth. Nothing is said which is new, and anything in these modern teachings which appears to be new is in fact the old presented in a more palatable form to our twentieth century taste.

Because modern psychology is largely based on so little certain knowledge, and because the ancient teachings appear to be more comprehensive in theory and more efficient in practice, I have found it necessary to return to the older teachings in order to establish a working hypothesis of types. Naturally, I have not hesitated to employ such psychological concepts as appear in my own experience to be based on accurate observation, but on the whole I have preserved the rich and ancient connotation of 'types', which results with certain modifications in an eight-fold classification. It cannot be overstressed that 'types' are merely abstractions in our mind which must be used to give guidance in the attempt to determine a life pattern of what is ultimately an individual person. 'Types' as such do exist. As Collin observes in relation to the classification of types in terms of glandular secretion:

If we study the so-called 'types' it thus only means that we try to find extreme or even pathological cases of the dominance of one or another gland, in order to determine its special nature. Even so, there is something distasteful and unreal about such descriptions, as there is about the 'average man' of statistical investigation. They both remind us of those we know, and at the same time omit all that is alive and interesting about them.

Before proceeding to examine the complex, though highly practical, system which I have evolved, we shall examine one or two of the most useful teachings which relate to chirognomy and which experience has shown me to be accurately based, for these will help towards a general understanding of the basic principle behind chirognomy. Each of the following 'teachings' will, in one way or another, enrich and deepen our understanding of the hand types we shall examine.

At this stage I feel that I should point out that whatever method of classification is employed in an attempt to gain a general impression of the subject's temperament, there are certain general characteristics of the hand, independent of variations of form and shape, which can modify in one way or another the interpretation due to a hand type. Skin texture, for instance, forms an excellent guide to the degree of sensitivity possessed by a subject. A fine, soft texture, only slightly more rough than that found in a baby's hand, is always indicative of a refined emotional sensitivity. Such a skin indicates a person who is opposed by nature to physical exertion. On the other hand, a skin which is rough, coarse and leather-like always indicates the presence of the opposite qualities: a coarse and unsympathetic sensitivity and a love for manual labour. Benham's maxim 'Refined texture softens everything: coarse texture animalises it' is worth remembering. A skin texture between these two extremes is sometimes called the 'elastic' skin. It is neither fine nor coarse, but elastic in texture, and characteristic of the hands of active people such as doctors, lawyers and the more refined kind of businessmen. Thinkers who have the ability to translate their ideas into terms of action have this kind of skin texture.

Properly speaking, the papillary ridges fall within the category of skin texture, but because these ridges have been shown to be so important in the assessment of an individual's character, they have been accorded a special chapter of their own. It is sufficient at this stage to mention the 'sensitive pads' which are sometimes found on the finger tips. When present, these pads always show a great sensitivity on the part of the subject, and are very often found in the hands of musicians, poets and creative artists.

The consistency of a hand, which is marked by its resistance to pressure, is a sure indication of the quantity of energy possessed by the subject. A hand which offers little or no resistance is of the 'flabby' type: the hand of a dreamer with insufficient energy to put his dreams into action. Such a person desires a life of mental and physical ease, and his main aim in life is comfort. A hand which offers some resistance, but is still soft and boneless, is found on a person still deficient in energy, but not to the full extent as with the flabby-handed types. This type of hand usually suffers more from a lack of desire to act, rather than from a definite inability. The elastic hand — one which resists pressure in a lively way, rather like hard, springy rubber — is found in active people whose energy is abundant and flows naturally in mental and physical work. 'The elastic hand,' says Benham, 'puts vitality into all human qualities.' The truly hard hand is comparatively rare. It is a hand which will not give to any extent under pressure: an obstinate, unreceptive hand, indicative of a person filled with a physical energy which must be expended in physical labour. There is an immense store of energy at the disposal of such hands, but it is always of a very coarse nature, most suitable for manual labour.

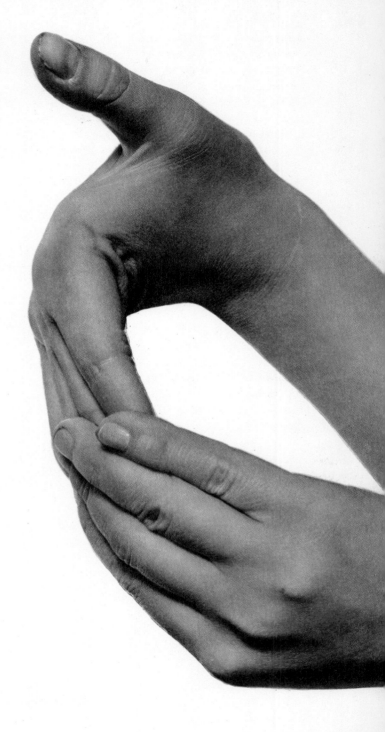

21 A very flexible hand

On the whole, people with hard hands tend to project their imaginations outward — that is to say that they may exaggerate easily, and often have a facile tongue. A hard hand should always be examined in order to determine the degree to which lying plays a part in its owner's life. Spier observes that hard-handed people have a tendency to acquire complexes through shutting themselves off, through hardening themselves to the outside world. Soft-handed people are generally speaking more receptive to the outside world, and fit more easily within their environment. They have a tendency to project their imagination inwards in the form of daydreams: they tend to lie to themselves, and to have a more egocentric concept of their own lives and abilities than the harder type. It is almost as if the hard hand tends to lie outwardly, to other people, as a result of the pressures caused by the immense energies at their disposal by passing their energies inwardly.

22 *The hand of a 16-year-old schoolgirl, with sensitive pads particularly noticeable on the fingers of Mercury and Apollo*

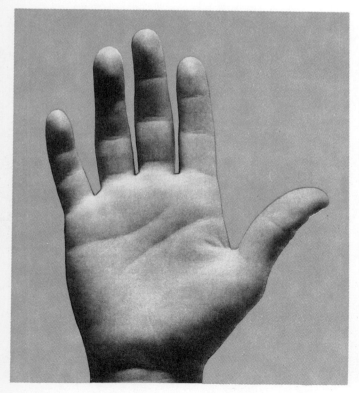

The flexibility of the hand denotes the flexibility of the mind and emotions. A highly flexible hand is always a sign of an interesting personality: it is the hand of a person agile in thought, and often gifted with a high intuitive grasp. The hand at [21] illustrates extreme flexibility. It is the hand of a French student of psychology, whose mental and emotional agility is remarkable. She is particularly distinguished by an ability to sum people up even after a short acquaintance, and by an uncanny ability to go straight to the truth of a matter, even when the truth is being intentionally obscured. In other words, it is quite impossible to pull the wool over her eyes — she misses very little, not because of any particular brilliance of intellect but because of her intuitive perspicacity. A very stiff hand is most usually found amongst elementary types, and can always be taken as intensifying elementary characteristics. The stiffest hand I have ever encountered was that of a Northern mill worker, whose hand would bend backwards little more than half an inch.

Most books on palmistry insist that the colour of the hand is a guide to certain aspects of temperament. However, no hand retains one colour for very long: the action of the heart, which is mainly responsible for hand colour, varies as a result of the demands made on it. A distinctly white hand, or one tinged with blue, is a fairly certain sign of weak heart action, and this will naturally reflect itself in the life of the individual in many ways. I have observed a normally quite pale hand turn bright blue in the space of two hours during an acute attack of bronchitis. One has only to bear in mind the 'accidental' factors which contribute to hand colour, such as light, room temperature, and tan, to realize the foolishness of drawing any definite conclusion from colouring. It is more advisable to draw one's conclusions from the more stable hand features rather than from such variables as colour. In practice it will be found that the colour of the nails records the fluctuation of heart action with much more reliability than that of the hand.

There is a very old palmistic tradition which presents a most interesting 'rule of thumb' for rapid and simple assessment of type. It is sometimes called 'The Three Worlds of Palmistry', for it divides each hand into three parts, traditionally called 'worlds' [23]. The sizes and qualities of these three worlds are indicative of the basic disposition of the subject, and the classification is founded on the assumption that a person is chiefly occupied either by the mind, or by the affairs of every day, or by the baser animal qualities. This trinity was supposed by some to relate to the trinity within man, Spirit, Soul and Body, or Mind, Emotions and Instincts. The teaching has its origin in the Aristotelian trinity of soul:

> *In diverse bodyes the soule is sayde to be three fold, that is to saye,* Vegetabilis, *that giveth lyfe and no feeling, and that is in plants and rootes,* Sensibilis, *that giveth life and feeling, and not reason, that is in unskilful beastes,* Racionabilis *that giveth lyfe, feeling and reason, and this is in men.*

The first world (*Racionabilis*) is represented by the fingers, and is sometimes called the mental or ideal world, and is supposed to relate to the spiritual nature of the individual. Hence, if the fingers are long, the subject may be said to live in a more spiritual world than if the fingers were short; such a person would be fitted for abstruse mental work, for study of complicated theory, or for a job in which the higher sensibilities of good taste and refinement come into play. The hands of lower anthropoids have very short fingers, and we can, by analogy, expect short fingers in man to be an indication of a less refined nature. Very short fingers must be regarded as being to some degree regressive.

The second world (*Sensibilis*) is marked off at the top half of the palm by an imaginary line running across the hand from the top of the mount of Moon to the top of the mount of Venus. It is called the Material world, and is supposed to relate to the business capability of the individual — to his position in life, and his relationship to practical affairs — but it is in fact more directly related to his emotional background. Thus, if the area is particularly large, the individual's inner life may be regarded as being largely identified within the emotional plane, allowing little to escape from the practical considerations of finance, ambition and other everyday emotions.

The third world (*Vegetabilis*) is contained in the lower half of the palm, below the imaginary line described. This is usually called the Baser world, and is supposed to denote the qualities and characteristics of the basic instincts of the individual. Within its area is contained the mount of the Moon, the seat of the imagination in all its forms,

and the mount of Venus, which Spier suggests is related to the Id — the 'structural unconscious' which determines our life's course.

I have observed that a high percentage of neurotics have very long palms — long and narrow rather than long and heavy. Such a palm shape is usually accompanied by an elongated mount of Moon which protrudes well below the mount of Venus. It is significant to observe that the hands of many criminals — particularly those of sadists — have hand formations with the lower worlds markedly prominent. Carus observed that the skeleton of the palm forms almost all of the hand in a brute animal. One can be sure that a person with such a developed lower world is bound up with base desires. A description of this type is very accurately drawn by Benham:

> *He can appreciate nothing high or elevating. If he acquires money he does not know how to make a refined use of it. He loves beauty, but it is vulgar, showy kinds that attract him: he is fond of eating, but with the gluttony of the gourmand, not the delight of an epicure. He has no mental recreations; mind is not a guiding*

23 The three worlds of palmistry

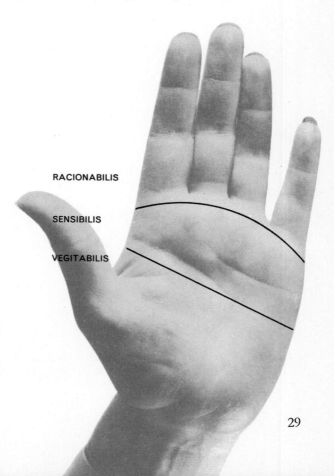

RACIONABILIS

SENSIBILIS

VEGITABILIS

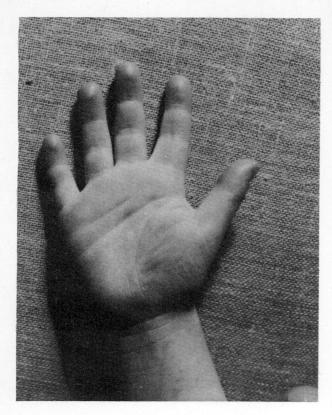

24 Short fingers; the hand of a six-year-old boy

25 Long fingers; the hand of a 17-year-old girl

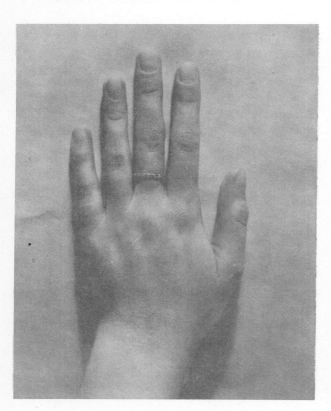

force with him. He is sometimes shrewd, but with the instinctive cunning of the fox, not the talent of a high and lofty mind. He loves display, and in his home will have profusion, not taste; glaring colours, not harmony.

It is not surprising that this ancient three-fold division, which is remarkably accurate as a general theory of types, has been preserved to some degree by a modern school of psychological palmistry:

It is essential to observe the relative size of the back of the hand and of the fingers. If they are of relatively equal size a certain harmony and balance is indicated, but should the back of the hand be much larger and wider than the fingers we can infer that the practical, the material, the realities of life preponderate at the cost of the intellectual, the spiritual, the capacity for development and emotional sensitivity. On the other hand, if the fingers are longer than the back of the hand, the sense of reality is curtailed and the practical abilities are neglected to the advantage of feeling, imagination, intellect and spirituality, which leads to conflicts with the world of realities and generates a tendency to live in a world of emotional phantasy and imagination. (Spier)

This teaching of 'the three worlds' has been included here because it throws much light on the four types we are about to describe. There are, in addition, one or two other old teachings which augment to a degree the types we shall analyse, and which are I feel worth mentioning here.

According to Desbarrolles, the nineteenth-century French chiromancer, short fingers [24], particularly when smooth, are apt to form hasty judgments with little regard to detail. 'In the business of life, in the excitement of speculation, they seize the whole question at a glance — sometimes correctly, for they judge by a sort of inspiration . . . Should the fingers be pointed, although they may indicate a tendency to indulge in metaphors and images, the *ensemble* is never lost sight of; for that, with them, is the great object to be secured.' Long fingers [25] are, on the same authority, irresistibly attracted towards detail. They prefer the details of a plan to a broad and sweeping statement of its intentions. 'Should you ever seek the patronage of a man endowed with long fingers, take care that you betray no neglect in dress . . . Such a one, if he be an orator or a writer, is apt to indulge in ornaments, and minutiae, to the injury of argument; and which, by exalting the value of certain parts, lead to a neglect, even to a forgetfulness, of the point of departure and of the end to be attained.' Desbarrolles' observations to some extent complement the theory of the three worlds, if we can imagine the emotional world, which is the source of intuition, as being highly developed in the lower anthropoids.

The manner in which the fingers end is also accorded some importance by the Frenchman. Pointed fingers [26] strengthen the imagination, squared fingers [27] the reasoning faculties, whilst the spatulated fingertip is supposed to indicate activity. None of these characteristics must be isolated from the more general understanding of the hand. It would be ludicrous to say that a hand giving every indication of the subject living purely in imagination is in any large way affected by one or two square endings. It is essential that the student learn by experience the distinctive 'shape' of the finger endings before pronouncing on the character they are supposed to represent. Jupiter is usually slightly pointed, Saturn slightly squared, Apollo slightly spatulated, and Mercury pointed.

Knotty hands, that is hands with the finger joints noticeably developed [28], are according to the old traditions supposed to confer a degree of 'reason' to the hand. I have not found this tradition to be based on accurate observation. Spier's suggestion that knots indicate great staying power is more acceptable — they grip fast to objects, and show a quality of tenacity. My own observations show that knots are often a sign of exactness of method in every undertaking. The hands of almost all scientists have a 'knotty' character, and this is probably the basis for the old contention that 'knots lend reason'. We can see, however, that method is the basic demand of science: an artist may be just as rational as a scientist, but is rarely as methodical, and rarely needs to be so. Knots on fingers tend to mitigate the swift intuition natural to smooth fingers, and they add an element of 'deliberation' to the subject's actions. Long fingers of the knotty kind naturally attracted to detail by their length, become almost too preoccupied with methodicity in the details and minutiae which take their interest.

Amongst the most interesting attempts to correlate hand types with temperament are the ones made by the Frenchman D'Arpentigny in 1843 and by the German morphologist Carl Gustav Carus in 1848.

The classification suggested by Carus is the more

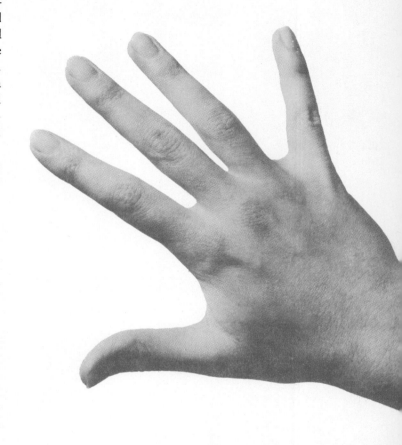

26 *Pointed fingers on the hand of a 22-year-old typist*

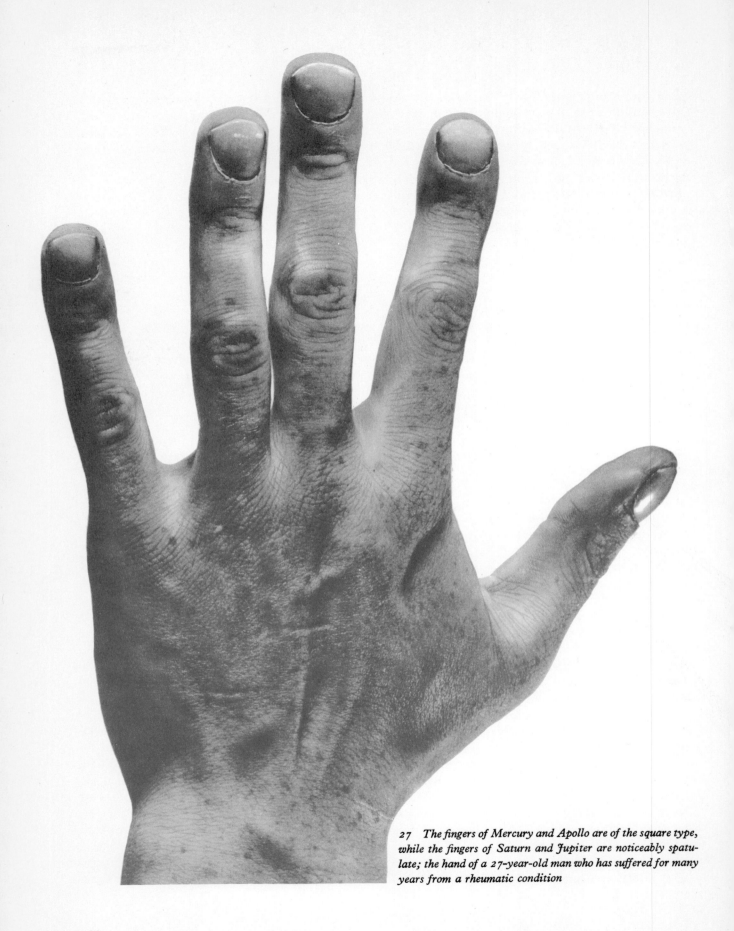

27 The fingers of Mercury and Apollo are of the square type, while the fingers of Saturn and Jupiter are noticeably spatulate; the hand of a 27-year-old man who has suffered for many years from a rheumatic condition

simple, and is more scientifically based than that of D'Arpentigny. It merits our attention here not merely because of its historical importance, but because in itself it forms an excellent general classification which may be used practically in chirological research. In the following analysis of the classification originally proposed by Carus, I have altered and expanded where I have felt necessary. No one can expect that a division of all the bewildering variety of hands into four groups can lead to anything more than a rough and ready assessment of temperament, but there can be no doubt that a general classification can be very useful in rapid assessment of character traits and personality. The main practical thing to remember is that no final conclusion as to temperament must be made from such a general classification without each aspect of the temperament being substantiated by other signs in the hand.

It will be found that this four-fold classification in no way invalidates any of the later systems of hand interpretation. In fact, on the contrary, it will be quickly seen that this simple classification will considerably enrich the later and more complex one with extra shades of meaning.

The classification suggested by Carus describes simply the relationship between temperament and the form of the hand in terms of its 'functional appearance'. Carus distinguished two main types of hand — the *Prehensile*, which in form and structure was fitted for grasping and holding objects, and the *Touch* type, which is adapted by its nature for feeling and sensing objects. These two divisions in terms of functions he further sub-divided in terms of quality of function. The prehensile was subdivided into the *Elementary* and *Motoric*, whilst the touch was separated into the *Sensitive* and *Psychic*.

The Elementary hand [31] is, according to Carus, large, thick and heavy in appearance, and corresponds in description almost exactly to the one classified by D'Arpentigny under the same name. It is on the whole a coarse hand, not very flexible, with short fingers, and usually marked with only the main lines, whilst the papillary ridges are comparatively thick and heavy. The hands of all anthropoid species are markedly 'prehensile' in character, and this association is worth bearing in mind when examining an elementary hand which has any definite signs of degeneracy shown in it. The palm of a gorilla is remarkably like the palm print of a degenerate elementary hand. In a palm print this hand, unless very hard indeed, shows up to advantage: the skin ridges are clearly defined, and the line markings have a characteristic 'thickness' which suggests a strong, if turgid, energy flowing through the hand. The prehensile elementary hand, as its name suggests, is possessed by a 'down-to-earth' type of person, usually a worker of the artisan class, or a farmer, bricklayer or millworker. In Chinese palmistry this hand type is referred to as the 'hand of the earth', and is supposed to relate to the Saturnalian qualities in a man, such as practicality and seriousness. The print shown at [44] is the hand of a thirty-two-year-old farmer who is temperamentally well fitted to his job. This type of hand does not always indicate a low intelligence; on the contrary, many people showing elementary features are extremely intelligent, and adapt themselves well to their life circumstances, but their mentality is always bounded by a strict, earthy commonsense. They are usually extroverted, and prone to a cycloid emotional temperament, which is to say that they oscillate between extremes of excitement and depression. An introverted elementary type is always a 'difficult' person, but fortunately rare. This type is discussed more fully in my later classification.

The other prehensile type, the Motoric hand [32] is more refined than the elementary; the fingers are longer, more flexible, and because of the fleshiness of this type of hand which results from its muscularity, it tends to be softer to the touch. The palmar zone shows a greater number of crease lines than the elementary types, and there is found a corresponding richness of emotional life. This type of hand is found on an extroverted person who is disposed towards the pleasant aspect of life, to good food, wholesome entertainment and jovial company. The Chinese tradition refers to this hand as the 'hand of wood', which suggests something of the resilience and endurance of this type. It is equated with the Jupiterian characteristics of largeness of outlook and expansiveness. He tends to be an egotist, but is generally of a kindly disposition when things are going in a direction which suits his own personal plans. Although possessed of a better intellect than the elementary types, he is not over-brilliant in abstract thought, for he is a practical man, and intellectualism in itself, with no foundation of actual

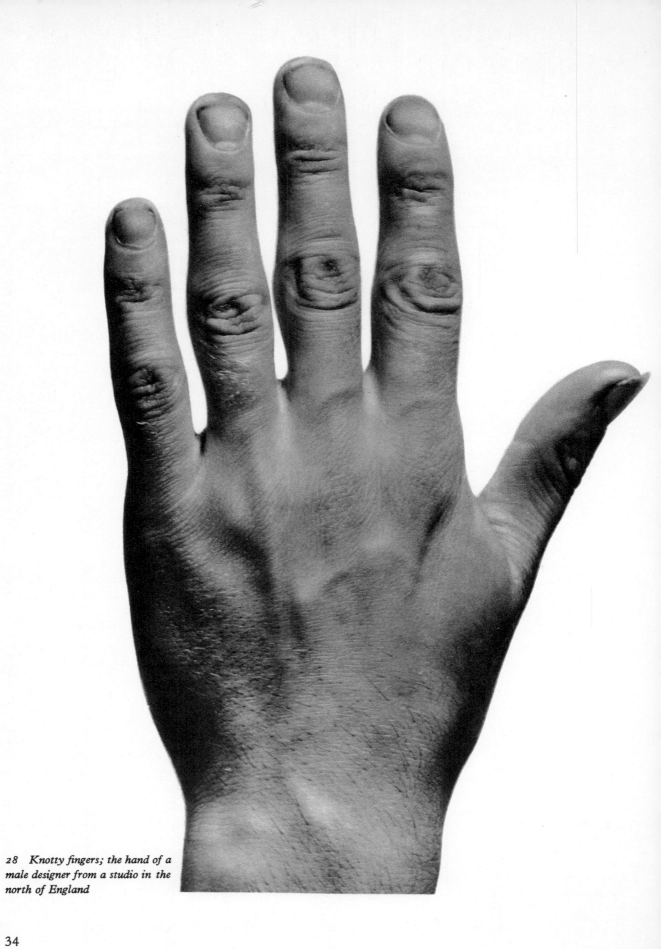

28 *Knotty fingers; the hand of a*
male designer from a studio in the
north of England

reality, would be repugnant to his commonsense mentality. He is best fitted to a job of an active, thoughtful nature where he can use his hands in an intelligent way and where an outlet for his natural common sense and strong energies can be found. Engineers, sportsmen, soldiers, businessmen and certain types of artists may often be found in this hand type: the one uniting factor being their healthy ambition to succeed in their own particular sphere. The print given as an example of this hand type is that of a trade journalist in a fairly responsible position.

The Sensitive hand [33], which is the first within the second classification, is described by Carus as being small in proportion to the body, flexible in movement and usually possessed of a small thumb and slender fingers. The palm of this type is always well marked with lines of a fine and energetic quality. Such quality of lines are indicative of a rich, though not entirely impractical, emotional attunement to life. This type of person always has a childish side to his or her nature: one part of him is an eternal Peter Pan. Such people are rarely active in a physical sense for long periods, but they make up for this by a natural receptivity in emotional matters. Actors, dancers, designers are often found with this hand type: they have a tendency to be schizoid, unstable and subjective. The Chinese palmistry refers to this as the 'hand of water', and associates it with the Mercurian characteristics of quickness and versatility.

The second type in the touch classification is the Psychic [34]. This is described as being slender and flexible, with tapering fingers and small thin thumb. It has been aptly described as the 'aristocratic' hand, suggesting something of its languid appearance. It is always soft to the touch, sometimes flabby, and is therefore difficult to print. The lines on this hand create a fine, net-like mesh which is particularly bewildering to the chiromancer. The numerous lines suggest an over-indulged emotional system, which leads to, or is directed by, a strong imagination, and results in many cases in a schizoid lack of contact with life. Most people exhibiting the psychic hand type are 'mixed-up' emotionally and, as the name suggests, live on such a heightened plane of reality as to be divorced from the normal level. They tend to be lethargic, have very little sense of practical affairs, and suffer from slight aboulia. This type can hardly be described as intellectual —perhaps imaginative and able to express strong imagination—

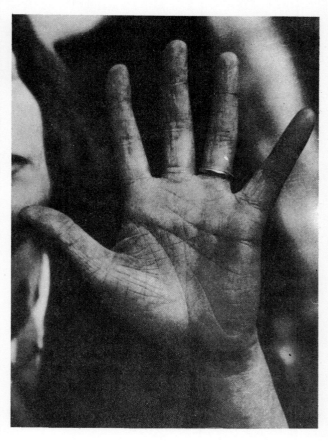

29 *A female hand with smooth fingers and pointed tips*

but hardly intellectual: what mental energy they have is usually poured into day-dreaming. They are 'intuitive' types who tend to take refuge in 'watery' mysticism. Their sensitivity and weakness tends to make them easy prey to imagination, which they readily embrace in the face of a 'hard' world. The hand as a whole does not exhibit sufficient energy to belong to a creative type, but it is frequently found amongst the dilettante class of artists. The Chinese describe this hand type as the 'hand of metal', and associate it with the Venusian characteristics of placidity, companionability and tendency to laziness. The print given as an example is that of a man of twenty-eight who is 'drifting' through life, creating many difficulties for himself, and finding it almost impossible to orientate himself to the

35

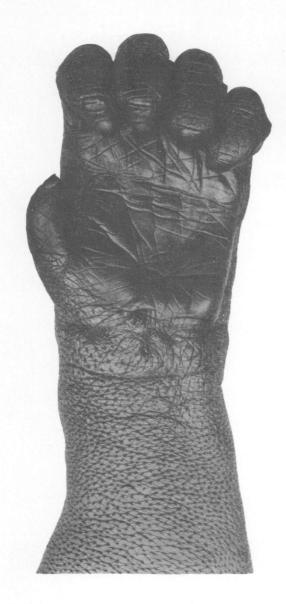

world. He has no fixed job. Observe how badly the soft hand has printed.

D'Arpentigny, and later Heron-Allen, arranged the various types of hand into six distinct groups: the Elementary, Spatulate, Conic, Square, Knotty and Psychic [219]. This classification, which is basically descriptive in character, has been employed by almost all palmists ever since the day of its invention. Unfortunately, even a simple analysis of the classification shows that D'Arpentigny knew very little about the principle of logical division. D'Arpentigny originally attempted to describe his hand types in terms of their shape (either square, conic or spatulate) and the length of the fingers in relation to the palm. Had he pursued his classification with any awareness of the laws of logical division he would have arrived at six pure hand types, each of which excluded the others, and all of which, taken together, would comprise the whole of hand types. However, his list of hand types, although based on acute observation, was not the result of sound reasoning. This has led to very many difficulties, for certain hand formations were not included in his classification, whilst others were included twice under different headings.

To remedy the inadequacies which were apparent in his system, a seventh group, described as a 'mixed' class, was included in the classification, and to this was allocated any hand type 'of which the shape is so uncertain, as to resemble, even to the possibility of confusion, more than one type'. Obviously, had the classification been exact and carefully thought out, there could be no 'confusion' of types of class. There could, of course, be 'border-line' cases, but this is an entirely different problem, for it is not surprising that living organisms should be difficult to pigeonhole. Each hand is different, each hand is as unique as the person to whom it belongs, and difficulties in classifying them are to be expected.

At any event, D'Arpentigny's classification led to several difficulties owing to the weakness of this classification, and few people were thoughtful enough to discover the real reason. One man, writing in 1892, hinted at the 'cross division' of which D'Arpentigny was guilty, but no one took any serious notice of the argument. The result is that today, over a hundred years after the classification was first formulated, it is still commonly used in palmistic circles, despite its obvious absurdities.

30 The hand of a chimpanzee. Observe the marked simian line which has the distinct appearance of being a 'crease line' folded into the epidermal layer. The area of papillary ridges is particularly defined here. It covers much the same area as on a human being, but there is a greater contrast between it and the surrounding ridgeless skin. Note the degenerate thumb, which is incapable of versatile movement. The low-set position of the thumb, 'a simian insertion', is occasionally found in degenerate humans. (Photograph by courtesy of Dr. John Napier, Royal Free Hospital School of Medicine)

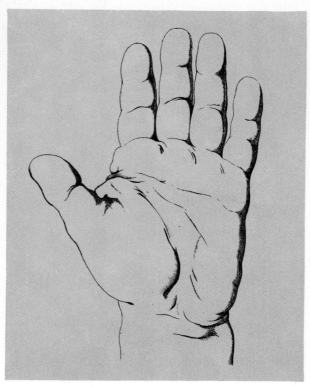

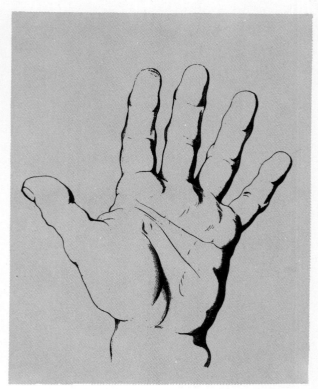

31   *The Elementary hand*

32   *The Motoric hand*

33   *The Sensitive hand*

34   *The Psychic hand*

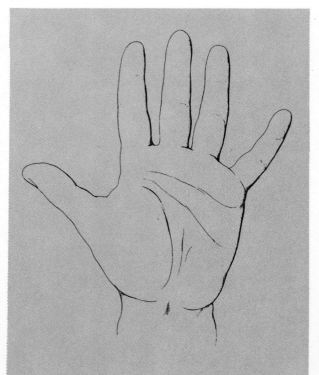

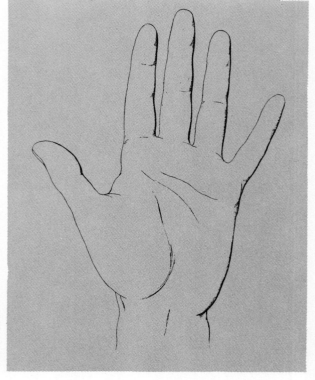

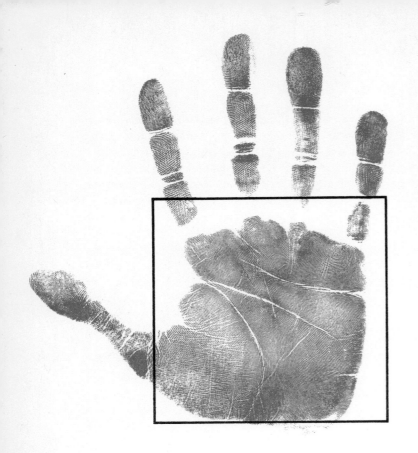

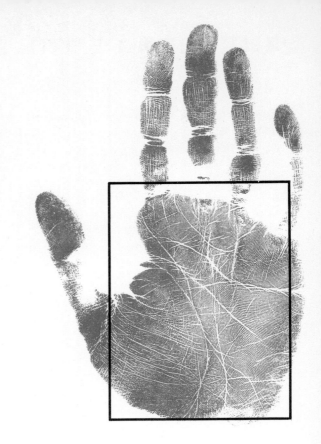

35　*A square palm; the hand of a 30-year-old Spanish artist*　36　*An oblong palm; the hand of a 30-year-old English female artist*

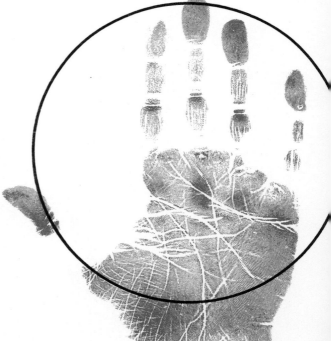

37　*Long fingers; the hand of an English artist*

38　Right: *Short fingers; the hand of an eight-year-old boy*

THE FORM OF THE HAND

The classification of hand types which I use myself is quite different from any other. It is based on a logical division which enables one to recognise a general hand type quite easily after practice. My first main division of hands is made in terms of the subject's *sex*: my second division is in terms of the *shape* of the palm, and my third division in terms of the *length* of fingers in relation to the palm.

All hands, to some degree, are conic in shape: that is to say that the fingers, when closed together, are between them narrower at their broadest part than is the palm at its broadest part. The degree to which the hand as a whole is conical reflects the person's inner psychology; and I have found it necessary to evolve a method for determining this degree. It is necessary first of all to estimate whether the palm is *square* or *oblong* in shape. This can best be done by actually drawing on tracing paper over the palmar area of a print, taking care to allow for deficiencies in the printings. If the width of the palm is approximately equal to its height, we have an example of a square hand [35]; should the width be less than the height, we have an example of an oblong hand [36].

To determine the length of the fingers in relation to the palm it is only necessary to draw a circle with a pair of compasses, centre at the base of the lower phalange of Saturn, and radius the length of Saturn. Care must be taken to allow for the inevitable shortening of the finger as a result of printing. In some cases, the fingers will be long in relation to the palm and the drawn circle will enclose almost the whole of the hand [37]. In other cases, the fingers will be noticeably short, and the lower half of the palm, sometimes including the thumb, may not fit within the circle [38].

Using this method of measurement we arrive at four distinct types of hand. The first has a square palm and short fingers: this hand, regardless of the sex of the subject, I have designated the *Practical* hand. The second type has a long palm and short fingers: this I have called the *Intuitive* hand. The third type, with a long palm and long fingers, I have called the *Sensitive* hand; whilst the fourth type, with a square palm and long fingers, I have called the *Intellectual* type. It will be observed that very rarely does a hand have fingers which are longer than the palm. The terms 'long fingers' and 'short fingers' are purely relative. It will be found later on that the four basic hand types are in fact characterised by other particularities, and experience enables one to quickly determine the hand type without having to make actual tracings and measurements.

I consider the four basic hand types I shall describe to be analogous to the four elements, or the four *triplicities* of astrology. The four elements of Fire, Earth, Air and Water have a rich association in astrology with distinct human types. I was first struck with the idea of trying to draw parallels between these astrological associations and hand types after reading the book on Chinese palmistry by Soulie de Morant, and I was surprised to find how excellently the two went together. The Practical hand is related to Earth, the Intuitive to Fire, the Intellectual to Air, and the Sensitive to Water.

The four Elements of Empedocles — Earth, Fire, Air and Water, 'the four-fold root of all things', was the fundamental basis underlying astrology, alchemy and medicine from the very earliest times. Hippocrates is supposed to have originated the teaching of the medical humours, but they were in fact derived from pre-Ionian teachings which came from the East, probably by way of the Sabaean tradition.

The teaching of the humours in relation to the four elements propounded by Galen is represented in the diagram [39]. This teaching was much more subtle than modern thought is disposed to picture it: in its original form the humours were descriptions of the 'mental and emotional colour' of an individual. Illness was the result of an imbalance or lack of unity between these four humours. In this respect the teaching, like modern psychology, recognised that diseases were a result of an exaggeration of one or more functions or attitudes.

The body of man has in itself blood, phlegm, yellow bile, and black bile; these make up the nature of his body, and through these he feels pain or enjoys health. Now he enjoys the most perfect health when these elements are duly proportioned to one another in respect of compounding, power and bulk, and when they are perfectly mingled. Pain is felt when one of these elements is in defect or excess, or is isolated in the body without being compounded with all the others.

So wrote Hippocrates in his book *On the Nature of Man*.

C. G. Jung is one of the few modern investigators to have recognised the importance and basic truth of the four-fold classification handed down to us from

39 *The four Humours of Galen*

40 Below: *An early attempt to relate the elements to the*
temperaments; with an approximate translation

Farben	Aschen-Farb.	Dunckel-Grün.	Roth.	Citronen-Gelb.
Planeten	☿	♄	♃	♀
Zeichen	♊	♒	♐	♉
Temperament	Wässericht mit schwartzer Gall vermischt.	Melancholisch mit Geblüt vermischt.	Gallisch mit Blut vermischt.	Geblüt mit Schleim vermischt.
Element	Wasser mit Erde vermischt.	Erde mit Lufft vermischt.	Feuer mit Lufft vermischt.	Lufft mit Wasser vermischt.

Colour	Ash colour	Brown	Red	Yellow
Planet	☿	♄	♃	♀
Sign	♊	♒	♐	♉
Temperament	Water with Gall	Melancholy with Blood	Gall with Blood	Blood with Phlegm
Element	Water + Earth	Earth + Air	Fire + Air	Air + Water

ancient times. It seems to me that the classification is at least as valid as any of those submitted by modern psychologists: the classifications (they can hardly be called 'systems') put forward by such men as Freud, Kretschmer and their followers are not, to my mind, as satisfactory as the ancient system. Unfortunately, since the development of empiricism in the past 200 years, the ancient system has been rejected out of hand; one suspects that this happened because the full significance of the theory was not grasped by those people who were responsible for its rejection. The eighteenth and nineteenth century scientists, delighted with their cold and mechanical ideas of the universe, had no time for analogical thought unless it could be projected in diagrammatic form in terms of cog-wheels, pulleys and levers.

Solomon Diamond has made an interesting attempt to correlate Galen's four temperaments with modern psychological ideas, and has come to the conclusion that so-called Hippocratic temperaments 'may be regarded as resultants of the interaction of two basic dimensions of behaviour'. The two basic dimensions are the Activity-Approach graphs, and the whole correlation between the ancient and modern teachings is best illustrated in diagrammatic form [41].

It will be noted that the Element Water may be equated with Withdrawal and Air with Approach on the horizontal line, and that Fire may be equated with high activity and Earth with low activity on the vertical line.

We shall now examine the four Elemental types in detail, remembering that no person is a pure type, and every person contains within him some degree of the qualities of all types. Each element partakes, to some extent, of every other element; the combinations are infinite, and no person belongs exclusively to one type. The particular elemental combinations within a hand, and therefore within a person, can be determined almost exactly after a thorough analysis of the hand. For the moment, however, we shall limit ourselves to a general classification aimed at determining the basic disposition and nature of the individual, before attempting to add the refinements which a detailed analysis would naturally bring.

Within the four-fold classification we shall, of course, examine the male and female hand, so in fact we shall find eight distinct types of hand. No one is a pure type, but the descriptions contained under each division will form an excellent basis for a detailed study of a person's hand, however complex his character.

41 Solomon Diamond's attempt to correlate Galen's four temperaments with modern psychological ideas, illustrating how the four Hippocratic temperaments may be regarded as resultants of the interaction of two basic dimensions of behaviour. (Diagram reproduced by courtesy of Harper Bros. from Personality and Temperament, *1957)*

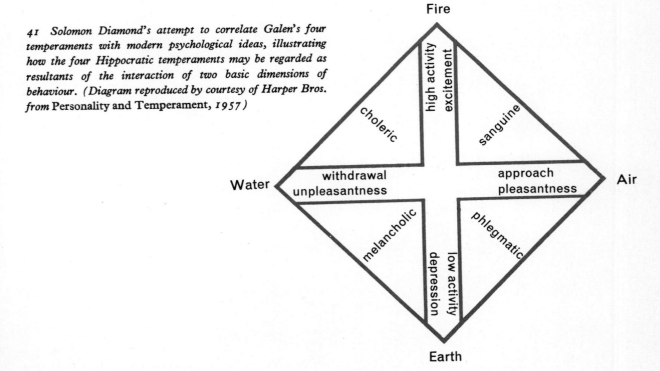

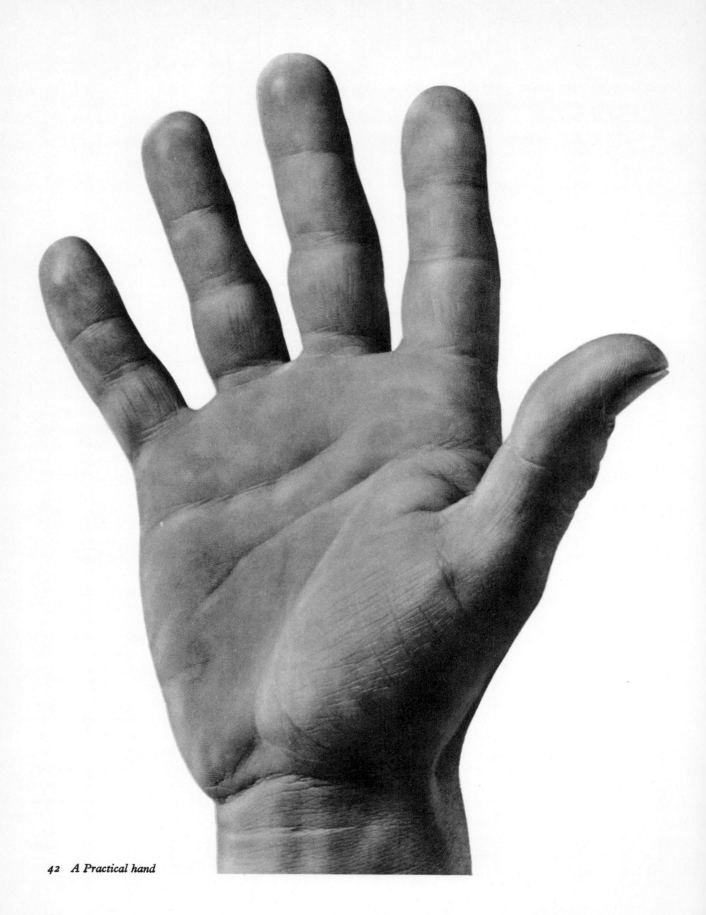

42 *A Practical hand*

THE PRACTICAL HAND

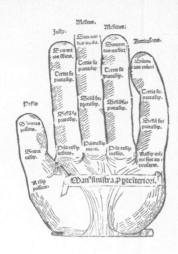

Earth is gross and porous, specifically heavy, but naturally light ... In this element the other three, especially fire, are latent ... It receives all that the other three project into it, conscientiously conceals what it should hide, and brings to light that which it should manifest ... Outwardly it is invisible and volatile.

Basil Valentine (16th century)

The Practical hand is distinguished chirognomically by a square palm and short fingers. It is usually heavy, solid, tending towards coarseness and, in its less complex types, marked only with the three main lines of Heart, Life and Head. In its extreme form the palm is thick, large and heavy, with an accentuated mount of Venus, whilst the fingers are stumpy, unrefined and knotty. The skin is coarse, and the thumb, which is usually quite short, is inflexible and heavy. The palmar surface shows few lines, but they are usually strong and vital in quality. A palm print [43] reveals well-defined skin ridges, and there is the characteristic 'thickness' representing the strong flow of energies found in this type. The hand corresponds in many respects to the prehensile elementary hand described by Carus, and the points of similarity between sub-human hands and this type have already been mentioned.

This type of hand pertains to the element of Earth. The large palmar surface suggests that the basic disposition of its owner is directed towards the 'animal-like' and 'worldly' life; whilst the short fingers and coarseness bring to mind the simian nature of the hand. Its symbol is ♁ for the male and ♃ for the female.

Earth itself is solid. We rely on it for support, for food, indeed, for our very existence. Earth is motionless, dry, and tends to be regarded as being merely a functional thing which gives freely of its produce when rightly tended. Above all, the earth is *productive*; whether it is as arid as the desert or as rich as a tropical forest, beneath its surface there is always a quick ferment of life. Seen from the narrow life span of man, the earth is motionless on the surface, but underneath its thin crust the earth is alive, and compressed under fantastic pressures which are continually adjusting themselves and occasionally escaping in magmatic fury.

All these characteristics of earth may, by strict analogy, be seen in certain types of individuals. Such individuals are reliable, 'solid', one might say. Their practicality keeps their feet on the ground, they tend to dryness and like repetitive, hard, practical work in which they find pleasure in direct contact with earthly things. They are careful, guided by an innate knowledge of the rightness of things; they are trustworthy, for their natural sense of justice enables them to realise that crime does not pay. Hard work, honesty, effort and integrity of purpose combine to make the Earth type the essentially productive person in the realm of physical effort, such as building, carpentry, etc. They are, to the more blithe spirits of Air, Fire and Water, rather uninteresting. Their adherence to natural rhythms, like the rhythm of the seasons to the farmer or the rhythm of work to the craftsman, tends to make them in their turn suspicious of the other three Elemental types, whose lives are characterised by either quick, jerking movements, lacking in productive direction and aim, or by a lethargy which prevents hard work and any rhythm at all.

In the ancient tradition Earth is cold and dry, and therefore of a melancholic disposition. The farmer's boy of Gray's Elegy ('Melancholy mark'd him for

43 The Practical palm of a 23-year-old lorry driver; the break in the life line at approximately 22 years of age is contemporary with damage to the right hand in an accident. The few simple lines and the wide ridges are typical of the Earth hand

her own') springs to mind, typifying the simple, torpid, moody sincerity of the Practical temperament, which requires no recognition for talent and is in no respect an exhibitionist type: 'A Youth to Fortune and to Fame unknown'.

Paracelsus, in his table of alchemical correspondencies, links the element of Earth with *firmness, the body, mass, the visible and the tangible*, connoting the essential heaviness and strength of the type.

Just as the earth is motionless, dependable and reliable on the surface, but seething like a cauldron underneath, so is the Earth type a duality. Break through his reserve, his sense of justice and his adherence to rhythms, and destructive energies may be released.

Earth is attracted to water, which refreshes its dryness. Earth does not like parching fire, nor drying air, for they are blown about by the winds hither and thither without seeming purpose and without any basic rhythm of their own.

Astrologically, Earth is related to Taurus, Virgo and Capricorn, who form the Earth triplicity and whose governing planets are Venus, Mercury and Saturn. The possessive, conservative, steadfast and careful Taurian; the slightly reserved, practical and intelligently critical Virgo, and the prudent, quietly aspiring, orderly and almost utilitarian Capricorn, are all different aspects of the Earthly nature. The temperance and harmony of Venus, which gives a love of natural beauty and of beauty in the home, relates to the feminine aspect of the earthly type. Without Venus, Earth would be too dry, too solid,

too set in its ways. The adaptable, exciting and changeable Mercury affords a safety valve for the type, for just as the earth needs its volcanic channels to prevent it from disintegration, so does an earthy type need its ways of escape from routine and hard work. Saturn, cold, restrictive and melancholic, adds thought, meditation and moodiness to the Earthly sense of tenacity and purpose. Between them all, these factors create a fascinating type, no less interesting than any of the others, and certainly the more reliable — more, as it were, 'down to earth'.

Earth is the balance wheel of personality. Each of us contains within a little of each one of the triplicities, and this is particularly true of Earth.

Psychologically Earth gives a sense of concrete reality without which a person must of necessity lack all mental ballast and become a visionary or a child of sensation, according to the prevailing Triplicity and planetary influences. (Carter)

This is the hand which suggests the reliable, 'down to earth', commonsensical person. He tends to be impatient of small details, and has a penchant for out-of-door work. It is the hand often found on a labourer, farmer or factory worker, where there is a rhythm of motion and seasons as a background to the work. Physical labour and constructive work with the hands is very attractive to the type, and he does not like problems which cannot be solved by hard work or exertion. He would, as it were, prefer to chop down a dangerous tree rather than attempt to discover some way of preserving it — not because he is naturally destructive, but because he would prefer not to make the effort with his mind. Signs of a good mentality would suggest an occupation where *practical* thinking would be relevant: I have observed that many hands of this type are found among mechanical engineers, high-class craftsmen and similar artisans.

In its really severe form, that is to say when the hand is particularly elementary in appearance, it may be regarded as belonging to the lower grades of the human race. The short fingers give no love for detail, and a certain rashness of action is usually an aspect of their psychology; whilst the developed lower world indicates the animal-like direction of emotions. Knottedness in such a hand is not a pleasant feature, for it adds tenacity to unreason, which

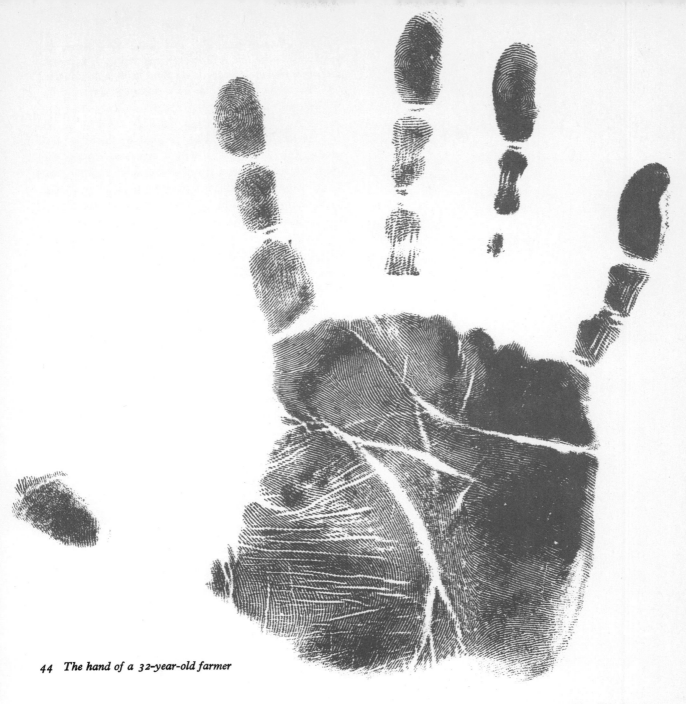

44 The hand of a 32-year-old farmer

leads to bigotry and crude superstition. It is the hand of the peasant, of the unintelligent worker, who is incapable of originality, and fitted only for menial tasks in which the inherent sense of bodily rhythm is given a opportunity for expression. The emotional life of such people is not so simple as one might think, but it is directed mainly towards the 'herd' instincts of life — their efforts being at best towards the primitive essentials in terms of mass conformity, and at worst towards crimes of an asocial nature.

D'Arpentigny gave the alternative name of 'Necessary' to the Practical hand type, thereby suggesting that its owner would spend his life identified only with the basic necessities of life, oblivious to anything higher than earthy animality.

The Practical hand delights in physical effort, and has a basic craving for rhythm. The tendency in modern civilisation to destroy slow natural rhythms is having its most disastrous results amongst this type of Earthy person, who, although not disposed naturally towards neurosis, is, like the Earth itself, slowly being contaminated by many of the modern changes in manner and tempo of life.

We have already noted that the basic solidity of

the earth can easily be disturbed if it is probed too deeply, or if it is not permitted its natural rhythm and its natural 'volcanic' safety valves. This is a hint that the psychology behind the Practical hand is not quite so simple as one might at first expect. In fact the possessors of such a hand can be divided into two related personality types — the one relatively simple, the other very complex and difficult to classify. The first type corresponds in its essential form to that already described as the temperamentally extroverted down-to-earth person, possessed of a dull balance of emotions which is not easily disturbed in the course of ordinary life.

The second type is chirologically distinguished by certain atavistic markings such as a highly developed whorl on the mounts of Moon or Venus, a simian line, a clubbed thumb or some malformation of the finger of Mercury. This is the type in which the outer simplicity hides the inner complexity of the subject, and within its grouping we find such widely differing types as low-quality musicians, painters, criminals and lunatics; all characterised by a definite schizoid temperament which tends towards social hostility.

There is usually something infantile about the possessor of such a hand. Sometimes the infantilism is mental, in which case we find the coarse boxer, wrestler and athlete, whose developed physique compensates for lack of mental development, and who find expression in bodily rhythms. Sometimes the infantilism is physical, in which case we find an overdeveloped emotional system accompanying the sensitivity of the artist and creator. Sometimes the infantilism is emotional, in which case we find the criminal type of madman.

Perhaps the social aberration resulting from this particular schizoid grouping is produced by the individual being disposed by nature towards life within a group — the certain characteristic of a simple Elementary type — but by some freak of psychology (manifest in the atavistic marking which singles him out with some distinctive characteristic) being quite unable to adjust to that group. The consequent behaviour is the resultant of the inner stresses created by these two different forces. The unhappiness of such people is largely engendered by their being outsiders who want to 'belong'.

In his *Laws of Scientific Hand Reading*, Benham preserved two very interesting prints from this schizoid elementary group: that of Ira Marlatt, the 'prison demon', who was serving a life sentence for murder at the time when the impression was obtained; and that of Albert J. Franz, who was convicted for murder and electrocuted in 1898. Both these men had hands of the elementary type, but each had special characteristics which marked them as being of the complicated and schizoid type.

At first glance the hand in [47] is of the simple Practical type, but the atavistic marking of the finger of Mercury (deficient in the lower phalange), allied to the forceful thumb, reveals the subject to be of the more complex Practical type. This is the hand of a most remarkable person who, until his conversion to Christianity a few years before the print was obtained, was a degenerate with strong criminal tendencies. It is regretted that there is no print of his hand made before his very abrupt change of life. His case history makes fascinating reading in relation to his hands.

As in all hand types, once the basic characteristics which indicate the Practical hand have been noted, and once the Earthy connotations have been associated with it in a very general way, it will be necessary to examine the rich variety of factors which indicate the individual psychological trends of the particular hand.

In the Practical hand there are three factors which are worthy of close observation. The first is skin texture, which can best be determined from a print. The refining role of smooth skin reflects the agency of Venus, the planet of Taurus. It imparts a quality of femininity to the hand type, and one is led to suspect a deficiency of thyroid hormone which leads to mental, physical and emotional sluggishness and to bodily fatness.

Fingers are the second most important aid to determining the nature of the individual type. Very short fingers are fairly common amongst Earth types, but if they are smooth, a most interesting individuality arises, for a strong intuition is revealed, and the Mercurian characteristics which, though properly being an aspect of the Earthly triplicity, is strictly speaking too Fiery, too changeable to appear to any large extent in an Earthy hand without danger. The hand in [49] is of course of a basically earthy nature, but the short, smooth fingers add a dissonance to the whole, which leads one to suspect some sort of psychological difficulty. The hand does belong to

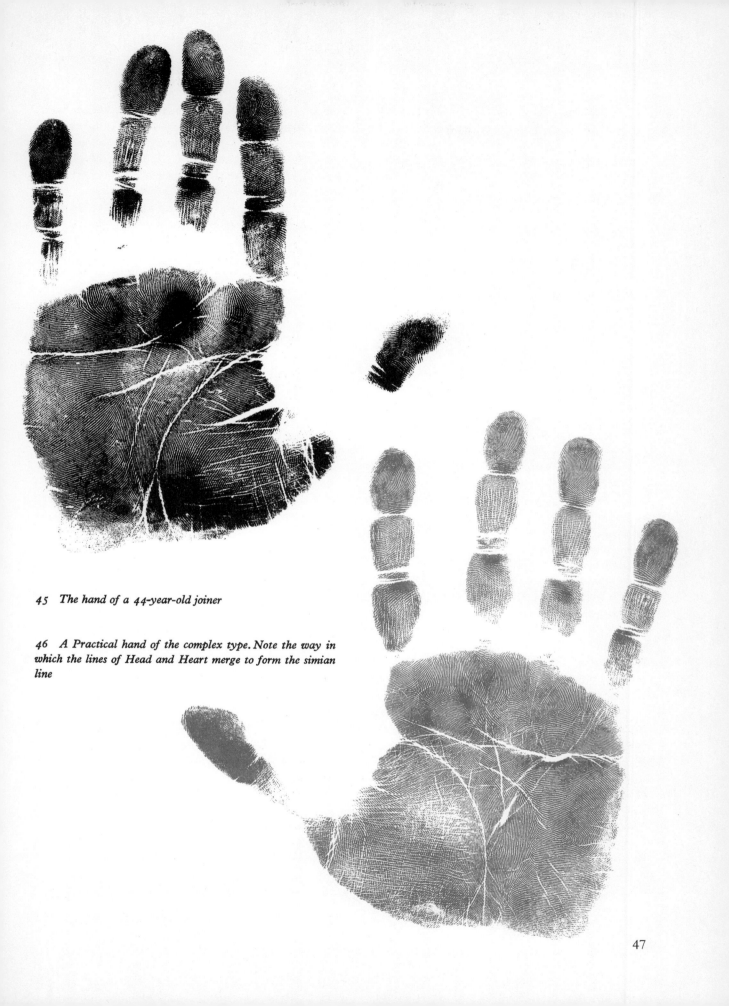

45   The hand of a 44-year-old joiner

46   A Practical hand of the complex type. Note the way in which the lines of Head and Heart merge to form the simian line

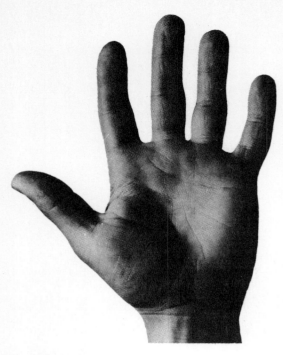

47 *This man was an alcoholic fairground pugilist until converted to Christianity; he is now a youth group leader, an active member of the Church, and rapidly becoming an authority in a specialised branch of engineering*

a type whose endocrine system is regulated by a too free flowing of the thyroid glands. He is very active, energetic, and indeed may be associated with the Mercurian type. The personality represented by such a hand is extremely individualistic, for it represents an excess of Mercury, which is the escapist quality of Earth, in an evidently earthy hand. Such a hand as that is, however, very uncommon.

The third aspect of the Practical hand which is a certain indication of the basic individuality underlying the Earth type is the linear conformations on the palm. Most commonly the hand is characterised by three, deep, vital lines of Life, Heart and Head (four if Fate is included), which suggest something of the basic simplicity and vast reservoir of physical energy. Occasionally one meets up with a practical hand which shows numerous lines, all of the 'vital' quality which is so hard to describe but so easy to recognise. Such a hand is of course a sign of a complex Earthy type. In general one can presume a tendency towards a neurotic and restless disposition, which is not common to the type, and which reveals the traditional and most unexpected association of Mercury with the type. The precise nature of this disposition must be determined by a detailed analysis of the actual lines and other morphological considerations.

The female Practical [49] hand is not as commonly found as the male, though a survey in a factory of female workers established a 65% occurrence of the hand type in that particular milieu. It is not surprising that the female Practical hand should be rare, in fact, for the type is of an active and masculine nature.

In comparison with the male hand, there are one or two differences worth noting. The general squareness of the palm is mitigated by a general roundness of form — particularly in the area of the mount of Moon which in a print is almost always rounded. As one would expect, the skin quality is finer in a female hand; the papillary ridges, which are still clearly discernible, are closer together, more delicate, and consequently tend to produce dark areas in prints, where the ink fills up the fine spaces between the ridges. The lines on the palm are always more numerous, though the three or four main lines of Life, Head, Heart and Fate are well distinguished. Perhaps the most noticeable difference, however, is the size of the hand: the female Practical hand is always *small*. One is led to the conclusion that a small male hand of the Practical type will reveal a character which is to some extent feminine.

The square-palmed, short-fingered female hand reveals a temperament which is of a homely nature. This is the female aspect of Earth, the provider in the home, the solid, unintellectual, well-balanced kind of worker. She, like her male counterpart, has a dual nature; on the surface she is self-possessed, realistic and down-to-earth, but there are underground springs which may under probing burst into life.

Venus governs Taurus, which is of the Earth triplicity, and it is this feminine planet which tends to manifest most strongly in the female Practical hand. The practicality and cautiousness of the type are somewhat mitigated, and directed towards the home, consequently the type is best occupied in the actual routine of keeping the house clean and spruce, and will exhibit here cautiousness in the business of economical shopping. She tends to be 'over economical', and the earthy cautiousness will lead her to buy cheap foods simply because they are cheap, and to avoid any exotic foods, not so much because she cannot afford them but because she is instinctively suspicious of anything not common or ordinary.

It is the female Earth hand which reminds us that the very origin of the word 'economical' was

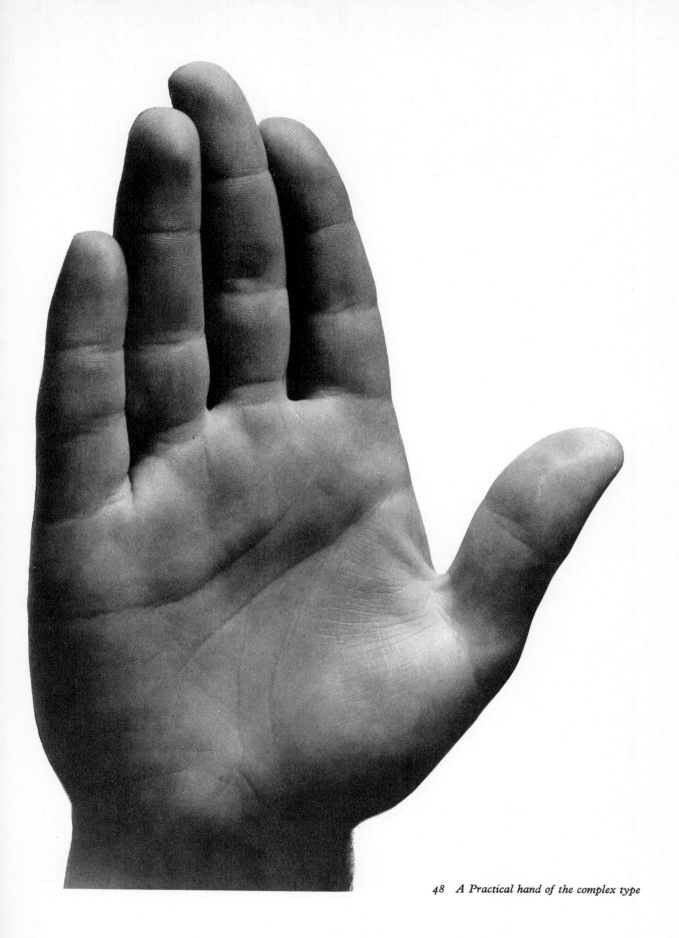

48   A Practical hand of the complex type

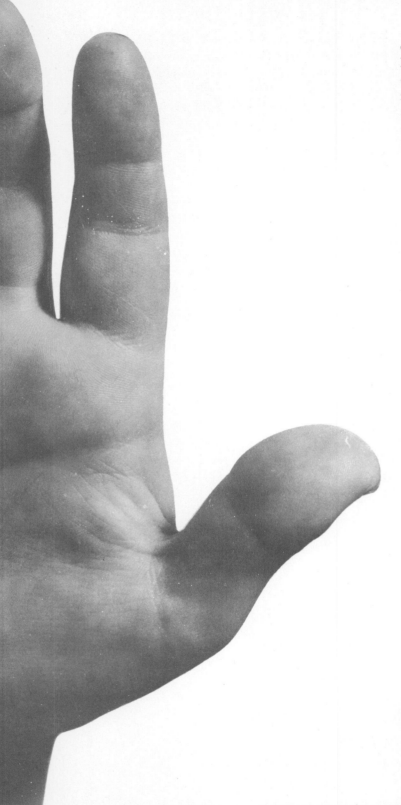

connected with the Greek concept of running a household. The whole life of such a person will centre around running the home, which will give food both for her over-possessive nature and for her sense of orderly routine. She will enjoy 'having someone in for a chat', which is the Earthy equivalent of hospitality. Above all she will find her best self-expression in the country, ideally as a farmer's wife, where the natural rhythm of farming, the sense of possession and security in owning land and animals, and the practical activity demanded of her during the day, would give the most complete satisfaction. The type is not happy in the town, and if compelled to live in one, as so many are nowadays, she will continually dream of the day when she can 'get away from it all'.

When economic factors demand that she should work for a living, her narrowness of outlook, dislike of active thought, and addiction to routine will lead her to work in a factory, where naturally enough she will be basically unhappy. The one thing which will make such work acceptable to her will be the companionship of people similar to herself, which will feed her group-instinct. The ironical fact is that it is one half of her Earth character which leads her to seek financial security in working, perhaps to supplement her husband's income, and another half of the same character which makes the work repugnant to her.

A girl with a Practical hand would do well to marry a Practical male; boredom could be the outcome of

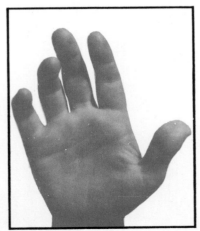

49 *A female Practical hand; the bulbousness of the thumb, and its low insertion, place this hand in the complex class*

such a marriage, but Earth types are well adapted by temperament for the sort of monotony which other types would find unbearable.

Marriage is based on expectancies: some people expect a husband to act in a certain way, to fulfil his obligations in a definite manner. His wife is expected to act in a particular manner. The ideal is that in marriage a relationship of mutual interdependencies should be established in which the needs of each person be satisfied by the needs of the other: that, for example, the passivity of the female should be assuaged, balanced and compensated by the activity of the male. Modern psychological research indicates that 'like poles attract' in marriage — this is certainly true so far as the triplicities are concerned, but 'likeness' of type must always be refreshed by a different admixture of another Element to give life to the relationship. Earth types, with an admixture

of Fire in the male, for example, will tend to escape the monotony and to give the married pair, seen as a social unit, a higher degree of activity.

At best, marriage between Earth types tends to be steady, orderly and tied to strict routine of events. When a schism does occur it is 'volcanic' and abrupt, both sides tending to bear grudges for a long time. Marriage with a Sensitive male, of the right intellectual level and of the right emotional strength, would 'refresh' her natural dryness. In extreme cases, the contrast between Earth and Water, which would be in essence a clash between imagination and practicality, can result in a quagmire, in which both partners are sucked down. In any event, marriage between an extreme Earth type and an extreme of one of the other three elements could only result in disaster, but a natural law of attraction seems to operate, and few such marriages actually take place.

50   The hand of a masseur

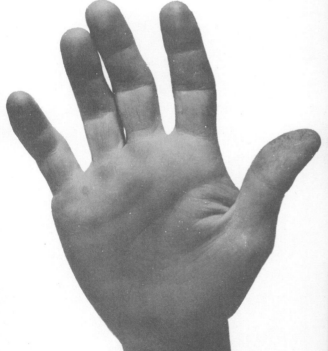

51   Detail from The Incredulity of St. Thomas *by Guercino (1591 — 1666) in the National Gallery, London. An excellent example of an Earth hand. The gesture is a little 'staged' as one might expect in a baroque painting; an Earth type would not be given to such an exuberantly dramatic posture*

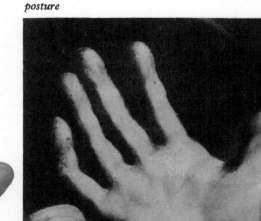

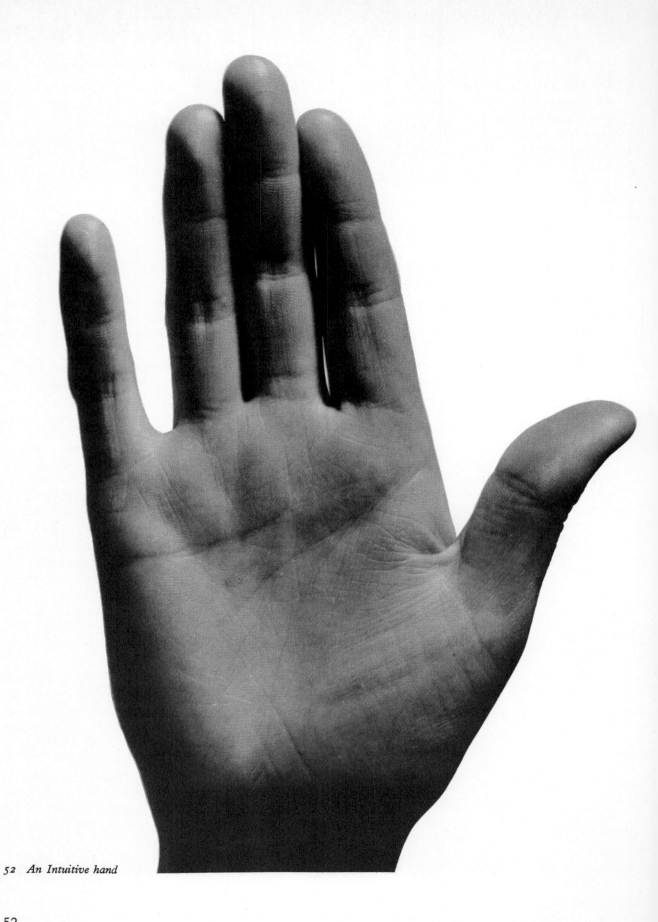

52 An Intuitive hand

THE INTUITIVE HAND

Fire is the purest and noblest of all Elements, full of adhesive unctuous corrosiveness, penetrant, digestive, inwardly fused, hot and dry, outwardly visible, and tempered by the earth. This Element is the most passive of all, and resembles a chariot: when it is drawn, it moves; when it is not drawn it stands still.

Basil Valentine

The Intuitive hand [52] is distinguished chirognomically by a long palm and short fingers. It is usually agile, flexible and of an elastic texture. Because the length of the fingers is measured in relation to the length of the palm, the short fingers of the Intuitive type are usually a little longer than those of the Practical type. They are always more refined, and never as heavy or stumpy as the Earth fingers. The hand, which is predominantly a masculine type, is always lively in appearance. The palmar surface is usually covered with a multitude of fine, energetic lines, and a palm print [54] reveals fine quality skin ridges. There is a highly characteristic 'liveliness' about the crease lines themselves. This type of hand pertains to the element of Fire. Its symbol is ♂ for the male, and ♀ for the female.

Fire burns, it is alive with energy. We rely on it for heat which excites and delights our bodies. Fire penetrates into things, warming from the outside inwards. Fire is also destructive in places where it is not under control; when not performing its function of warming, of keeping alive and active, it can be too consuming, and even lethal.

By strict analogy these characteristics may be seen in certain types of individuals. Such individuals are active, keen, full of movement and excited life. On a level of society they *warm* us with their life and talents. On a level of individual relationships a Fire type will warm another, passing on something of his own enthusiasm, astonishing him with his brilliance and versatility. The Intuitive type is predominantly emotional in make-up: even the intellectual capacity depends on the emotional life and almost any argument offered by a Fire type in an intellectual way is basically an elaborate justification for emotionally held viewpoints. Just as fire uncontrolled can be dangerous, so can the Intuitive type of a too fiery nature be dangerous both to himself and to others. He can 'sear' others with the heat of his energy. A strong Intuitive type lives at a rate of intensity which many others find impossible to bear. His innate enthusiasm can often be tiring to other people of a less ardent disposition: an Earth type, for instance, will be completely overwhelmed by such a person, for he will be made to feel intellectually inferior and emotionally slow. The quick Fire type would have little patience with an Earth type: practicality is too slow for his liking. Impatience with other people is one of the chief faults of a Fire type; this is often seen as a tendency to superiority.

An Intuitive type is always active; he must always be doing things. He has no basic rhythm like the Practical type, and his way of doing things has a flame-like quality which is highly characteristic of the type. The many-tongued flame suggests his versatility, and at the same time his inability to stick at one thing very long — the flames flicker up and down, rapidly and without rhythm and, as the Earth type would say, without purpose. In fact, rapid movement and change are in themselves purposeful to the Intuitive type, for they help to rid him of his incredible store of emotional energy. A need for constant activity, combined with a strong need for variety, results in a 'changeable' personality. For this reason, a Fire type tends to be unreliable.

As the sixteenth century alchemist Basil Valentine said, behind all its volatile movement, the Fire type is very passive 'and resembles a chariot; when it is drawn, it moves; when it is not drawn it stands still'. The Intuitive type is utterly dependent on emotional stimuli which must come from the outside world. It is moved easily, and it is difficult to stop once it is moving, but at no time can it move by itself. The Intuitive person must always have some aim and incentive to keep him going. Whilst the Earth type might be likened to a donkey, moving steadily forward in its attempts to reach the carrot dangling before its nose, the Fire type might be likened to a charioteer in a race where fame and adulation are the prizes. A Fire type always needs *recognition* for his abilities and it is this need which motivates most of his actions. Ambition is one of the strong forces behind the personality of this type.

Fire types never settle easily to authority. They tend to be unhappy when restricted either in place or time. Fire wants to spread and consume all around it. The ideal position for a Fire type would be as a leader of a small group of individuals where his natural enthusiasm for life can be communicated and his own sense of importance be gratified. His position of leadership or authority must not, however, be too restricting, and he should feel free to come and go as he pleases.

Intuitive types have a tendency not to fit easily into society. This is not a result of open hostility as in the case of a degenerate Earth type, so much as of the Apollonarian attitude which Freud, in a different classification, summed up as springing from the feeling that 'the world owes them a living'. The Apollo type is, according to some authorities, associated with the thymus glands, which are closely related to growth. As Collin pointed out, Peter Pan, the little boy who didn't want to grow up, is simply the thymus type, with its transparent milk and roses skin, its delicate teeth and bones, and its particular air of beautiful frailty. The mental attitude of 'not wanting to grow up' and of refusing the responsibilities proper to one's age is often manifest in the Intuitive type. The mental attitude is best seen in criticism of society, or in retreat from society by way of an art form or craft. The creativity of Apollo, the active planet, always carries with it artistic ability.

The Intuitive type can, in many respects, be associated with Kretschmer's description of the leptosome individual, excitable, nervous, sensitive and withdrawing — popular and tending to the egotistical in nature; vigorous in activity and hypersensitive. He is caught between the desire for active participation in human affairs, and the desire to escape from contact with the world. This duality is most conveniently managed by the individual developing an art form or 'craft' which presents a way of escape from the world and at the same time employs his vital energies.

In the Paracelsian correspondencies, Fire is associated with Sulphur, Oil, the soul, feeling and energy. Each word is a key to the different sides of the Intuitive temperament.

Fire is attracted to Air, which is its source of oxygen, and which fans it and helps it to spread more quickly. Fire does not like the dry weightiness of Earth which would restrict it; nor does it like Water which would extinguish it. (The photograph at [53] shows the hand of a writer who is married to an Air type.)

Astrologically, Fire is related to Aries, Leo and Sagittarius, who form the Fire triplicity and whose governing planets are Mars, Apollo and Jupiter. The energetic initiative 'battering ram' Aries, so directly incisive, satirical and invective in speech; the powerful organising leadership and self-assurance of Leo, and the intellectual freedom-loving Sagittarius, are all different aspects of the Fiery nature. The manifest energy of Mars reinforces the Arian invective with a belligerence which is often well hidden from the subject himself. Apollo relates to the versatility of Fire, to its many tongues of flame; Apollo is the Sun planet and emphasises the *creativity* of the Intuitive type. The expansive fire of Jupiter leads to a certain opportunism, but accounts for the wish of the Fire type to become a leader in his field. Between them, these factors create a type remarkable both for his diversity of talents and for the quick energy which springs from some deep reservoir of emotions.

Charles Carter writes that the triplicity of Fire: *undoubtedly corresponds to the manifestation of life as an outgoing energy born into the world of nature, and therein seeking to maintain and develop itself, and reap experiences of a positive kind in the field of action.*

In many respects this hand corresponds to the

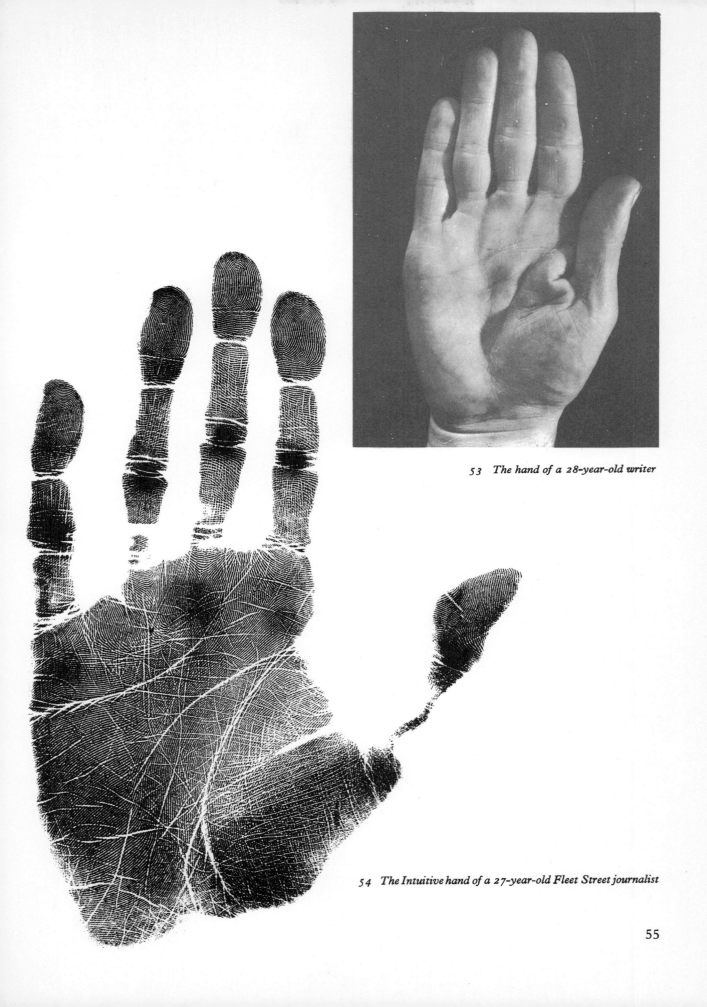

53 *The hand of a 28-year-old writer*

54 *The Intuitive hand of a 27-year-old Fleet Street journalist*

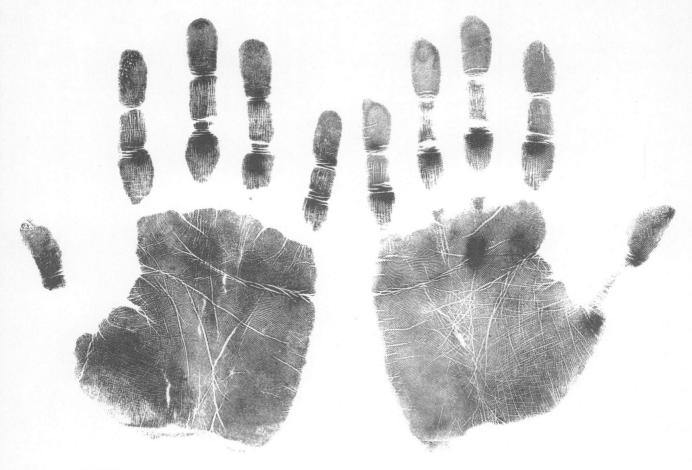

55 The hand of a highly individualistic Fire type

56 The Intuitive hand of a designer

Conic, or artistic hand described by D'Arpentigny, who outlines the type as follows:

> *Inclined to enthusiasm, he will live in constant need of excitement, and the activity of his mind will render domestic life heavy and uninteresting to him. In a word he will be a man of sentiments rather than ideas.*

This type of hand belongs to a 'creative' person, to a designer, a dancer, actor or artist [56], to someone who demands variety of occupation, emotional scope, an outlet for intuition and above all self-expression. The Fire type can range in ability and temperament from the gifted artist both intelligent and versatile to the glib jack-of-all-trades, but the 'quality' of the type can easily be determined from other aspects of the hand.

The short fingers suggest that such an individual will tend to have little care for minutiae, and that his mind will tend to move in wide-sweeping plans rather than in petty concerns. However, I have observed that within the sphere of creativity or self-expression these individuals often exhibit an incredible attention to detail, which they recognise as being essential to their art. Their natural distaste for detail is overcome by their desire to excel in their own particular field; ambition curbs their impatience. In all other matters, such as personal appearance, appointments and method of thinking, little or no attention for detail is found. At best, detail is regarded as a necessary evil, to be avoided wherever possible

One aspect of this repugnance for detail is the type's dislike of problems that cannot be solved quickly. He tends to be impatient of drawn-out arguments, of slow people, and this impatience often reflects itself in his abruptness of action in dealing with people, particularly his subordinates. He prefers to solve problems 'intuitively' rather than intellectually. The Fire type is not disposed naturally either towards physical or purely intellectual pursuits, and the first thing to be established on seeing a Fire hand is to determine the direction and motivation behind the intuitive force, which is bound to be the predominating characteristic.

A very long palm usually indicates a neurotic type. We can understand this to some extent when we try to picture a combination of an excessive development of the lower world, with the natural fire of the type. The conflict between these two opposed directions can only result in neurosis.

The hand at [55] belongs to a highly individual Intuitive type. He is the head of a Design studio, full of an unbounded energy (note the double Life line), widely talented, as the lines of Apollo would suggest, and highly intuitive in his approach to people. The strong line of Mercury, and the lines directly off the mount of Mercury, emphasise his natural ability to respond intuitively, whilst these lines, taken together with the straight, calculating Head line, point to an interesting way of dealing with people. There is a slight inferiority complex shown in the short finger of Jupiter and consequently this highly individualistic person (the five whorls) would shy away from directly dealing with other people. However, the possessive finger of Jupiter, and the line between the Heart and Head show that the natural disposition of the Intuitive type towards ambition is in fact present in this case. In order to achieve his ambitions, which must run, in accordance with his type, in some artistic field, he must deal with people. In order to hide his inferiority feeling, he tends towards undue self-assertion, and he must, in terms of his type, easily become impatient with others. This impatience is given expression in a particularly witty, often brilliant, flow of invective criticism. Such a typically Intuitive way of coping with a basic inferiority feeling is taken lightly by other Fire types, but Earth types will feel scorched, whilst Water types will become uncomfortably hot. Air types will be particularly attracted to him.

In this particular hand the emotional instability, common to a Fire type and clearly manifest in the line of Heart, is counteracted by the strong and sympathetic line of Head.

The Intuitive hand delights in variety. His job of work must have variety, he must have constant

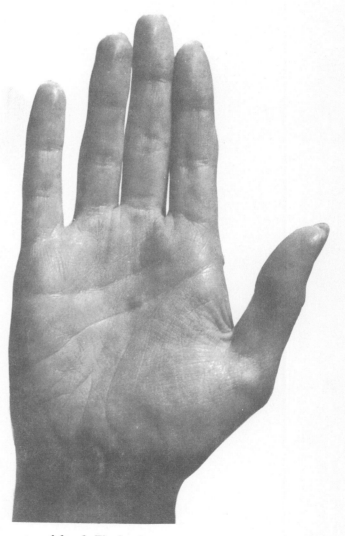

57 *A female Fire hand*

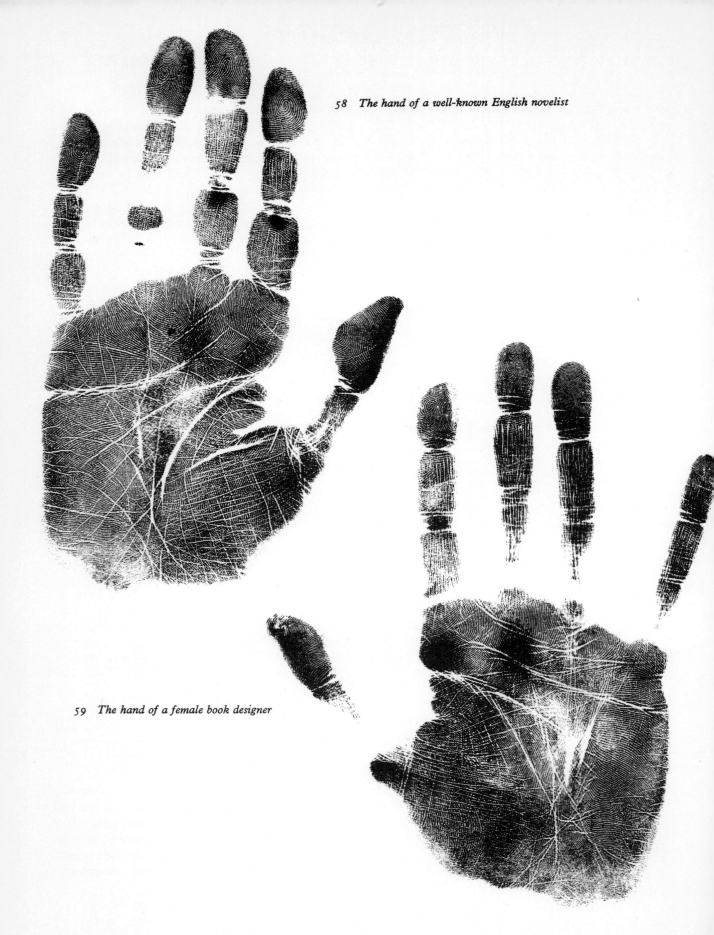

58   *The hand of a well-known English novelist*

59   *The hand of a female book designer*

variety amongst his friends, and tends always to be changing friends, going to parties to meet new people and to establish new contacts. His home life must be filled with variety, and a strong Fire type does not settle down easily to marriage unless a great latitude is allowed by the partner.

Within the general description of an Intuitive type, there falls a wide diversity of types, ranging from the vital, talented artist to the profligate and extravagant criminal. This type of hand, as one might expect from the quality of energy, tends easily towards a neurotic condition resulting from a thwarting of natural tendencies.

Many creative artists have this hand form, particularly those in the field of graphic art. A recent survey of a design studio in the north of England consisting of twelve men and seven women revealed only one hand which could not be ascribed to this type. In general the artist's hand is of the Fire type, with a refined skin texture, a well-developed line of intuition (line of Mercury), several longish lines of Apollo, and whorl-type patterns on the finger-tips. The line of Heart is almost always badly island-ed which, as we shall eventually discover, is signifi-cant of the fire-like quality of this type's emotional energy. It must be clearly understood that the 'artistic' class to which I refer does not necessarily relate to the creative painter. Such individuals often do fit into this class, but mainly they have hands marked-ly degenerate in quality, and they will be dealt with separately. In fact the type of hand which can prop-erly be called Intuitive relates to the less 'creative', but none the less artistic type such as the graphic designer, typographer, visualiser and layout artist. A truly creative hand is often of the complex Earth type.

In an attempt to reach into the individuality of an Intuitive type there are several factors which are particularly worth observing. The girdle of Venus suggests a state of hypersensitivity common to the type. If this is missing or consists only of a short line running through the mount of Saturn, then the basic instability of the Fire type is to some extent mitigated, and the person will tend to be a little more reliable and hence able to accept responsibility more easily than is common to the Intuitive type. A very strong girdle of Venus, or one which is long, broken and many-lined, is a dangerous sign of imbalance in an Intuitive hand.

Fire hands have, as experience will show, a dis-tinctive quality of linear markings. There is normally a unity of liveliness about the lines, and if this is not found on a hand which in other respects belongs to a Fire type, grave complications must be assumed. In a hand with a long palm and short fingers we should expect a lively energy to back its natural ambition and artistic temperament. If the lines are few we can presume this lively energy to be absent, and expect neurotic symptoms resulting from the clash between desires and performance.

Both the lines of Apollo and Mercury have a great modifying effect on the Intuitive hand, but it will be best to examine their roles in relation to the hand type when we actually deal with these lines later on.

The thumb also permits one to determine the character of an Intuitive type more precisely, for the thumb relates to the staying power of an indi-vidual, and the natural enthusiasm of a Fire type without staying power leads to purposelessness. However, a more detailed analysis must be left until later, when we deal with the thumb itself.

The female Intuitive hand [57] is much more commonly found than the female Practical, and for this reason alone one must take pains to distinguish the specific hand traits which single out the indi-viduality of any given person.

In comparison with the male hand there are one or two differences worth noting. As in the case of the female Earth type, there is usually a general rounding of form, though the mount of Moon tends to be low set, and a little more angular. The skin quality is almost the same as the male, though the palmar area is always broken up or 'disturbed' by numerous clear, and often disorderly, lines which emphasise the nervous activity common to the type [58]. The female hand is smaller than the male.

The characteristics of the active, Intuitive male are, in a modified form, present in the female of this hand type. She is full of energy, and possessed of an alert, vibrating emotional life which warms with excite-ment her relationships with other people and her environment. In the home she may be compared to the fire in the hearth which lends warmth and cheer to the room. In her job she will be confident in her own field of work, though tending, like the male type, to be slightly overbearing. Her natural versatility, vitality and emotional scope compensate for any faults.

60 *The hand of a 30-year-old Israeli lady journalist; the intense raying of the lines suggests a restless degree of hyperactivity*

The modifications of the male characteristics are the natural outcome of the female passivity which dampens the exuberance and energy which is so strong in the male, but the female Intuitive is the most active of the four types. Her activity finds its most fitting expression in the home, and her particular enjoyment comes out of 'arranging things' whether it be in the office, where she will make an excellent secretary, or in the home, where tidiness and beauty will be her main joys. Like the male, she loves to be surrounded by beautiful things, and lacking the thriftiness of the Earth type, she tends to have little sense of money values. She might be accused of having expensive tastes, because her love of beauty is not modified by a sense of economy.

Whereas the Earth type will regard the home practically, as a place in which she and her family must live, the Fire type regards the home more personally, as a reflection of herself and of her own personality. Her home, like all her actions and conscious attitudes, must exhibit her own tastes, cultural background and individuality. Thus the positive energy so characteristic of the type is largely expended in making the conditions of life beautiful and pleasing to the senses.

Personal appearance will be regarded from much the same point of view as the home — yet in strict accord with the hasty disregard for detail common to the type. Whilst detail will be ignored, the more 'emotional' and 'sensitive' factors of colour-matching, texture and fashion consciousness will be considered very important. In this way both the desire for attention and for beauty of expression will be satisfied.

Fire types, male or female, tend to be strongly individualistic, and this often quite naturally leads to partner trouble. A Fire hand of either sex must always be examined for signs of such difficulties.

Many female hands of the type do not confine their creativity to the home, but turn towards self-expression in art and literature. The print at [58] is the hand of a well-known English novelist, and that at [59] the print of a highly proficient and gifted book-designer. One can see at a glance that, of the two, the book-designer is the more neurotic: the marked girdle of Venus, the well-defined mount of Moon with its large arched pattern, the individualistic ridge markings on the finger-tips and the broken lines of Head and Heart, point to a highly-strung nervous system which often accompanies the artistic sensitivity.

The fingers, which are quite long for the type, suggest that she will be able to give attention to detail, and that the general impatience with things which is so common to the type will be mitigated to some extent.

Like the male type, the female takes a pride in her own individuality: there is no feeling for a repetitive or uninteresting job. She craves variety in all things, and for this reason does not settle down easily to an uninteresting married life. Ideally she should marry a Fire type of much the same mentality: there will, no doubt, be a danger, speaking figuratively, of an explosion, but even this is more preferable to the type than a mediocre drabness which lacks variety and excitement. Whilst it is entirely satisfactory for a male Intuitive type to marry an Air type, it is not advisable for a strong Intuitive female to marry a male Air type, unless, of course, she finds one who likes the constant excitement and variety she demands. One cannot help feeling that the male should dominate and lead in marriage — at least externally — and the only man capable of leading a female Intuitive type would have to be of the same fiery nature himself. The Fire type of both sexes wants to lead and to 'be the boss' — probably due to a combination of the Jupiterian sense of leadership, the Martian aggressiveness and the strong desire for the recognition of individuality which is found in such a person.

It is interesting to note that Sarah Bernhardt, the famous French actress, was a Fire type. Her hand has been preserved for us by Cheiro in his *Language of the Hand* [61]. The versatility, magnetic personality and boundless energy of the 'divine Sarah' reveals her as an extreme Intuitive type. Although she is chiefly remembered for her versatility as an actress she was a talented artist, a sculptor and writer, playwright and stage director. Widely travelled and widely educated, she was of indomitable courage; even the amputation of a leg in 1915 did not prevent her from appearing on the stage again and again afterwards.

Besides Sarah Bernhardt, several other famous people appear, from their preserved hand-prints, to have been perfect Fire types. They include Sir Edwin Arnold, the British poet and journalist of the last century who worked for over forty years on *The Daily Telegraph*; his most widely known poetical work is *The Light of Asia*. Mark Twain, the American author and humorist, was also a Fire type. Versatility showed through the whole of his life; his various occupations ranged from being a type compositor to piloting steam boats, newspaper reporting, mining and, of course, writing. Mark Twain appears to have been interested in palmistry himself, and it was probably this alone which enabled Cheiro to take a print of his hand.

61 The hand of Sarah Bernhardt, from Cheiro's collection of prints

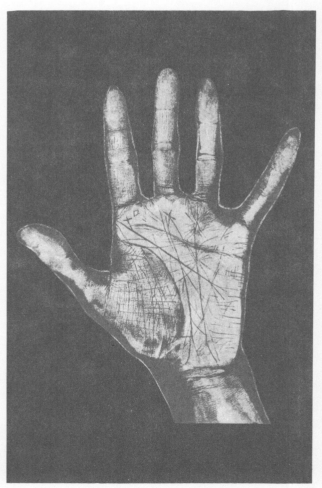

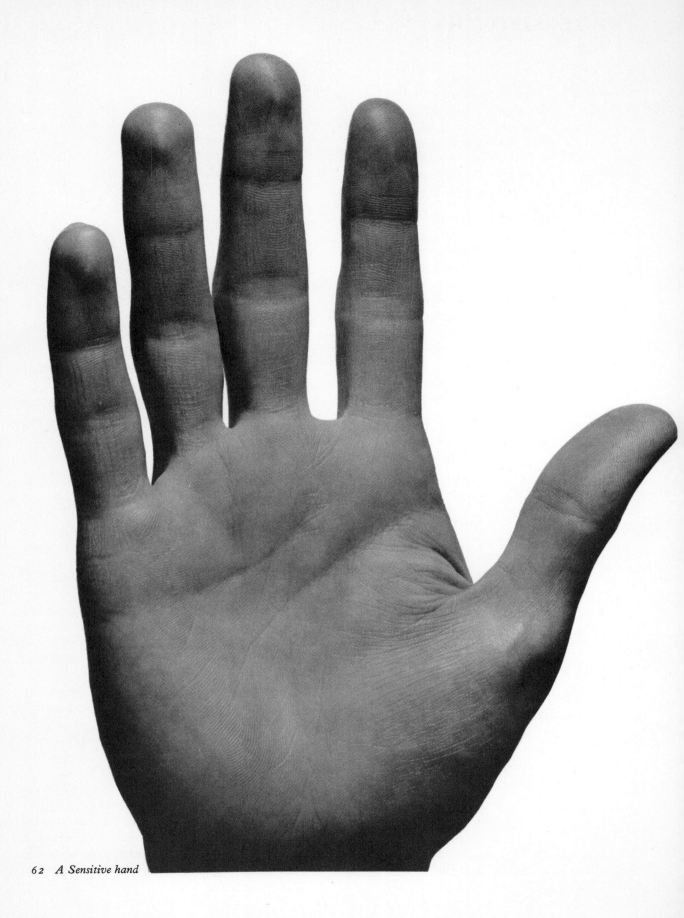

62 *A Sensitive hand*

THE SENSITIVE HAND

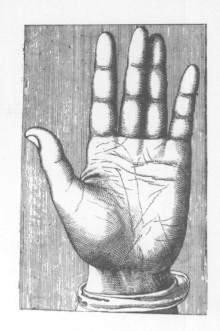

Outwardly Water is volatile, inwardly it is fixed, cold and humid. It is the solvent of the world, and exists in three degrees of excellence: the pure, the purer, and the purest. Of its purest substance the heavens were created; of that which is less pure the atmospheric air was formed; that which is simply pure remains in its proper sphere where it is guardian of all subtle substances here below.

Basil Valentine

The Sensitive hand [62] is distinguished chirognomically by a long palm and long fingers. It is usually soft and flexible: sometimes it may be 'elegantly aristocratic' in appearance, with long, tapering fingers, and a smooth, refined skin. It is often quite narrow, particularly in women. The palmar surface is usually covered with a great number of fine lines [63], with the four principal lines clearly standing out from the rest. The Head line always curves down towards the mount of Moon, indicating the strong imaginative tendencies of the type. This type corresponds to the element of Water. Its symbol is W for the male and W̅ for the female.

Water is fluid, restful if contained, continually seeking to escape yet taking its shape from that of its container. Its surface reflects all around it. Water is deceptive: a calm surface may hide strong undercurrents — a storm may only be surface deep. The sea is often seen as a destructive force in its unpredictability; but its rages are always caused by the other elements, for water is not itself destructive.

These characteristics may, by strict analogy, be seen in certain types of individuals. Such people are passive, emotional, unstable, sensitive, and often given to sullen moods: they find their best expression as 'reflectors' of stronger personalities, for they have a strong need to feel 'contained'. On a level of individual relationships a Water type will need to be dominated, to be controlled by others more active than himself. His surface life, so much a reflection of others, will be less meaningful to him than his deeper, subconscious life with which he is in close

contact. For this reason he gives other people the impression that he is 'dreamy'.

With this close relationship to his deeper levels, and with his natural sensitivity and strong intuition, he is highly introverted, secret and sealed up within himself. No one can ever reach into him, and he often gives the impression of being 'cold'.

Like the Intuitive type, he is a child of the emotions. The difference between them is the difference between activity and passivity. The emotions of the Intuitive type are always alive, moving, investigating and enthusiastic — in a word, they *act* upon life. The emotions of the Sensitive type are always less active, introspective, protective, secretive and lassitudinous — they are *acted* upon by life.

A Sensitive type, as his name suggests, is always impressionable: his surface moods are constantly being changed by changing conditions, and, like water, he is always flowing and never constant. The feminine principle of *receptivity* is largely the cause of this constant flux of moods. It might be well argued that all types are changeable and depend on their environment for their particular manifestations, because the inability to change and to adapt can only mean an inability to live. This is true, but a Water type is particularly changeable and fluid, having none of the stability of Earth, none of the ambition of Fire, and none of the intellect of Air to keep him on a set course of action. Whereas the Fire type is constantly changing because of the energies which are forcing their way through his body, the Water type is constantly changing because external

63 *A male Water hand; the chief interests of this 30-year-old man are astrology and religious theory*

energies are forcing their way into him.

It will be seen from these considerations that the environment in which the Sensitive type lives is of the utmost importance. A calm and peaceful environment is essential to his emotional balance and stability, but even in relatively settled conditions he is easily upset emotionally.

Astrologically Water is related to Cancer, Scorpio and Pisces, who form the Water triplicity, and whose governing planets are the Moon, Jupiter and Mars. Certain modern schools of astrology suggest that Pisces is governed by Neptune and not Jupiter, and that Pluto, rather than Mars, governs Scorpio. The sensitive and protective Cancer, the emotional and deeply penetrating Scorpio, and the idealistic and 'confused' Pisces, are all different aspects of the Watery nature. The fluctuating Moon, with her reflected light and her traditional link with femininity, the impressionability of Neptune, and the capacity for regeneration of Pluto, emphasise both the changeability and receptivity of the type.

In astrology the Fourth and Twelfth houses, which are Water houses governed by Moon and Neptune respectively, represent places of retirement and escape. The Fourth house represents the home, the womb and the grave in particular, and anything which surrounds and protects in general. The Twelfth house refers to the retirement into the inner being, into the subconscious and the psychic sensibility; it also refers to hospitals, prisons and asylums, and was at one time called 'the house of sorrows'. All these astrological considerations emphasise the Water tendency to 'escape' and to seek protection from the outside world. Each Water type will seek to escape from life in terms of his own particular strengths and weaknesses — these must be determined from other chirognomical factors.

A girdle of Venus must be regarded as deepening the desire to escape and the wish to live in fantasy. This hand corresponds to the Psychic hand which, Carus claimed, when found on a man is a sure indication of a strong tendency to femininity.

The Water type is predominantly imaginative, 'the reason being', Carter writes, 'that its natural

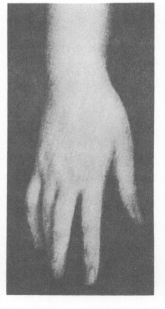

64 Far left: *The hand of a wooden statue from Easter Island*

65 Left: *The hand of Lady Rich from Van Dyck's portrait in the National Gallery, by permission of Lady Lucas; clearly a Water hand in form and posture*

reserve and caution check freedom of action in the outer world, and so drive it back upon itself and its own resources'.

This imagination allied to extreme sensitivity enables the type to be a sympathetic friend, instinctively feeling the need in another for protection, and being drawn by this need to help.

Strong imagination and a desire to escape from life results in the dreamer, the subjective and unproductive individual who passes most of his waking life in the clouds. His method of thinking, if it can be called thinking, is of an extremely passive nature — 'fantasy-thinking', as Jung called it:

We have . . . two kinds of thinking: directed thinking, and dreaming or fantasy thinking. The former operates with speech elements for the purpose of communication, and is difficult and exhausting; the latter is effortless, working, as it were, spontaneously, with the contents ready to hand, and guided by unconscious

motives. The one produces innovations and adaptation copies reality, and tries to act it; the other turns away from reality, sets free subjective tendencies, and, as regards adaptation, is unproductive.

Jung's comments throw much light on the temperament of the type, the connection with the subconscious (in dreams and fantasy the sea or a large expanse of water signifies the subconscious mind — which is chirognomically expressed by the mount of Moon), the escapist attitude to real situations and relationships which leads inexorably to a schizoid personality. The type is not talkative by nature, being so immersed in dreams, but conversation is always emotion — he will say 'I feel' rather than 'I think' — and the matter tends to be unrelated to 'truth'.

The Water type often gives the impression of being a liar. He is so lost in his own web of day dreams that it is impossible for him to know what 'truth' is. It is here that Neptune's power is most clearly seen; the intangible is often more real than the tangible. What may appear to be a clear-cut issue to an Earth type may well be a complex and ill-defined issue to the mind of a Water type. He sees things more deeply than the other types, and consequently things are not quite so simple for him.

Inspiration, direct contact with subconscious workings of the mind, is one of the chief characteristics of the Sensitive type, and although the natural laziness is usually too strong to permit active creativity, a Water type may sufficiently rise above his nature to be productive. However, since the type is essentially passive and uncreative in the sense that he does not act on life, it is best to think of the pure type as merely the dreamer, the creator of imagined

66 *A female Water hand; the sensitive mesh of fine lines, and the gentle curve of the Head line towards the mount of Moon, are typical of this type*

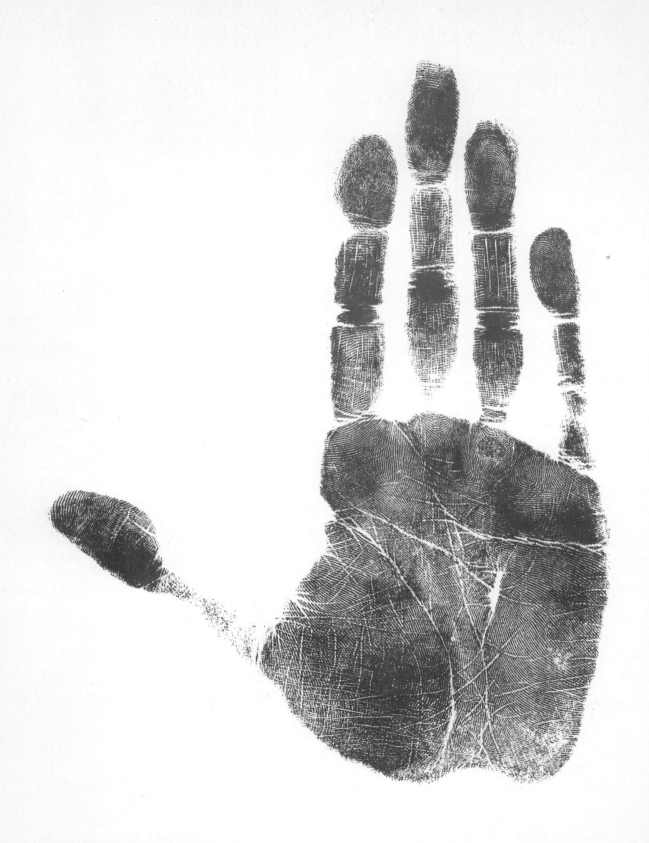

67 *The female Water hand of a 22-year-old nurse*

Utopias, fine deeds and mental acts of greatness.

Water types do not get on well with Fire types, whom they find too 'hot' and too active — Water does not want to boil, and thus to lose its own nature. Nor does the element like Air, for it is too 'dry' and absorbs water in evaporation. Earth, however, offers a resting place for Water, it contains it, gives it shape and form.

Of the four types, the Sensitive hand is the least adapted to the business of living life. It cannot come to grips with life because its whole nature compels it to flee from reality into dreams. It is not adaptable in itself, but the highly adaptable surface life of the personality changes rapidly and sufficiently well to enable a contact with life to be simulated, and this in itself is sufficient to prevent too much friction between the person and society. There can be no real friction simply because there is no real contact: the Water type, in his pure form, is too immersed in dreams to have contact with life — he is rather like a skin-diver happily exploring the rocks and pebbles at the bottom of the ocean, oblivious of what is going on in the world above the waves.

The print at [68] shows the hand of a Greek small-part actor who lives in Paris. He very rarely has any work to do, and how he keeps alive is a wonder to all his friends. He is highly imaginative, full of an inner lethargy, and is in constant difficulties owing to his egocentric and highly unreal attitude to life. He is sufficiently intelligent to realise that he is 'drifting through life', but he says that there is some force which keeps him on this course. The force is, one can be sure, his passivity which is constantly fed by his strong imagination.

As I have already remarked, the Sensitive hand is essentially feminine — it plays a passive role in life, taking its form and energy from its surroundings. 'The maternal significance of water', wrote Jung, 'is one of the clearest interpretations of symbols in the whole field of mythology.'

The female hand is generally thinner than the male. It usually exhibits the roundness of form and softness of texture so characteristic of the female hand. The skin texture shown in a print is delicate but the whole of the surface is covered with numerous fine 'nervous' lines. Often a very high degree of flexibility is found in the hand as a whole. The female hand is smaller than the male, but because of its narrowness it often gives the impression of being very long. She

68   *The hand of a young part-time actor*

is essentially a reflector on a superficial personality level, but beneath the surface she is 'deep'. She makes an excellent wife by virtue of her ability to put herself in another person's place and thus to be sympathetic; we must not forget that the Fourth house of astrology, governed by the Moon, is the house relating to the home and the womb, where protection from the world is possible.

In the home, comfort and ease of living will be her main aim and, given a pleasantly quiet and undisturbed home life, she will lead a peaceful and inactive life. She will worry a great deal, as her overactive imagination will seize at every little daily

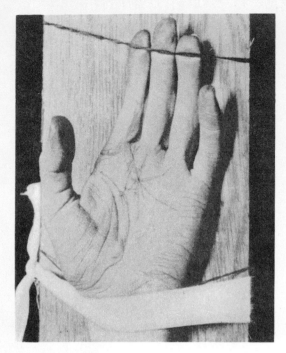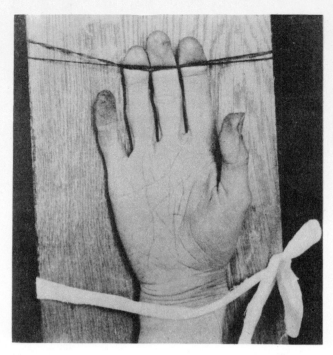

69 The Chittenden Hotel Suicide (from The Laws of Scientific Hand Reading *by William G. Benham, 1902)*

event and magnify it beyond all proportion. She may, for example, worry a great deal about her own passivity, her reluctance to start the daily round of keeping the house clean.

The happiness and personal well-being of the female Water type will depend almost completely on her relationship with her husband: she will reflect his moods, his anxieties, even his activity. The main demand she will make of marriage is to feel wanted, that her sensitive and protective nature is appreciated by her husband and family. The Water type is not at all independent, and she is always prepared to submerge her own individuality in the cause of harmony or unison.

Long fingers suggest that she will not easily become impatient when dealing with minutiae. She is not like the Earth type in demanding repetitive work, nor is she like the Fire type with a desire for variety. Her wish is more for an occupation in which her love for quiet slowness and her imagination can play an important part. She will be fond of poetry or music of a 'reflective' kind which appeals to the imagination, and which the active Fire type would find boring, sentimental or merely lethargic. She will enjoy the theatre and cinema particularly, because this creates an opportunity to remain passive and to be stimulated with relatively little effort.

Two historic examples of this hand type represent between them the opposite poles of Watery 'escapism'. The hands of the Chittenden Hotel Suicide [69]

are markedly Watery hands which show complete instability. Benham, who reproduced a photograph of both left and right hands in his book, has the following to say:

In November, 1898 a well-dressed, fine-looking woman came to the Chittenden Hotel, engaged a room for a few days, absolutely destroyed every clue to her identity, and killed herself. She took an enormous dose of morphine, supposedly to deaden the pain of the carbolic acid with which she completed her destruction. Her only request was for a respectable burial, to pay for which she left one hundred and fifty dollars in her purse. She lay for ten days at the morgue, her picture was printed all over the United States, but she was never identified. The pictures of her hand were taken the day before the burial. The Life line shows a most remarkable confirmation of her death. The hand also shows the diseases which produce the mental condition necessary for the act.

The *Praying Hands* [70] of Albrecht Dürer, in the Albertina, are of the Sensitive kind. Dürer was one of the truly great artists who understood the emotional and intellectual meaning of hands: there is not one picture by him which does not show an acute understanding of the human hand. His was a time when palmistry was at its height, and it is safe to assume that this understanding was consciously expressed in his art. His *Praying Hands* is the archetype of a Sensitive hand manifesting the link between subconscious needs and the religious impulse.

70 The Praying Hands *by Dürer in the Albertina, Vienna*

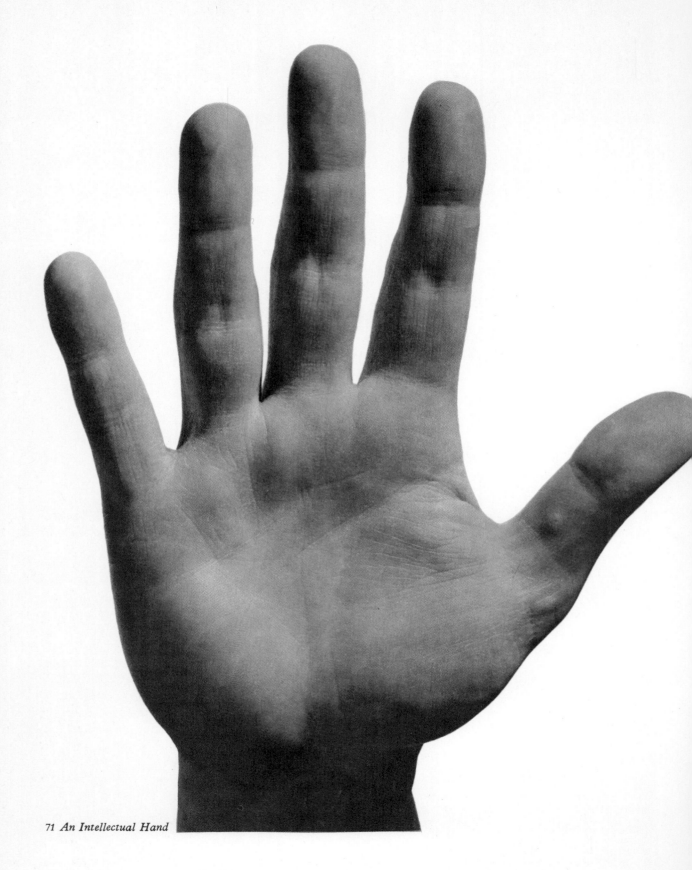

71 *An Intellectual Hand*

THE INTELLECTUAL HAND

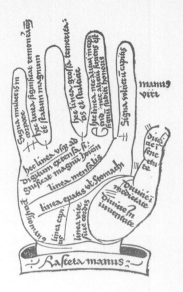

The most noble Element of Air is volatile, but may be fixed, and when fixed renders all bodies penetrable. It is nobler than Earth or Water. It nourishes, impregnates, conserves the other elements.

Basil Valentine

The Intellectual hand [71] is distinguished chirognomically by a square palm and long fingers. It is usually flexible, and in a print has characteristically spread-out fingers. The skin texture is usually very fine. The masculine hand is always large, with thick, though delicate fingers, whilst the feminine hand is small, with delicate long fingers. The lines of the hand [73] have a definitely healthy feeling about them, and little of the neurotic feeling of the Water or Fire types will be seen. The thumb is long and strong.

The long fingers and refined skin suggest that the type is an evolved Earth — that is, that the basic Earth qualities have been refined by intellect to produce a higher type of man. This type of hand pertains to the element of Air. Its symbol is ♂ for the male and ♀ for the female.

Air is essential to communication: it carries speech from one individual to another, enabling the highly complex system of communication which is so characteristic of the human race. Air is free, not contained, and easily moved. Without air no life on Earth could be possible.

The characteristics of Air, chiefly relating to communication, may by strict analogy be seen in certain types of individuality. Such people lead lives which stress, in one way or another, the art of communication: they tend to be intellectual, and they tend to express themselves in terms of thought. They like to be free, and in their movement they wish to 'connect' things, places, and ideas. They have an innate distrust of emotions.

Air is very adaptable and an Intellectual type will, within the field of thought and communication, be able to move easily from one job to another. Whereas the Intuitive Fire type tends to be versatile emotionally and is often intellectually superficial, the Air type will be versatile intellectually and is often emotionally superficial. He tends to be too much bound up with the intellect, and may be described at times as 'having his head in the clouds of theory' — a very different thing from the dreaminess of the Water type.

One great characteristic of the type is the wish for order: in every activity or situation he will attempt to establish order, which is, after all, a prelude to exact communication. In society, in the realm of politics, he will attempt to establish his own sense of order, categorising intellectually and often making the mistake of not taking the emotions into account. His theories have a certain 'dryness' about them, and it is this dryness or abstractness which makes many of his theories unworkable.

As one would expect in a person with long fingers, infinite patience and attendance to detail will back his attempts to communicate ideas. The softness of the hand parallels the softness of his nature, and he will rarely be belligerent about his ideas — for this would be to let sentiment and emotion take the place of reason. He is, therefore, a very gentle person, preferring a quiet though active life to the constant excitement and change of the Fire type.

In the ancient tradition Air is moist and hot, and therefore of a sanguine disposition. This connection with blood emphasises the healthy energy which accompanies the type. To Paracelsus Fire and Air were closely connected, and found their closest connection in this strong energy. The difference between the types corresponds to the different uses to which they direct their energies: speaking broadly the Fire type directs his energies towards self-expression, and the Air type directs his energies towards communication.

Air is attracted to Fire, which gives it added life by virtue of its heat. It does not like to be wet by Water which represents undisciplined, unordered emotions and sentimentality. Nor does it feel attracted to drying Earth, which would slow down communication and reduce its thinking to mere pedantry.

This type of Hand is most often found on a person who delights in intellectual work, in theories, and in organisation. He must work within a sphere where his originality and love for freedom are given expression. He is a lover of problems, finding actual enjoyment in the unravelling of complicated knots and improving relationships between people. One would expect the type to be best represented by a good public relations officer, or some other person whose job deals with communication between people. Print [73] shows the hand of a p.r.o. of one of the largest industrial concerns in Great Britain.

Astrologically, Air is related to Gemini, Libra and Aquarius who form the Air triplicity and whose governing planets are Mercury, Venus and Saturn. Certain modern schools suggest that Aquarius is governed by Uranus and not by Saturn. The quick-witted, intelligent, versatile and inquisitive Gemini, the companionable and attractive Libra, and the original-minded, independent and freedom-loving Aquarius, are all different aspects of the Airy nature. The quickness of Mercury (the gods' messenger), and the temperance and harmony of Venus, linked by tradition with Saturn, indicate how closely the triplicity resembles the Earth type, and how conveniently the Air type might be regarded as being a refined and evolved Practical type. Uranus is generally regarded as the planet of disruptive change, and this adds an element of rebellious freedom to the type which often springs from originality of thought. It is interesting to observe that, as Hone pointed out, the symbol for Uranus is almost the shape of the

H television aerial, the perfect example of advanced communication, and a reminder that communication can be for the good or bad of civilisation.

The word 'Intellectual' comes from the latin *intellectus* which connoted perception, discernment, the ability to perceive objects in their relations. To choose between things, to discriminate, is the specific function of the mind and, provided that the emotions are kept in check, there is a certain objectivity, a certain dispassion in the activity. This is the function of the Air type, who acts as an intermediary between two parties, whether they be two ideas which must be related to produce a third or two people who must be related in order to create understanding between them. It is this connotation of the word 'intellectual' which is applicable to the Air type. Mere intellectualism, without any attempt to relate ideas or things, and with little regard for order, does not represent the Airy temperament.

The Air triplicity governs the Third, Seventh and Eleventh houses of astrology. The Third house relates to communications, particularly to mental communications, such as writing and reporting. The Seventh house refers to relationships with other people; the role of communication in such a house is self-evident. The Eleventh house relates to distant connections and interests — groups of people in clubs and societies — in fact any group of people with a set plan and purpose in view. Part of the 'orderliness' of the Air type demands that his viewpoints be regularised and set down in some form of credo. His desire to propagate his ideas leads him to seek the company of others with similar credos so that an organised dissemination of ideas may be facilitated. Air types often like to belong to clubs and societies.

In his attitude to Nature and the world around him an Air type exhibits a healthy curiosity. 'Nature is perceived as something to be understood,' writes Carter of the Air type, 'as well as utilised, the understanding being the condition for its complete utilisation. Hence the joint rulership of Mercury, Venus and Saturn over the Earth and Air Triplicities.'

In comparison with the male hand, the female hand [74] shows one or two differences worth noting. The hand is not only smaller in size, but 'lighter' in feeling. There is the 'rounding' of forms which we find in all female hands. Perhaps the chief characteristic, however, is the smooth long fingers,

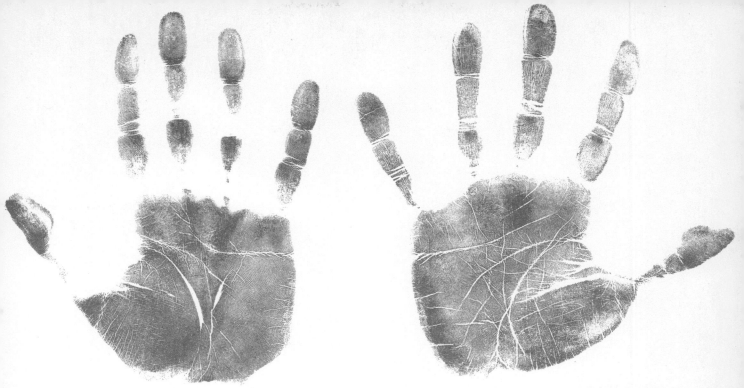

72 *The Air hand of a French psychology student, who is doing research into the symbolism of language*

73 *The hand of a public relations officer of a large industrial concern; the widely spread fingers, and the general roundness of the whole hand, are typical of the Intellectual type*

74 *The hand of a 23-year-old pianist*

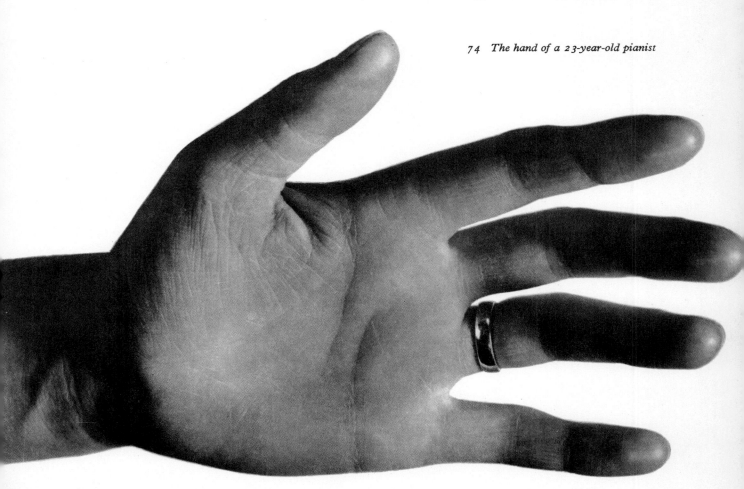

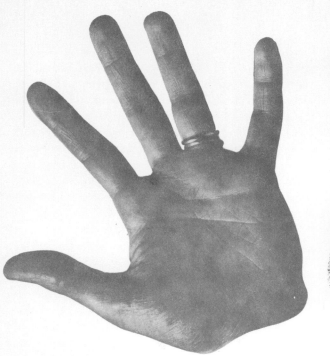

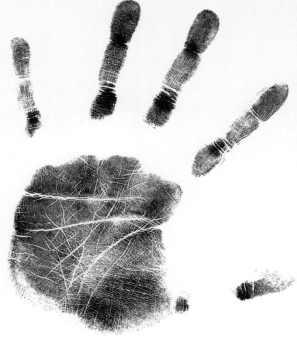

75 *Photograph and print of the Air hand of a young fashion editor*

76 *Detail from Caracci's* The Dead Christ Mourned *in* The National Gallery, London; *a fair example of the Air hand*

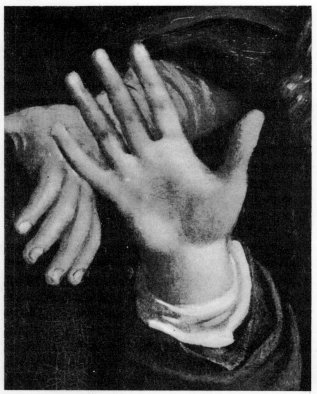

which are usually printed open, giving the impression that the hand would fit in a circle. The beauty and harmony of the hand form is the perfect external sign of the internal beauty and harmony.

The female Air type, like the female Earth type, finds her best expression as a subject of Venus, the planet of Harmony and Relatedness. Venusians are adaptable, tending towards arty-crafty. The wish to communicate often takes the female out of the home into some job where her intellect and versatility may be utilised. The hand at [75] is that of a young lady who is a Fleet Street journalist.

Like the male type, she will be original in thought, and though not as emotionally deep as the Fire type she will have a woman's intuitive understanding of relationships and people to complement her natural thoughtfulness. With Venus strong she will be more sympathetic than the male who, as we have already observed, tends to be scornful of sentiment.

A girl with an Air hand would do well to marry an Air male; both being orientated towards the establishing of good relationships, harmony and peace would be the result. Marriage with a Fire type is a little more precarious, a little more exciting and lively, and she, with her natural open-heartedness and desire for peace, will be prepared to play second role to her more active husband. A marriage will tend to tie her down unless she can carry on working in a job which favours her independence of spirit and originality of mind.

SUMMARY

A completely pure hand type in terms of the preceding classification is, of course, quite impossible. Every person contains within himself a little of each element, and it is the palmist's task to determine the exact proportions of this mixture in each case before moving on to analyse the more specific indications of character afforded by the individual aspects of the hand.

After a little experience it becomes much easier to establish the predominating characteristics by judicial combination of hand factors. One may, for example, find a hand which should be placed in the Fire category in view of measurement, but by virtue of its softness and flexibility may be more usefully classified as a Water hand. Only experience can enable one to sort out such difficulties. In that particular example, where there is a clash between two opposed elements, one can be assured that the person's life would be completely unbalanced and this lack of balance, resulting in a rapidly changing emotional life, would be the chief characteristic of the person's temperament. Such extreme cases are rare, however, and it is more difficult to determine the presence of other elemental characteristics in a hand which is predominantly of one type. The most common thing is to find a definite hand type with the wrong linear characteristics: one might, for example, discover an Air type with the simple lines more proper to the Earth type. In such a case, much care must be taken in order to establish the precise point at which the natural frank openness of the Air type will be affected by the suspicious, rather jealous and practical nature of the Earth type.

Palmistry is so much a matter of combination that a series of twenty volumes would not suffice to indicate the possible combinations of the subtleties involved. The past few pages contain sufficient material for ordinary practical purposes, however, and as one's experience widens, one's understanding of the interplay of forms becomes more complete.

77 Detail from Rijmerswaele's Two Excisemen *in the National Gallery, London*

78 *The zodiac superimposed on the human hand to show something of the relationship between astrology and palmistry*

76

THE FINGERS

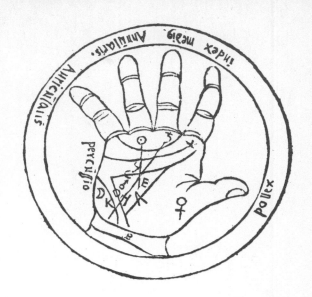

The realm of the fingers is that of differentiation. Their significance is that of aim, of aspiration, of willed and conscious action, and these of a personal quality which rises above the merely instinctive levels.

von Mangoldt

Whereas the general hand formation marks out the class of the individual's mental, emotional and instinctive life, the fingers, comprising the first or spiritual world of palmistry, mark out those factors which make him unique as an individual. Because of this a careful examination of the fingers in terms of the basic hand types can reveal more about the subject than any other aspect of the hand.

It is not wise to generalise too broadly about the hand as a whole, still less about the individual fingers. Those systems of traditional palmistry which strictly classify types of fingers are not very convincing, but within limits the following *dicta* may be held to be true. Long fingers are a sign of patience, and love of detail; short fingers indicate impatience and reliance on intuition. Thick fingers have a taste for 'wordly pleasures' and luxury, whilst thin fingers tend to be more removed from the world, more 'idealistic'. Knotty fingers, as I observed earlier, confer exactness of method to understanding, whilst smooth fingers suggest a highly developed intuitive ability.

In the tradition, pointed fingers are supposed to suggest imagination, square fingers positivism. This kind of generalisation leads nowhere. Each of the five fingers has its own particular ending, and it is only when there is some excessive deviation from the normal that a serious investigation is worth while.

The thumb is, quixotically enough, a finger; though as Benham put it, 'the thumb cannot be called a finger, because it is infinitely more'. Its

significance in relation to man's position in the evolutionary chart is almost inconceivable. Something of its importance can be grasped from the ancient practice of conquering kings who used to cut off the thumbs of their princely captives and thus reduce those who were once so high to a grovelling state lower than that of a beggar.

The thumb and the index finger between them dominate that quarter of the hand which I related to 'the externally directed factors of an active and specifically human nature'.

If one imagines the hand as a miniature zodiac [78] (and this, I believe, was how palmistry attained its present pregnant nomenclature), one finds some very interesting correlations. The thumb would lie in the First house, the place of the individual, his self-interest and position in life. The finger of Jupiter would lie between the Eleventh house, the place of detached contacts, aspirations and life aims, and the Tenth house, the place of honours, ambitions and morality, sometimes called 'the house of careers'. The finger of Saturn would lie between the Tenth house and the Ninth, which is the house of philosophy, journeys and deep mental activity. The finger of Apollo would lie between the Ninth house and the Eighth, the houses of feelings and possessions. The finger of Mercury would lie between the Eighth and Seventh houses, the place of marriage, sex and close relationships. The astrological connotations achieved in this way are a perfect summary of the significance which may be attributed to each finger.

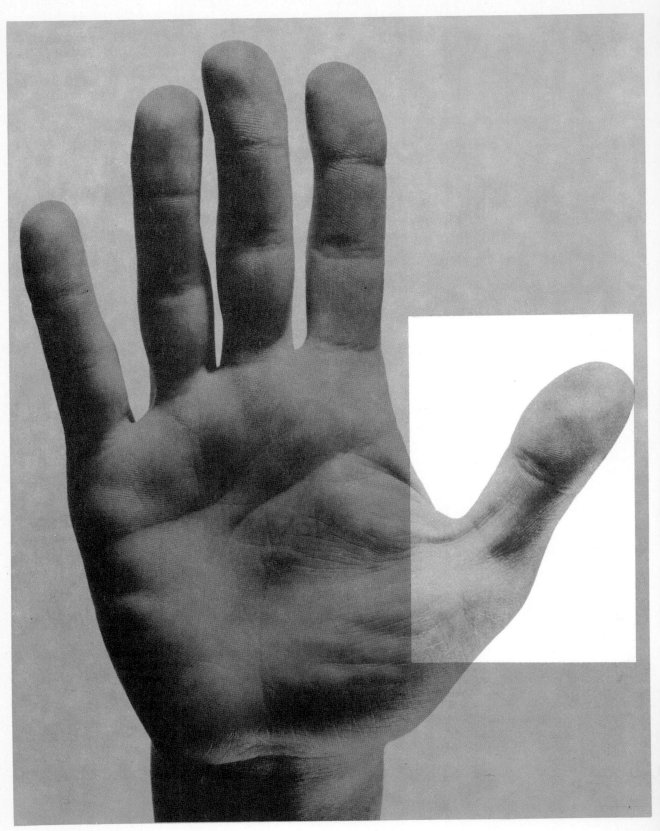

79 *A strong nail phalange on the thumb*

THE THUMB

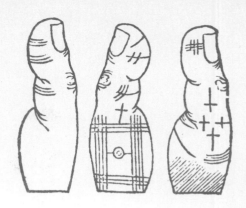

*Have you a thumb large and overbearing; on the
contrary, you belong to yourself, and you have then, as
Henry IV said, 'only a foolish master'.*

Craig (*1867*)

The thumb is located on that side of the hand which
relates to conscious life, and is in itself representative
of the life-force, of vitality and energy.

The importance of the thumb chirognomically is
perhaps best illustrated by the fact that certain Hindu
palmists restrict themselves to the thumb alone when
making their observations and predictions. Benham,
who wrote the most exhaustive study of the thumb
in print, claims that 'the Chinese have a most minute
and intricate system based solely on the capillaries of
the first phalanx; and all gypsies use the thumb for
a large part of their chirognomic work'. The range
and dexterity which its anatomy affords cannot be
overstressed: it is a peculiarly human feature, which
governs to an enormous degree the form of our
external lives. 'The hand,' says D'Arpentigny, 'denotes the superior animal, but it is the thumb which
individualises the Man.' Newton, who in common
with Danton, Descartes, Leibnitz and Voltaire, is
said to have had enormous thumbs, remarked: 'In
want of other proofs, the thumb would convince me
of the existence of a god.'

It is hardly surprising that the thumb, so intimately
connected with the externals of our life, should represent that quality and quantity of energy which we
divert towards that life. Babies, cretins and people
under certain types of severe emotional disturbance
hide their thumbs in their clenched fists; they are in a
state of mind where they are incapable of dealing
with, and thus controlling, their lives. All the
external characteristics of the thumb are worthy of
attention and, properly interpreted (particularly in
conjunction with the finger of Jupiter), will give an
indication of how the individual relates himself to
the external world, which is in itself a clue to his
hidden psychological workings. Not only the size,
shape and strength of the thumb, but also the more
abstract qualities of 'vitality' and 'expression', must
be taken into account before valid judgments can
be made.

As a whole, the size of the thumb is an index of the
basic energy of the individual, whilst the two phalanges reveal the manner in which this energy is
used. D'Arpentigny claimed that the thumb was
'an index of talent or genius', and most certainly a
large thumb is found on the hands of individuals
manifesting a special adaptability in relation to life.
A large thumb is a capable thumb, which reveals not
only a deep well-spring of energy, but also a forceful
personality. 'So in taking hold of a hand and finding
a large thumb you will know that strength and head
guide the subject, and that something pronounced
may be expected.'

Structurally the thumb is divided into three parts
— the first, or nail phalange, which is traditionally
called the phalange of Will; the second phalange,
called the phalange of Logic; and the bottom part,
the root or ball of the thumb, which is called the
mount of Venus. This last part will be dealt with
in the next section, for it bears quite a different interpretation from the rest of the thumb, and must
consequently be treated separately.

The nail phalange, which is traditionally linked
with the will power of the individual, reveals the

DE MONTIBVS DIGITORVM SIVE EO.
rum radicibus atque de ipſis digitis, & primò de pollice &
eius monte, quem Veteres Veneri dicatum voluere,
CAPVT XIII.

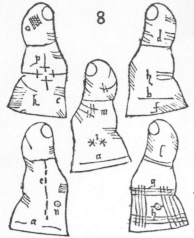

8

VBI habundè ſatis de literis diuinis & de characteribus, qui in montibus planetarum aliquã do inueniri poſſunt, tractatum eſt: ad digitos nũc meritò pro cedendum eſt, qui etiam ſuos particulares habent characte res, & de eorum ſignificatio nibus dicendum reſtat. Et pri mò de pollice, qui eſt dictus di gitus Veneris, eò quod monti Veneris ſupereminet, qui ſi ſit colore viuo, et rubenti benè diſ poſitus, bonam corporis quali tatem notat, & mulierũ ama torem oſtendit hominem, ve ſtitus pulchros appetentem, & munditijs ſtudentem. Quod ſi in eo breuiuſcula alia linea, ſecundum vit.æ lineam rectè diuoluatur, vt in li tera A quæ vitalis ſoror dicitur, ſignum eſt, hominem Venereis oblectari, per petuis diuitijs habundãtẽ, & quo longior ſine abruptione vitalem comitetur, eò melior, etiam ſi à ſummo tubere non incipiat, ſed fortè in medio, vt litera B aut non longè ab imo, tenuitatem quidem rerum in prima ætate, in ſequentibus E 2 copi-

quantity of energy at his disposal and the manner in which this energy is directed towards the external world.

A narrow, pointed phalange of Will indicates that the energy runs freely from the subject, perhaps too freely, and that he has a certain lack of staying power. Such a phalange betrays want of decision and a tendency to procrastination: in other words, the energy of such a thumb is poorly directed, vacillatory in quality and insufficient in quantity. A hand with a very weak phalange of Will [83] must be examined further in order to determine the cause of the maldirection of energy: quite often an inferiority complex, possibly brought on by parental over-indulgence, is the root cause.

A strong nail phalange [79] indicates a good clear passage of energy towards external life, in which

80 *Thumbs from Taisnier's* Opus Mathematicus

81 *A strong thumb; this is the hand of a man who, purely by his own efforts, has become a millionaire*

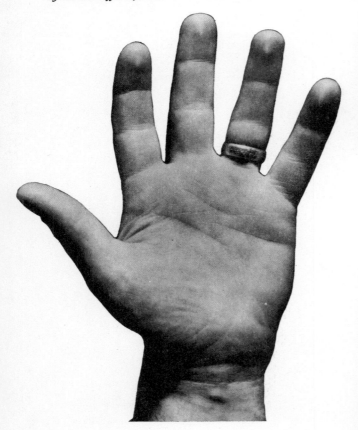

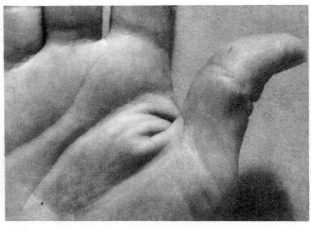

82 *An impulsive type of thumb*

83 *A weak thumb, typical of the Sensitive hand*

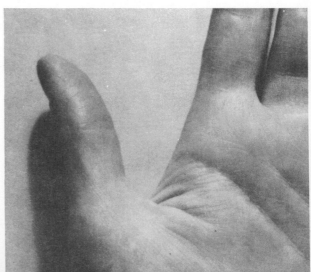

staying power is good. There is a tendency to translate all thoughts into immediate action — particularly when the phalange of Logic is thin or waisted, in which case a rash impulsiveness is revealed. [84] shows the hand of a writer with a well-developed thumb with a large Will phalange. He is compelled by a need to translate his thoughts into immediate action which often leads to his getting up in the middle of the night to put down his ideas: the generation of his energy is not even, and consequently he is a victim of insomnia. The indications of impulsiveness (note the thin phalange of Logic) is completely borne out by his life: he finds it almost impossible to organise himself or to be systematic over long periods, so that his life, work and financial position are constantly endangered by passing whims and fancies. The phalange of Will in photograph [87] is less developed: it is the hand of an engineer who is most careful and systematic in his approach to life: the application of his energy is infinitely more controlled, more evenly applied, than in the last case, and consequently his life is less subject to the bursts of energy which characterise the creativity of the writer's hand.

A deformed Will phalange is the so-called 'murderer's thumb', a bulbous Will phalange which gives the thumb a clubbed appearance [88]. If we bear in mind that this phalange represents vitality we can easily imagine the damming up of energies, and the tendency of the owner to lose his temper when some external stimulus causes the energy to flood out. This thumb marking, which is certainly atavistic, is characteristic of the criminal type in whose life violence and sudden, unexpected outpouring of uncontrolled energy play a predominant role.

Benham uses an extreme form of the clubbed thumb as an illustration of the type. He points out that the father of the subject was a sailor, who in a fit of drunken rage had beaten a companion to such a state of insensibility that he thought he had killed him. He escaped home to his wife, and that same night they conceived the child with the malformed 'murderer's thumb'. Thus, we can see that the clubbed thumb can be an atavistic sign: in almost all the instances where I have seen such a thumb in a non-criminal type there has been either a marked tendency towards infantilism, or degeneracy. The youthful self-portrait by Dürer, in the Louvre, shows that he had a markedly clubbed thumb.

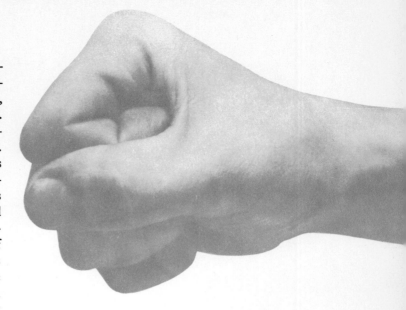

84   The hand of a writer with a strong thumb

85   A thick second phalange on the thumb of an eight-year-old girl

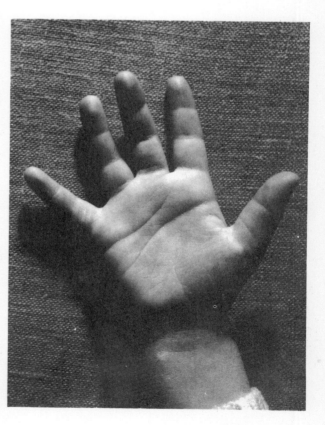

86 *Dürer as a young man; a self-portrait painted in 1493,*
in the Louvre

The thumb at [49] is from the hand of a young female student of psychology at London University. Although her thumb is of the typical clubbed type, she is neither given to tempers nor violence of any kind. Certainly her present mode of living suggests that her life energies are not flowing harmoniously, and she has a distinctly involutionary trend towards infantilism. Almost any atavistic sign, like the clubbed thumb or the simian insertion of a thumb is, *by itself* and unaccompanied by other regressive signs, an indication that there is a strong involutory trend in that person's life. However, it is worth noting that a clubbed thumb in a coarse Practical hand is a sign of degeneracy sufficient to suggest a strong, violent and uncontrollable temper. We shall discuss this aspect of palmistry in greater detail in the section on the simian line.

Reasoning power is traditionally ascribed to the second phalange, the phalange of Logic, as it is called. A large, thick Logic phalange suggests that the subject will think carefully before acting, for such a marking indicates the degree of control over the manifestations of life energy. A well-balanced thumb, with the two phalanges of equal length and thickness, will suggest a person given to careful consideration of action, and one unlikely to act too hastily. A phalange of Logic too long will tend to kill action, the more so if the top phalange is weak in appearance.

An entertaining illustration of how different attitudes, dependent on life energies, manifest themselves can be seen from the hands at [84] and [87] already discussed. The subjects are close friends, and I was amused to see how they both went about the business of buying a tape recorder. The writer [84] had vaguely felt the need for a tape recorder himself, but had never really been able to afford a good one — until his wife said that she wanted one for her birthday. Instantly, without reflection as to the financial outcome of his purchase, he went out and bought a very expensive recorder, with the inevitable financial difficulties. Now the engineer, the more careful type, with the strong phalange of Logic, had wanted a tape recorder for a long time, but had also

87 *The hand of an engineer*

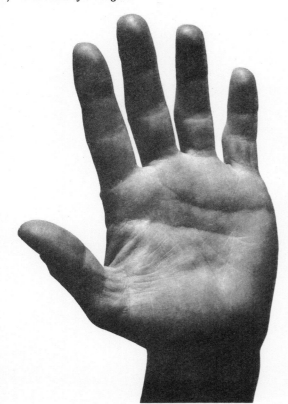

88 *A bulbous nail phalange, usually misnamed the 'murderer's thumb'*

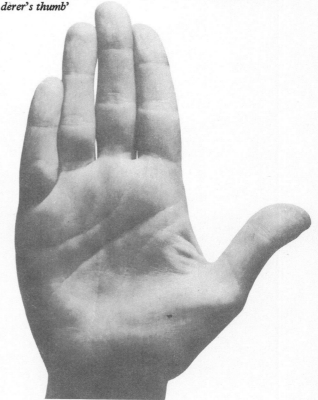

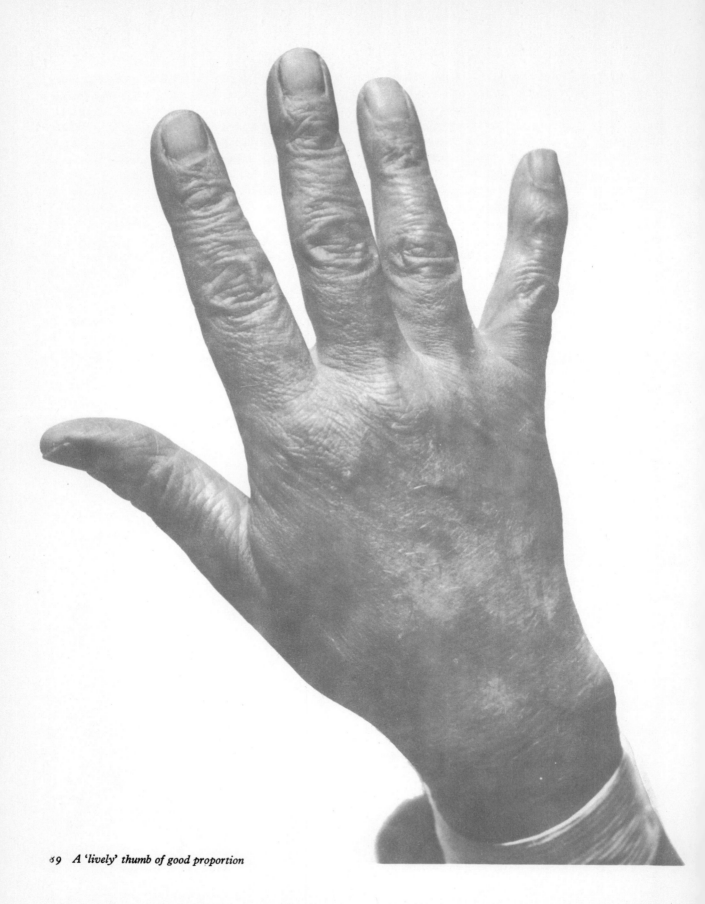

69 *A 'lively' thumb of good proportion*

felt that he could not afford one. He went into the subject of tape recorders deeply in an attempt to estimate their relative values, and for a long time turned the matter over in his mind, waiting until he had sufficient money to buy one. When he learned that his friend had bought a new machine he was a little surprised by the suddenness of the purchase, but spent an evening experimenting with the machine and discussing its technical points. A few days later he bought a similar model, completely assured that its value in relation to performance was excellent. Thus we have the two distinctive type reactions to the same urge: in one the energy came out without control, and the purchase was made quickly, almost blindly; in the other case the energy was well under control, a considered purchase was made after much delay and experiment. A rider to the comparison is that had the writer been prepared to wait for a few days before making his purchase he knew quite well that he could have saved himself almost a third of the purchase price. He preferred not to wait!

A thick phalange of Logic [85] will tend to kill action: the owner of this hand will be predisposed to act rarely, and then only with timidity and misgivings.

Spier remarks that the knot between the two phalanges forms a good basis for an estimation of the quality of energy expelled by the individual. A large knot acts as a sort of barrier between the controlling force and the raw energy, resulting in an unevenness of application: people with such joints will tackle a job with a great flow of energy which quickly dries up. Invariably such people never finish that which they set out to do if it demands evenness of application, or any staying power.

Psychological reason for this behaviour is an uncertainty, an unconscious fear of failing in their attempted purpose, which gives all their activities demanding an expenditure of energy a certain restlessness and uneveness. As the thumb, being the finger of life, represents the spring of vitality, it is not merely the dynamic expression of a person's display of energy but of the whole rhythm of his life. Thus, it is frequently observed that the various periods in the life of people whose thumbs have these hump-like protuberances are full of ups and downs.

Psychologically, the thumb represents the vitality, the will, the desire to live within a certain environment. A 'lively' thumb [89] full of vitality and expression with a degree of balance, suggests a person capable of tackling the problems of constant adaptation required by life. A bent thumb [90] indicates the opposite — particularly if it clings to the side of the hand, or is hidden under the fingers. Such a position in its more simple form [91] indicates a general unhappiness with life — a feeling that the problems of life are too difficult to be solved. The specific example given at [92] is the hand of a girl who, when this photograph was taken, was in an unpleasant emotional state for sexual reasons. She was quite unable to deal with the emotional demands of life, for she was lacking in vitality. In its severe form, the hiding of the thumb is a sign of a subconscious will to self-destruction which is paralleled by a toxic state of apathy. In such a case, there is an absolute lack of ability to transmit energy to the external world.

One often observes that a person in a state of despair or emotional upset will clench his thumbs in his palms, thus involuntarily signifying his wish to dissociate himself from the external world, and to withdraw his outward-directed energies [93]. This particular manifestation of apathy is frequent in cases of institutional neurosis in which a desire to lead a normal life in normal surroundings has been completely discarded, and a wish to 'retire' from life

90 The bent thumb of a 20-year-old engineer

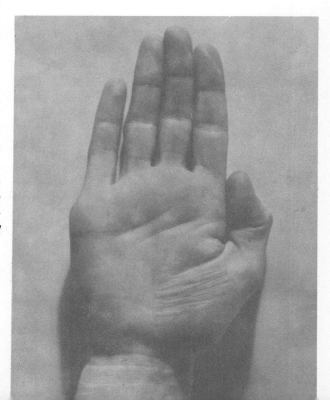

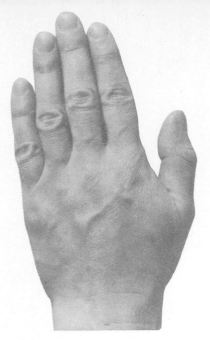

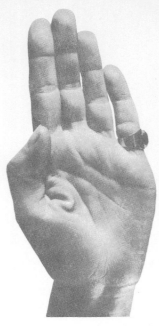

91 *The bent thumb of a 25-year-old Latvian; at the time of the photograph this man was out of work, and in great emotional difficulties*

92 *Thumb held in close to palm — a sign of emotional stress*

93 Below: *Hidden thumbs are often a sign of anxiety*

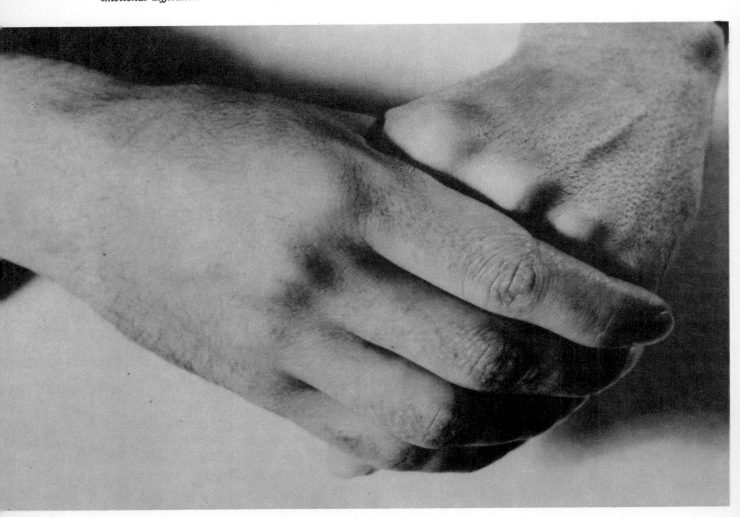

predominates. Astrologically speaking, a bent thumb is being forced from the First house into the Twelfth, 'the house of sorrows', the house of retirement and escape.

The insertion of the thumb can be highly significant. A low-set thumb [94], one which emerges from the lowest part of the mount of Venus, has a repressing effect on the quality of energy directed towards the world, whilst a high-set thumb has the opposite effect. Spier shows that a low insertion is a further sign of a parent fixation which holds a certain amount of the subjective energy in subjugation:

> To compensate for these arrested energies, these people cultivate an exaggerated ambitiousness in a domain outside their sphere of work such as sport, or they become inveterate collectors. Their ambitiousness is often combined with an almost childish and obstinate pride which does not permit them to accept other people's advice or guidance because they must always have the feeling that they owe everything to themselves. This over-sensitiveness is caused by the lack of self-reliance which was produced by their parent-fixation.

The low insertion at [94], allied to the inward bend of the finger of Jupiter, signifies that collecting would be a form of compensation for repressed energies. The subject's hobby is collecting ancient swords and armour. The things he collects, by virtue of their intrinsic value (he collects only valuable objects) act as an 'insurance' against the future, whilst by virtue of their actual properties (they are instruments of attack and defence) they pretend he really is able to deal with the problems of life, and constitute a neat rationalisation of his fear. The truth of the matter is, of course, that all the swords and other warlike objects he collects are of a nature and time removed from the demands of modern civilisation. He is quite evidently hiding his inferiority in his own dreams — he is a 'warrior in an outworn tradition', who will never be called upon to fight. His fear of life is thus hidden in a particularly interesting manner.

So important is the thumb in chirognomy that a whole book would not contain all the observations which have been accurately made in the past century. A good palmist must develop an instinctive 'feel' for thumbs if he is to understand the individual significance of the human hand.

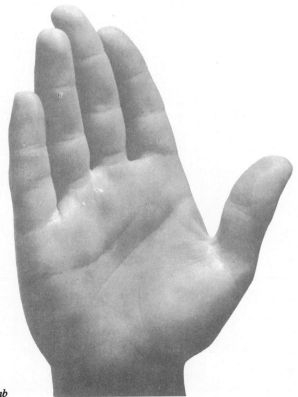

94 *A low-set thumb*

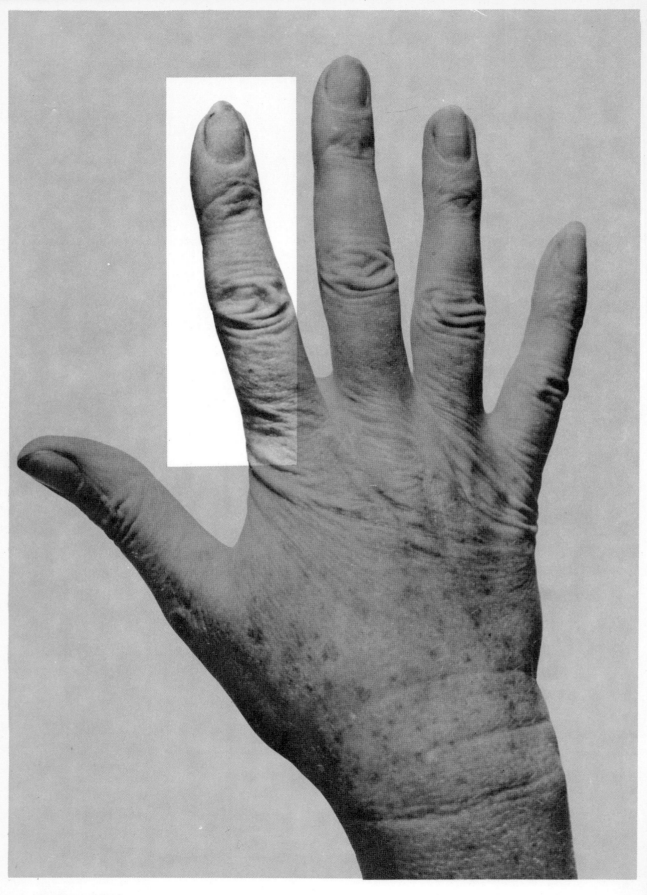

95 The finger of Jupiter

THE FINGER OF JUPITER

Jupiter

The index finger points at the outside world, and in itself is an indication of the subject's attitude to external life. A hand with its finger of Jupiter extended, as Professor Revesz has observed, need only be turned some ninety degrees to show a change in attitude so radical as to mark the difference between friendship and dislike. In one position the finger shows the kindly attitude behind a friendly attempt to explain the way or point out some object, whilst the same finger in the same position but with the wrist turned upwards shows an attitude of warning or threatening. Both the omniscience and the destructive power of Jupiter, chief deity of the Romans, are represented in these postures.

In traditional palmistry this finger was often called the finger of ambition, and in later times, the Napoleonic finger. Although the association with Napoleon is unfortunate (the Emperor had a very short index finger), the traditional associations are well based, for the finger reveals the particular way in which the subject relates himself to his environment. In this respect it is the most important finger to the chirologist for, in revealing the subject's basic attitudes to life, it forms the key to those aspects of his character around which all other attitudes are wrapped.

The finger, claims Spier (who chooses to call it the *World-finger*), 'is most actively connected with matters of the surrounding world', and for this reason alone its significance must always be evaluated in terms of the thumb which in itself represents the degree of energy available to the subject. Whilst the finger of Jupiter manifests the world-desires and aspirations of the individual, the thumb manifests the amounts of energy available to attain those desires. Medical research has shown a close cortical connection between these two fingers, and almost all palmists have insisted on their close chirological associations. It is obvious that a strong Jupiter backed by a weak thumb will lead inevitably to ineffectual frustration of life aims, whereas a strong thumb linked with a strong Jupiter can reveal degrees of ambitious striving ranging from a callous and egoistic domination to a refined and energetic desire to be brilliant (i.e. to dominate) in one particular field.

Whilst the thumb is a most important factor in evaluating the significance of Jupiter it must be remembered that the interpretation of its forms must always be made in terms of the hand type to which it belongs. Whilst one might expect a Fire type to have a longer than average Jupiter to back his ambitious activity, we might reasonably expect a Water type to have a slightly short, reticent finger. The natural practical acquisitiveness (speaking materially) of the Earth type would suggest a Jupiterian finger with a bend towards Saturn. An Air type would, in its pure form, present a well-balanced finger of even length and showing no malformations.

From the above it will be seen that the finger is not a key to the ambition of the subject but rather, by virtue of revealing his psychological attitude to life, a key to how well he is adapted to life. A well-adapted person is not necessarily one who is content

96 Dürer's St. Jerome, *in the National Gallery, Lisbon;
the moral that 'the fruits of life are death' is symbolised by
having the world-finger resting on the skull*

or secure or even happy: a well-adapted person is one who is achieving in his life what his basic temperament demands.

A good understanding of the finger of Jupiter in terms of the person's basic temperament will enable a complete estimation of how well adapted a person is in his own life. A middle-aged cretin [97] with the mental age of a child of four shows no Jupiterian deficiencies, and is, in fact, one of the happiest people I have ever met: she is perfectly adapted to her life circumstances.

Adaptability, 'the ability to conform to the necessities and facts of the outside world in an inwardly harmonious manner', has already been dealt with above, though Spier observes that if there is a noticeable space between the fingers of Jupiter and Saturn, the person is not very interested in the manifestations of the outside world — a sign of poor adaptability. Adaptability, to Spier's way of thinking, is indicated by the tip formation on the finger of Jupiter: his rule is that a conical form adapts more easily than a rectangular form. Length of finger permits an estimate of the degree of self-assertion: a long finger of Jupiter indicates a self-assertive type who will, if backed by a forceful thumb, go far in the achievement of his aims, whilst a long finger not backed up in this way is the sign of a person unable to translate his aims in terms of reality — a state productive of simple neurosis, such as stammering and claustrophobia. 'Thus,' Spier concludes, 'the discrepancy of a too long index and a weak thumb is a very essential factor in the search for the explanation of many a neurotic enigma.'

A finely proportioned finger of Jupiter firmly modelled and of even length is the theoretical 'norm'. It indicates the type of person who is well adapted to life, manifesting no undue self-importance, well liked, attractive as a companion and disposed to good living in terms of his social background. A smooth finger of Jupiter will reveal an intuitive approach to the external world, in which events and situations are examined from an emotional point of view rather than from an intellectual standpoint. Knotty fingers will slow up the perceptions to a degree, adding analytical concentration. Long fingers (in relation to the hand as a whole) will, of course, add patience, short fingers lack of patience and, specifically in relation to Jupiter, haste to **achieve an aim.**

Thick fingers add determination, thin fingers idealism in relation to life aims.

In relation to other fingers on the hand, the length of Jupiter has deep significance. An index finger which is distinctly shorter than the finger of Apollo [98] is a certain indication of an inferiority complex, either manifest or hidden beneath a mask of personality. A hand with a short finger of Jupiter is always accompanied by a fear of the external world which often prevents its owner from making any headway in life. This does not mean, as traditional palmistry would have it, 'failure in life' — some people, particularly Water types, do not want to make a headway in life. The short finger is found most often on self-effacing, perhaps rather timorous individuals, who prefer to take refuge from life in their dreams, hobbies or even in their job of work, provided that this does not bring them into too close a contact with other people.

The hand at [100] belongs to a deficient Jupiterian, whose index finger is almost a quarter of an inch smaller than the finger of Apollo. The subject is a highly sensitive, very individualistic type, who has, by reason of background and education, been forced into a fairly high-ranking position in the Civil Service. His official position demands that he controls a difficult department with a large staff, necessitating a degree of responsibility which his basic inferiority complex prevents. The result is that he dislikes his job intensely. He realises that he is unable to cope with it. His position in life is further aggravated by his fear of leaving the job which is 'secure' and which, should he reach retiring age without undue mental strain, will give him a pension. The irony is that it is the inferiority complex which is making his life in the office intolerable, and at the same time it is the inferiority complex which is preventing him from giving up his job and possibly thereby changing his way of life to some extent. A finger of Jupiter so markedly short would have been a very serious matter on a different hand-form, such as an Intuitive type.

As a generalisation we might say that an excessively short finger of Jupiter can often indicate a dangerous lack of self-confidence, and that some forms of inferiority feeling can be so severe as to completely paralyse the subject's relationship to ordinary life.

A long finger of Jupiter [99], which is to say one which is obviously longer than the finger of Apollo,

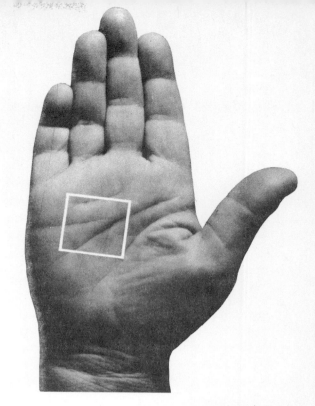

97 *The hand of a cretin; the disrupted line of Heart is a typical pattern*

98 *A short finger of Jupiter on the hand of a 25-year-old Indian*

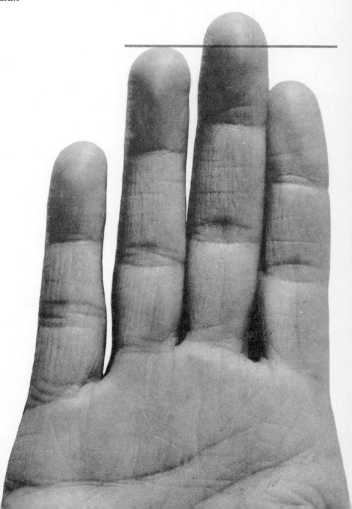

signifies a tendency to be dominating and ambitious. Such a finger belongs to the ambitious type, whose energy is directed towards dominating external life.

Occasionally one finds a long finger of Jupiter on an apparently self-effacing individual, but always other indications in the hand will reveal the person to have an over-developed concept of his own capabilities and importance. Some form of early conditioning will have resulted in a basic attitude which holds that he can best achieve his own aims by being 'self-effacing'. Usually such a person lacks the ability to project his own image of himself into the world, actually to do something to manifest his own self-importance. Such a state of affairs generally leads to a neurotic condition. Print [102] shows the hand of a beautiful woman who has no particular talents in any specific direction but who, like so many pretty girls, wants to be a model. Although she has spent

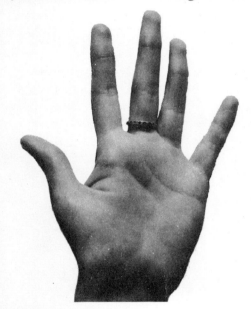

99   *A long finger of Jupiter*

much money on modelling courses she has found very little work as a model — other indications in the hand make it quite clear why this is so. Her problem is that she cannot find any way of projecting into real life the self-manufactured conception of her own abilities: the result is a neurotic disposition, which is clearly manifest in her hand.

Spier observes that this finger can be taken as representing the four features of observation, sense-perception, adaptability and the urge of self-asser-

tion, all four being aspects of the relationship between the individual and the external world. The sign of a well-developed power of observation is a straight index finger, whilst the sign of an inadequate power of observation is a bent index finger. A good observer is one 'who is able to quickly take in the phenomena of the outside world in contrast to the intuitive type who has a quick grasp of the phenoma of the inner world'.

An index bent in towards the finger of Saturn in a bow-like curve [101] (as opposed to the inward bend of the top phalange only) is a sign of an acquisitive tendency the strength of which depends on the crookedness of the finger. A markedly bent Jupiter is a dangerous sign of possessiveness, which can lead to states analogous to kleptomania. In a less severe form the bend will mark the collector; other signs on the hand (the thumb in particular) will enable one to establish more precisely the field within which the collection is made. In any form or degree a bent figure of Jupiter indicates a lack of free relationship with the external world.

The age-old tradition that the index finger is bound up with Jupiterian illnesses, like rheumatism, gout and sciatica, is well founded, for considerable investigation into this subject by many research workers has shown that the index is somehow linked with the functioning of the stomach, liver, gall and spleen. A disposition to the three illnesses may be perceived by a noticeable thickening of the lower phalange of the Jupiter finger, whilst the cause may be often attributed to a predilection for alcohol and an ill-balanced diet — both Jupiterian tendencies. One thinks automatically of Falstaff, the archetypal Jupiterian.

It is most usual for palmists to claim that the finger of Jupiter may be taken as representing the religious disposition of the subject. Looked at broadly religion is, in its internal and external phases, a doctrine by which a person may adapt inwardly to the mysteries of life, and from this point of view the traditional claims are well founded. Jupiter may, within limits, reveal the type of religion (or atheism) most suitable to the subject in his attempts to adapt himself to life and the mysteries of life. Within the obvious qualifications of the hand types, a smooth, intuitive finger will demand a mystical religion, whilst a knotty finger will demand a more philosophical religion based on intellectual analysis.

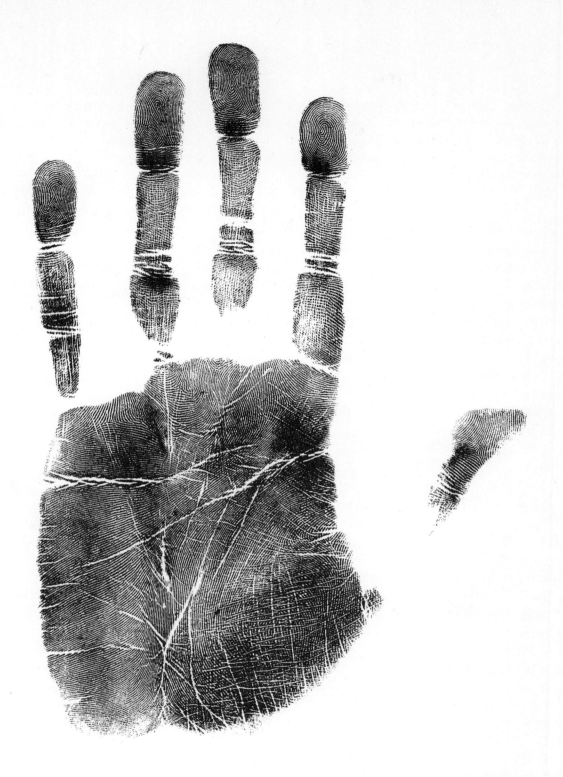

100 A short finger of Jupiter, commonly found on hands of the Sensitive type

101 An 'acquisitive' finger of Jupiter, on the hand of a research chemist at Oxford

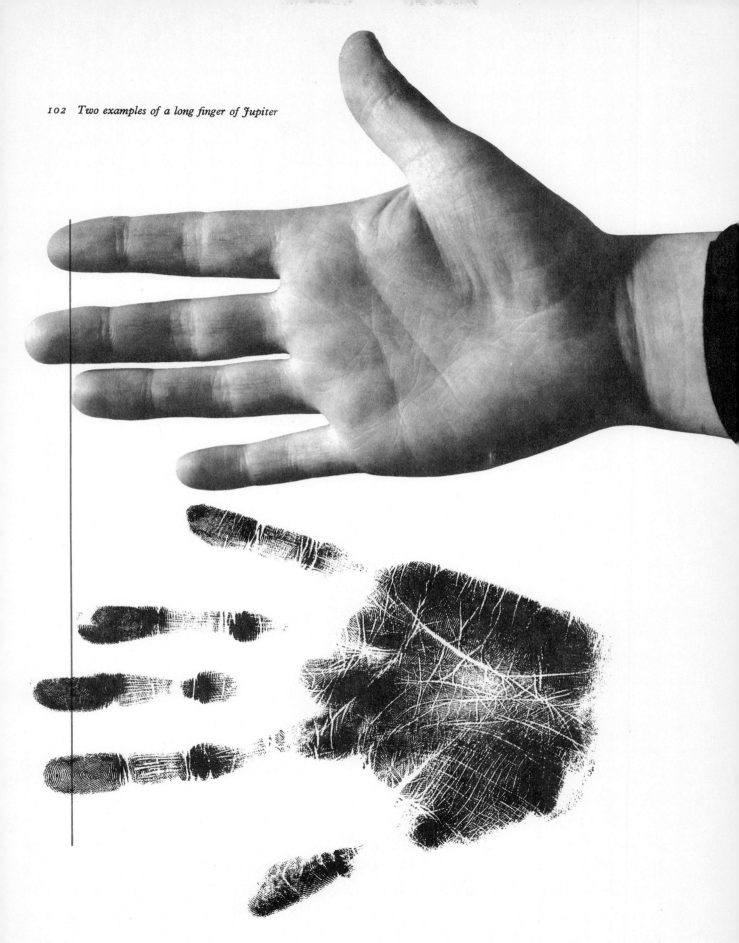

102 *Two examples of a long finger of Jupiter*

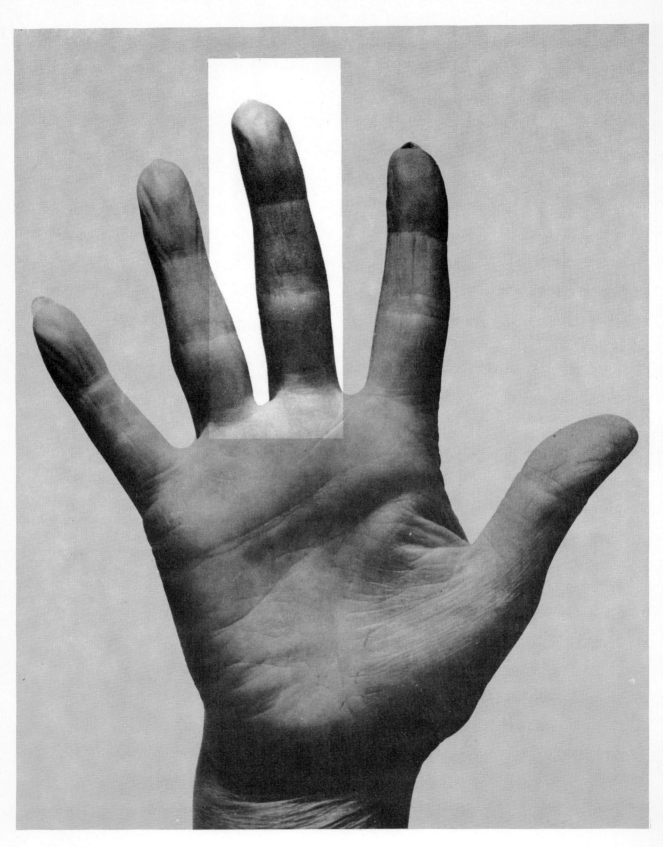

103   *The finger of Saturn*

THE FINGER OF SATURN

The third is called the middle finger, because in the middle, some call it Physitian, because that with it are touched the privy parts when something is amiss. This finger is Saturn.

Saunders

The finger of Saturn has always been the palmist's headache. Perhaps more than any other part of the hand it has presented difficulties, not least of which is its significance. The tendency with most writers on palmistry has been to preserve the traditional interpretation connected with the third finger simply because they have been unable to find a satisfactory alternative. Blood and thunder and all manner of evil prognostications have huddled themselves around Saturn, and have completely obscured its role. Even the comparatively restrained Heron-Allen has little to say concerning this finger which is not lurid and histrionic:

> *If on this finger the first phalanx is long, it betokens sadness and superstition, very long it betrays a morbid desire for death, and, in a weak hand with a small thumb, a horrible temptation to suicide. If the second phalanx is long by comparison with the others it denotes love of agriculture and mechanical occupations, or, if the joints are prominent, mathematics and the exact sciences. If the fingers are smooth the development of this second phalanx will give a talent for occult science. Lastly, if the third phalanx is long and large it denotes avarice.*

The reasons for this unpleasant connotation are complex, but it probably springs from the ancient belief that the 'morbid planet' of Saturn represented the evil characteristics in man.

To understand the true significance of this finger we must go back to classical mythology and examine Saturn independently of his astrological trimmings. Saturn was the son of Coelus and Gaia, the Earth goddess, and was, in terms of mythology, largely instrumental in civilising the people of Italy, introducing agriculture and various arts at a time when they were largely barbarians. Saturn emerges as a practical and beneficial god, and his reign is associated with the Golden Age of happiness and tranquility. This early picture of Saturn fits more closely into the present chirognomical interpretation of the significance behind the middle finger than does the later unpleasant picture, for Saturn is the finger of balance, of harmony.

In the preliminary analysis of the hand we saw that the finger of Saturn stands between those halves of the hand which represent the conscious and subconscious aspects of life. It is the meeting point of both worlds, and may be said to indicate the degree to which balance between the two is established. In this role, as a mediator, the finger of Saturn may be taken as a sort of referee between the *ego* and the *id*, standing sentinel, as it were, over the whole of the hand.

We can reasonably expect that a middle finger which is in any way abnormal represents some abnormal balance between the conscious and subconscious mind. It is significant, for instance, that a long finger of Saturn is usually found in the hand of an intellectual, and an excessively long finger is the sign of a person whose intellect tends towards such dryness as to cut him off from the rest of the world. The pedant who knows every detail about some period in history and is so far removed from the present as to be incapable of crossing the road safely

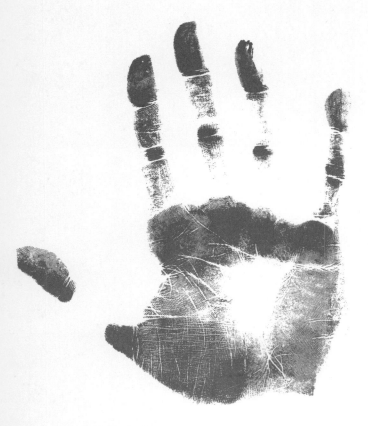

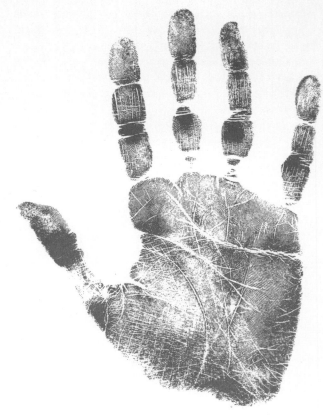

104   *A long finger of Saturn*

105   *A short finger of Saturn*

is an obvious example. Such a predominance of the intellectual function throws an individual off balance, upsetting the harmony of his life, and creating an uncontrolled state of affairs.

In general, then, a particularly long finger of Saturn is indicative of some sort of imbalance. The longest finger which I have ever seen was on the hand of a catatonic schizophrenic, but this must not be taken as being unduly significant, for the imbalance is rarely so strong. At [104] is the hand of a designer of considerable talent. In physique he is a typical Saturnalian and, as his middle finger (supported by a good Head line) would suggest, he is particularly brilliant intellectually. His emotional life appears to be one continuous series of breakdowns resulting from a clash between what his emotions demand and what his intellect needs: he is incapable of living up to the high ideals he sets himself. His lively intelligence and fine, penetrating

mentality have, to a certain degree, cut him off from ordinary life and have resulted in a moody disposition which permeates his whole inner life. The balance of his conscious and subconscious worlds is being disturbed by his inflexible theorising about how he should live, which seems to bear little relationship to the way he does live. In a hand less manifestly Intuitive the discrepancy between reality and self-made demands could lead to serious difficulties; as it is, basic intuition mitigates the intellectual dryness to a considerable degree. The result is a hyper-sensitive, over-emotional schizoid type of a rather precarious mental balance.

The short middle finger is usually found on a more intuitive, less intellectual subject. It is common among artists and people with highly tuned emotional sensitivities — particularly so if the tip of the finger is at all pointed. An example of this can be seen at [105] which is the hand of a young painter who refuses to rationalise about her art and relies completely on intuition. Her finest work was made 'as if in a frenzy' from bits of old canvas, plaster and newspaper glued to a piece of board, and during the act of painting she was in that trance-like state which seems to be characteristic of certain phases of artistic creation.

In relation to diseases, the finger of Saturn has been closely associated with intestinal disorders. This ties up well with the traditional picture of the Saturnalian type being regulated by excess of bile. Spier describes the outward signs of such enteric diseases as being a particularly thick lower phalange, and a bend of the top phalange towards the finger of Apollo. These two signs mark a disposition towards intestinal difficulties, and are not indicative of an illness itself. Photograph [106] is the hand of a girl with a family history of intestinal trouble.

106　*A bent finger of Saturn*

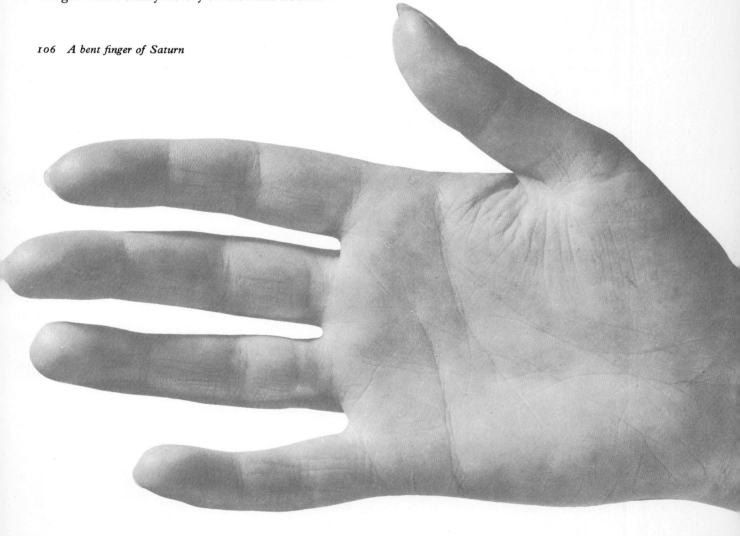

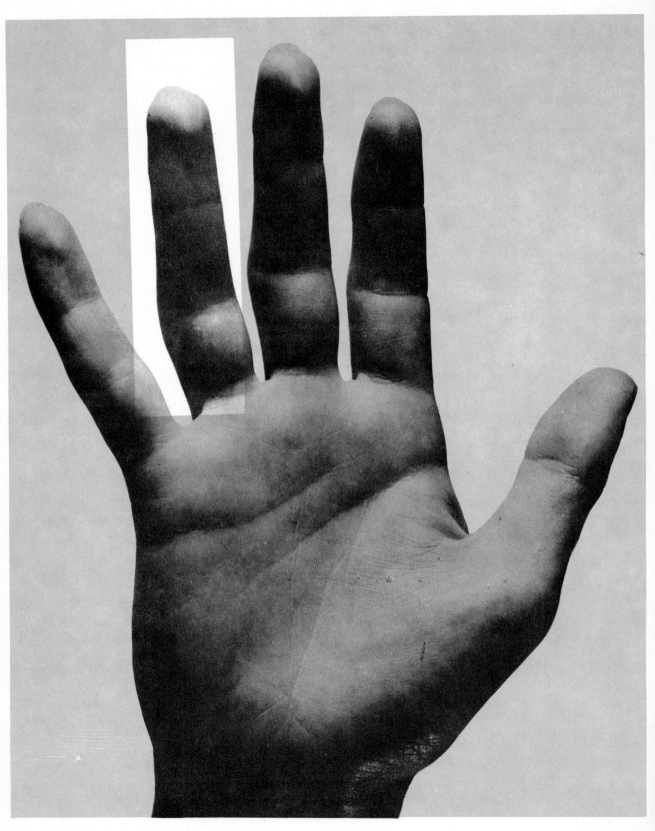

107   *The finger of Apollo*

100

THE FINGER OF APOLLO

As for the Ring finger, which is so called because commonly a Ring is worn on it especially in the left hand: the Physitians and Anatomists give the reason of it because in the finger there is a sense very tender and small that reaches to the heart wherefore it ought to wear a Ring as a Crown for its dignity. But besides observe, that in the Ceremony of Marriage, they first put the Matrimonial Ring on the thumb, whence they take it, and put it on everyone till they come to this, where it is left.

Saunders

The fingers of Apollo and Mercury mark between them the subconscious aspect of the 'externally directed' elements of temperament. Both fingers are intimately connected with relationships and attitudes of people. Apollo is connected with less proximate and less intimate relationships than Mercury.

A very ancient superstition about the Ring finger, preserved even by great medical authorities up to three centuries ago, was that the finger of Apollo is connected directly to the heart by a main artery:

So I observed in Gallia Belgica *that very many were subject to the gowt of their hands and feet, all whose joynts were swolln and in bitter pains, save onely the ring finger of the left hand which is next the little finger, for that by the nearnesse and consent of the heart felt no harm . . . Because a small branch of the arterie is stretched forth from the heart unto this fingev* (Saunders).

Derek Price comments on the curious association of the ring finger with medicine, and it is recorded that doctors were advised always to mix their drugs with the third finger by reason of its arterial proximity to the heart. Some old texts on palmistry refer to this finger as the finger of the Sun, thus recalling that Apollo was in origin a sun god, capable of destruction and of healing: Aesculapius, the god of medicine, was supposed to have been his son, whilst he himself was particularly renowned for his ability in prophecy, the Oracle at Delphi being one of his many shrines. Thus the name for this finger is not without significance: the sun is the creator and maintainer of life and earth, whilst creative energy

can, paradoxically enough, be used destructively as well as creatively. The creative ability is always intuitive, and prophecy can be seen as a heightening of the intuitive faculty.

Many writers have attempted to show, with admittedly good argument, that the finger of Apollo is related to the emotions. It manifests the type of creativity possessed by the individual, something of his reaction to emotional stimuli, and the degree to which histrionics play a part in his life.

Traditionally, this finger is supposed to denote the artistic ability of the individual, and to relate to his potentials of fame, ambition and wealth. Certainly these factors are intimately bound up with the emotional calibre of the individual, and to that extent, at least, the traditional viewpoint is well founded — it is however too exclusive an interpretation of the meaning which can be perceived from this finger.

A well-balanced finger, not unduly distinguished in shape, texture or formation, is found on the hand of an emotionally well-balanced person. The hand at [108] belongs to a young woman who is very well adjusted to life. She is an Air type — a kind, generous, good-natured individual, with a taste for fine living inherited from her parents. She has an important position on a fashion magazine as news editor, a post for which her breeding, great beauty and personal charm make her admirably suited. At home, her life is happy; she is married to a Fire type, who, though himself not well adjusted to life, finds the marriage extremely satisfactory by virtue of her understanding and kindness. The Apollo finger on

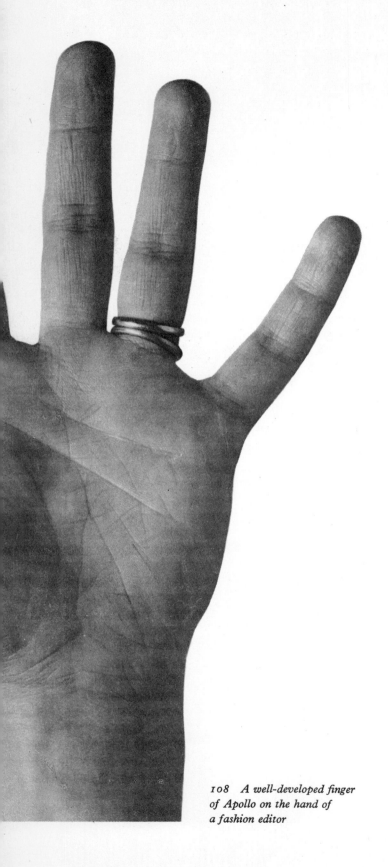

*108   A well-developed finger
of Apollo on the hand of
a fashion editor*

her hand is smooth and straight, indicating the fine emotional balance of her personality. The fact that she wears two rings emphasises her marriage, outwardly manifesting her contentment with the married state.

The hand at [110] also belongs to a happily married woman, but this time with a very different finger of Apollo. It is more waisted, thinner than the other fingers, and in its general appearance it seems hardly to belong to the hand as a whole. In addition to its formation, it is isolated, as it were, by the fingers to either side of it, so that one is led to assume that the emotional life which it represents is not at all integrated with her ordinary life. In fact, this is the hand of a ballet dancer, who before she retired to have a family, was a leading artiste with Sadler's Wells. Although her home life is satisfactory, she is emotionally 'off balance' because she still feels the urge to dance, and in particular to be part of a company. A partial solution to her problems would be to take up the teaching of dancing where, to a certain degree, she would be able to use her quite definite talents, but she feels that this will not be possible until her children are old enough to go to school.

A short finger of Apollo is quite rare, and is always a sure indication of emotional difficulties. I have seen several actors' hands with short ring fingers, but in each case other difficulties (mainly sexual) manifest themselves in the finger of Mercury. It is almost as if actors are heir to emotional problems of a subconscious nature. People with short ring fingers tend to be very individualistic — of necessity, for their emotional lives do not conform to the usual pattern. Consequently such people find it very difficult to adjust to normal lives.

A strong histrionic sense is indicated by a short finger, particularly if the top phalange is spatulate. A bend inwards of the top phalange towards the finger of Saturn is also indicative of emotional difficulties. Spier notes that such fingers are found with 'people whose lives seem to be an uninterrupted chain of disappointments, who inevitably find themselves in situations which lead to conflicts and difficulties in their own self as well as with others'. [111] shows the hand of a highly individualistic young man of twenty-seven with a relatively short finger of Apollo which has the top phalange bending in towards the second finger, leading us immediately to suspect a problem of emotional adjustment. He has had numerous jobs, all well below his intellectual standards, and inevitably he has grown tired of 'trying to get on in England'. A few days after his photograph was taken, he emigrated abroad where he hoped to find something more fitting to his own demands.

A long finger of Apollo is a sign of emotional imbalance in another direction. It indicates too great a preoccupation with one's own inner world, which leads to introvert tendencies not conducive to good emotional balance. Provided the introversion is directed by some inner discipline, a long finger of Apollo can be a strong sign of a schizoid emotional state. Photograph [113] shows the hand of a young housewife, who used to be a teacher. The excessive shortness of the finger of Jupiter, which reveals a severe inferiority complex, tends to emphasise the length of the finger of Apollo, but even taking this factor into account, the finger of Apollo is quite long. Fortunately this young lady has a certain conception of the meaning of inner discipline, in that she is an active Quaker, but without this her life could be affected by the regressive signs in her hand.

As a person she appears on first acquaintance to be reserved and shy, an appearance which belies her emotional strength. Her air of contentment is very much of a façade, for emotionally she is constantly tense and is easily disturbed. Her creative outlet was teaching, as the long upper phalange would suggest, and one of her pleasures, before she had her own child, was to organise school trips to art galleries and museums. The introvert tendencies shown by her Apollo finger are playing a very important part and, in fact, giving a purpose to her life. It is evident that without the internal and external disciplines afforded by her Quaker religion, her intuitive creative forces could run riot in a most unpleasant way.

Intuition is an inborn force which the modern system of education, with its predisposition towards an intellectual discipline, and with its little care for an emotional discipline, tends very quickly to suffocate. I have been astonished to find how many of the creative people I know have suffered to a great extent by conventional schooling. The best of these creative writers and painters have, by freaks of circumstance, escaped the usual stereotyped production line of education, and appear all the better for their escape so far as their emotional capabilities are concerned. A damaged, inhibited intuitive ability is

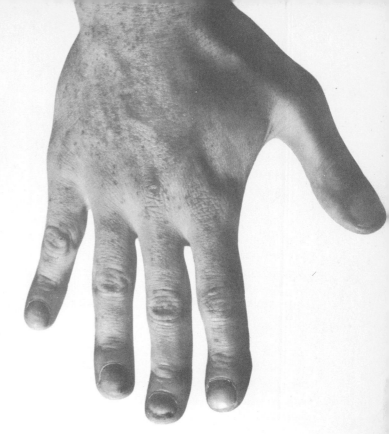

109   *A short finger of Apollo*

110   *The hand of an ex-ballerina*

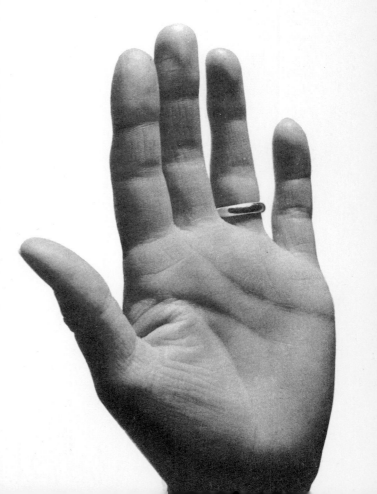

perceived by a bending in of the Apollo finger towards the palm of the hand. This bending can be slight or extreme, the degree of bend denoting the degree of damage. The most common forms of inhibition are shown at [111] whilst [112] shows an extreme case, in which the intuitive forces have been inhibited to a degree which has affected the sexual life of the individual. In this hand, the manner in which the finger closes over towards the palm suggests that the owner is trying to 'hide' his emotional life from view. Neither of these photographs was 'staged', each subject was invited to put his hand under the camera in the position which he found most relaxed and comfortable.

Regarding this inward bend of the finger of Apollo it is necessary to find out whether or not the position is a permanent one. If it is possible to bend the finger back, level with the other fingers, without causing pain and without undue pressure, then the finger may be taken as expressive of a temporary state of mind. The hand at [112] is that of a young girl who, when this photograph was taken, was in a state of great indecision concerning her future life. She had just completed a training in occupational

therapy, and was very unhappy about working any longer in mental homes, or even in hospitals — many of the cases with which she had to deal made her feel revulsion, whilst she felt herself to be quite inadequate for the demands made of her. It is evident that she is subconsciously trying to 'hide' her emotional life from the camera. In effect, the case is more interesting than it appears at first, for the above rationalisation is her own statement of her position, and is not quite accurate. The truth is that her sense of inferiority, allied to her basic fear of life, is manifestly refusing to take on the responsibility of the job for which she has trained for several years. That the revulsion against working with mental patients is not the real reason for her emotional state has been made quite evident by her consequent actions. She has entered university to study psychology! Thus the fatal reckoning, when she has to enter the hard world of reality, and to accept some responsibility, has been put off for at least three more years.

Physiologically, the Apollo finger is related to the heart. A crooked finger marks a disposition to heart troubles, such as poor circulation or more severe cardiac diseases.

111   The severe inward bending of Apollo, and the space between Apollo and Mercury, are indications of this young man's problem

112   A severe inward bending of Apollo on the hand of a young student of psychology

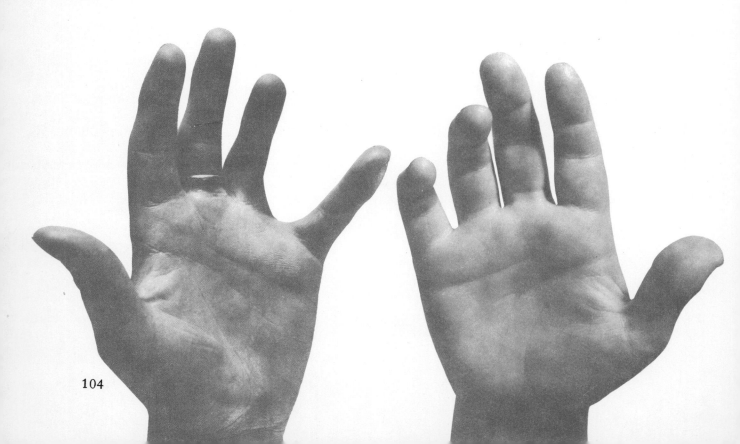

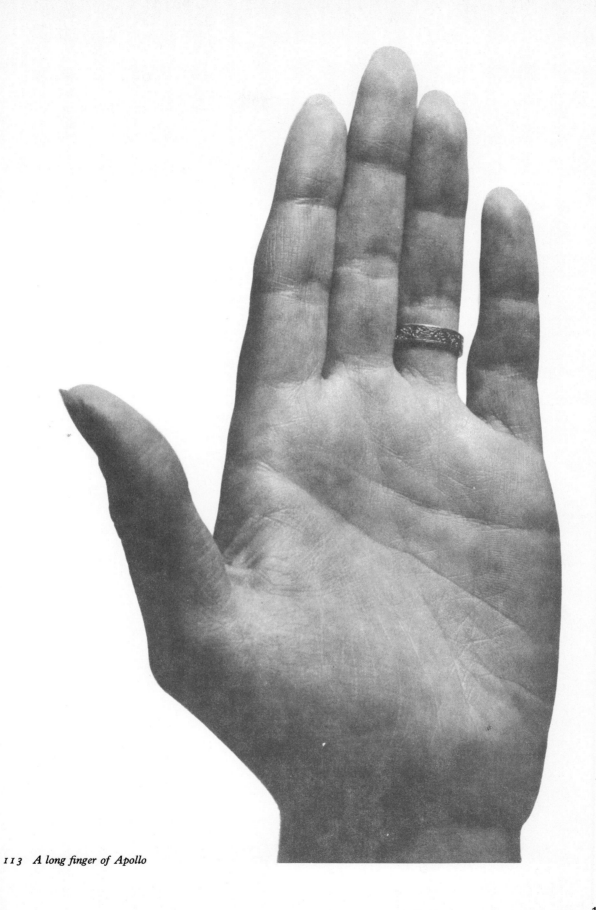

113 A long finger of Apollo

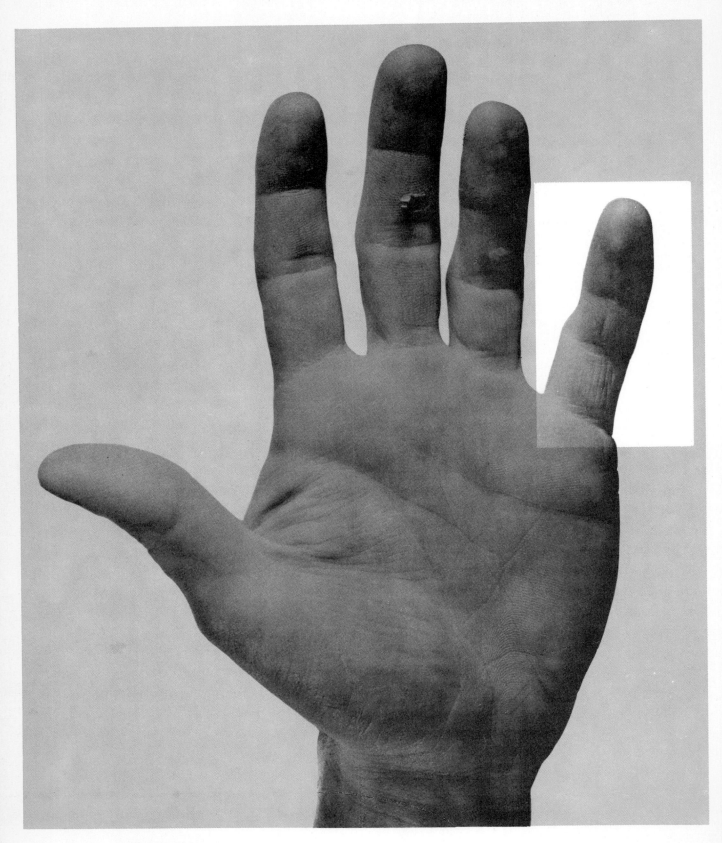

114 *The finger of Mercury*

THE FINGER OF MERCURY

Mercurius

The last and least of all is called the Ear-Finger, because commonly we make use of it to clean our ears, as if it were some instrument. We read that Dionisius or Denis the Sicilian Tyrant, would never make use of any other Instrument to cleanse his ears fearing they would give him some poysoned Instrument as being a Prince very fearfull and distrustful, whose life was miserable in his Tyranny, because of the fear imprinted on his Soul. This finger is attributed to Mercury.

Saunders

The only aspect of our emotional life not covered by the Apollo finger is that part which is devoted to our intimate relationships with other people. It is precisely this aspect which the finger of Mercury manifests, and for the sake of clarity its meaning must be examined from two points of view: partnership relationship with the opposite sex, that is sexual relationships; and parental relationships with immediate relatives, chiefly with mother and father. In addition to these two important aspects of an individual's life, the finger of Mercury is related to vocal ability in all its forms.

Sexual relations permeate our whole life, and the correct analysis of the place of sex in the life of an individual is an important step in the evaluation of his character and psychological disposition. Sex can be either an integrated part of an individual's life — though with modern educational methods this is rare — or it can cause disharmony in that individual's life. It can be either an immense force for creation or an equally strong force for disintegration. Disharmony in sex accounts for the majority of modern problems — and it is almost certain that sex, or more exactly, repressed sexual energy, is the basis for most crimes and mental diseases. An overemphasis of sexual functions can be as destructive as under-emphasis: they are both misuses of fine energy.

When the little finger is quite obviously isolated from the other fingers, difficulty in relationships must be immediately suspected [115]. A difficulty in relationships having been diagnosed it is necessary to give a more exact analysis by means of other parts of the hand in order to arrive at a more precise picture of the actual state of affairs. If, for instance, the little finger is isolated from the other fingers and there is a large, well-developed mount of Venus (see page 120) and a deeply marked, long and broken girdle of Venus (see page 150) then one can be certain that the root problem is too great a preoccupation with sex. It is then necessary to determine whether the preoccupation is imaginative in nature, or physical and carnal: a further examination of the Head line, the finger of Saturn, and Heart line should reveal all that is necessary.

The obvious alienation of the finger of Mercury in [116] is further emphasised by the ring, which shows without doubt that the subject's main problem in life is one of relationships. As the ring is on the left hand, one is led immediately to suspect a parental difficulty — a fixation on one of the parents. Other indications on the hand reveal the whole story: his right hand shows a strong inferiority complex, and a deep rift between his conscious and subconscious workings; other factors combine to place him in a state which can only be described as an almost continuous state of fear, which is well hidden from the outer world. He is the only son of fairly rich parents who have done all they can to help him on in the world, to the extent that now he is finding it very difficult to accept any responsibility for himself. Although in his middle twenties, he still lives at home, and most of his working life is devoted to making as much money as he can as an 'insurance' against the future. He is a very intelligent person, highly sensitive and cultured, and well aware, no doubt because of his training in psychology, of his problems. Unfortunately, a parent fixation of such strength is not easily mitigated. It will be observed that his present direction is evolutionary rather than involutory, for his right hand indicates a better state of affairs than his left.

The forward thrust of the little finger in [118] is a sure sign of a partner-relationship difficulty, in which problems of sex play too great a part in his life. In fact this man, who is not yet twenty years old, is living with a young girl. He is an interesting case of a schizoid personality, for he is trying desperately to be a 'bohemian' painter, though temperamentally not suited for such a way of life. This desire — more to lead the life of a painter than to paint — was probably grafted on him during a short stay in art school, and is resulting in emotional disturbances manifest in his hand. His problem is not that he is confounding conventional social morality, but that he has a subconscious guilt feeling that he should not be doing what he is doing. He is his own arbiter, for no one amongst the semi-bohemian class in which he mixes would ever dream of condemning him for his action. The indications are that he will settle down eventually, as his moral wanderlust is exhausted.

Palmists are fond of pointing out that the Old Masters invariably painted their Madonnas with the little finger divorced from the hand, and that this was probably a result of the sexual life of the models such artists used. This may be true, on the other hand it might well be a matter of aesthetics. Certainly true, however, is the equally common observation that women are constantly seen drinking their tea with the little finger much in evidence. Spier ties this down to a particular period:

At the end of the nineteenth century in the period of the emancipation of women, when equal rights were also demanded in sexual matters, it was considered as particularly fashionable and distinguished to hold the teacup with the little finger daintily jutting out, a symbolic gesture which manifested this particular demand very clearly.

However, one recalls having seen such 'symbolic gestures' in prints by Hogarth, and in many modern restaurants. Spier insists with good argument that a divorced little finger may reveal a desire for independence regarding the partner, a desire which

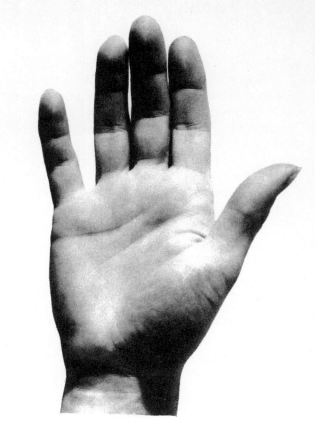

115　*An isolated finger of Mercury*

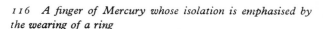

116　*A finger of Mercury whose isolation is emphasised by the wearing of a ring*

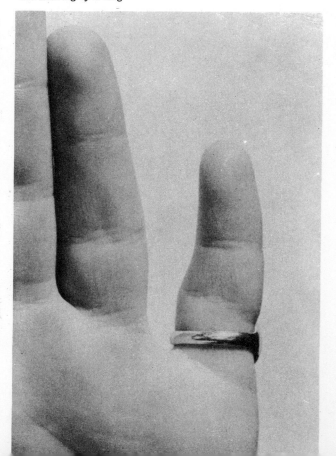

is often coupled with a fear of responsibility.

The hands of the Holy Mother from Crivelli's *Annunciation* [117], which show little fingers widely separated from the rest of the hand, are tenderly significant of the immaculate conception. Crivelli, steeped in neo-platonist thought, had too high a regard for detailed symbolism and too fine a dramatic sense to miss the subconscious significance of the alienated little finger. Just before Crivelli died, one of the earliest printed books on palmistry had appeared in Venice, and there was no doubt a strong oral tradition with which he was familiar.

While on the subject of paintings, we might note that Dürer's self-portrait (reproduced on page 82) shows, in addition to the clubbed thumb, a deformed finger of Mercury, which is itself an atavistic sign.

The deep-set finger of Mercury is a sign of a parent fixation which invariably leads to sexual difficulties with a partner. It is most often found in an infantile hand, and the Sensitive type, which is particularly prone to such difficulties.

If the little finger is long because the first phalange is very well developed it will, according to the old traditions, indicate a love of knowledge and a love of education. (See [113], the hand of a schoolteacher who, as we have remarked before, particularly loved teaching young children.) The hand at [119] is that of a civil servant, whose hobby is the study of occult sciences: he is gifted with a very good ability in oratory, with a fine vocabulary and convincing way of presenting an argument. When not in one of his moods of depression, his quick-witted humour makes him extremely popular. In fact, his linguistic ability is so good that he occasionally 'hides' from people behind a mask of elaborate circumlocution and verbosity. It will be noted that the square ending of his little finger adds a love of research and logic to his oratory.

The extremely long first phalange in [47] is very interesting: since this man's conversion to Christianity he has become one of the country's leading experts on fibre-glass structures. Note the third phalange, which is virtually nonexistent: this is always an atavistic marking, particularly interesting in this hand, which shows all the usual marks of degeneracy, and has by some outside force been granted sufficient power to turn its involutory force towards spiritual evolution.

The traditional view that the finger of Mercury

117 Crivelli's The Annunciation, *in the National Gallery, London. Detail*

indicates the honesty of a person is well founded. A twisted finger of Mercury is always the sign of an individual who tends to be dishonest in speech: in its more complex form it is the sign of the downright cunning liar. One wonders if it is an accident that this one finger should manifest both the honesty and sex of people, for it would appear that people lie about sex more than about any other subject.

In medical circles it has long been recognised that small or deformed fingers of Mercury accompany cretinism, and that at the very least such a finger is, rather like the simian line, a sign of degeneracy or thyroid deficiency. Again one must be wary of drawing too many conclusions from one sign; although a high proportion of cretins do show this atavistic sign, I have seen cretins with almost normal little fingers. Equally, of course, I have seen short Mercury fingers in people who, except for sexual difficulties, are reasonably well orientated to life.

Vocal ability in the realm of music is also attributed to the finger of Mercury, as well as the gift for speech. It is evident that there is a connection between the sex glands and the vocal cords. Photograph [118] shows the hand of an artist whose hobby is singing. He has a fine tenor voice, a great love of music, and a wife who is an accomplished pianist. Such a long Intuitive finger with sensitive pads on the first phalange can mean only a strong penchant for music.

Physiologically the finger of Mercury is connected with the abdominal organs, with the reproductive system, the bladder and kidneys. Spier writes that 'uterine illnesses, such as an indentation or dislocation of the uterus, can be recognised by an indented second phalange. A particularly thick lower phalange indicates that the ovaries are affected. Bladder and kidney troubles are revealed by an inward bend of the top phalange, and by the fact that it is the only finger without a nail moon'.

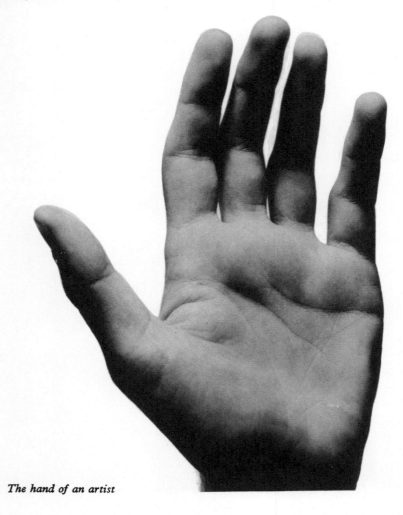

118 *The hand of an artist*

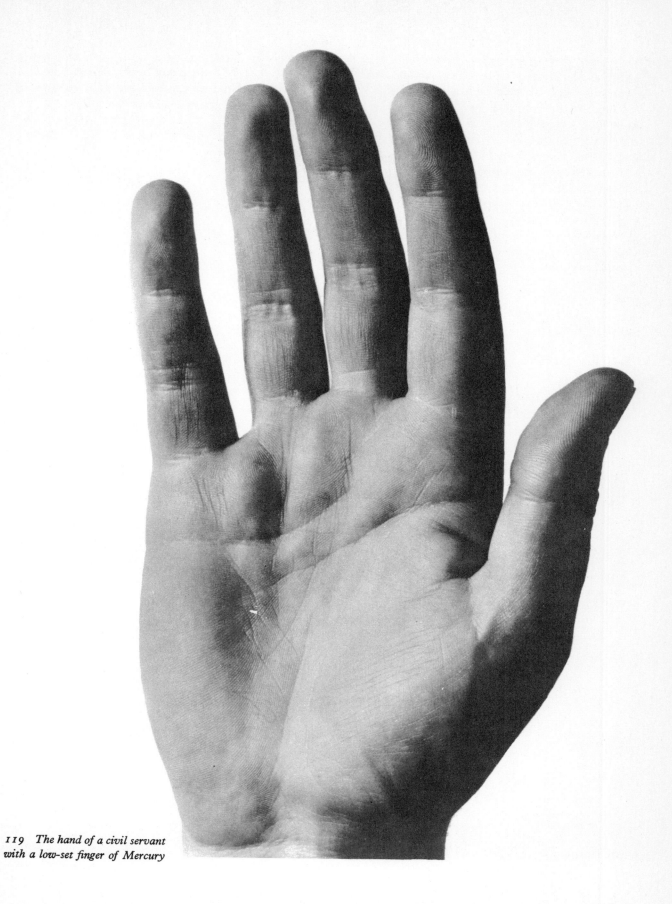

119   The hand of a civil servant
with a low-set finger of Mercury

120 *Matsys'* The Moneylender and his Wife *in the Louvre, Paris*

From a chirognomical point of view rings perform two distinct functions: they serve both to separate the finger from the rest of the hand and to draw attention to that finger. In other words a finger which sports a ring must be regarded with the same suspicion as a finger which is obviously divorced, either spatially or physiologically, from the rest of the hand.

The ring is an outward sign of imbalance in terms of the particular finger on which it is found. The disturbance in balance may be due to an excessive development or inadequacy of a specific function. We should expect a person who wears a ring on a little finger to have some imbalance relating to intimate relationships. It may be, for example, a confirmation of a strong parent fixation which is resulting in poor sexual relationships owing to identification with a parent image. This may result in a strong desire to 'collect', to accumulate money, as a compensation. It may result in a sexual abnormality. The ring merely points the way to a certain type of imbalance — other chirological factors must determine how the imbalance will manifest itself. In certain towns and cities there are groups of Lesbians who wear rings on their little fingers as a form of identity token. Many homosexuals wear such rings, as do many people, particularly businessmen, whose lives revolve around the accumulating of wealth.

A ring worn on the finger of Jupiter would suggest an excessive wish to dominate and to attain high position. Many Renaissance portraits of influential men reveal a 'fashion' for wearing rings on this finger [121].

An analysis of Quentin Matsys' *The Moneylender and his Wife* [120] in the Louvre is very revealing. The psychological 'tension' between the couple which is so apparent from the positioning of their bodies and from the simple compositional device is given further detailed significance by the rings which the couple are shown wearing. Matsys depicts the moneylender, obviously a man of the world and wrapped up in the world of finance, with a heavy ring on the finger of Jupiter, and a coin between the finger of Jupiter and the thumb. This in itself is an interesting act of 'unconscious' psychology by Matsys, but when it is related to the hand of the man's young wife, even deeper implications become evident. The banker's wife is only half turned towards her husband, and her expression shows no real interest either in him

121 Holbein's George Gisze, *National Gallery, Berlin*

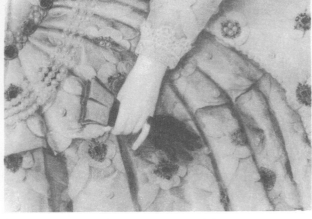

122 *A comparison between the hands of Henry VIII, detail from a drawing, and Queen Elizabeth I, from an anonymous portrait. In Henry's hands we see pride, force, certainty and vigour; note the rings on the Jupiter and Mercury fingers of* both hands. *The Queen's hand is uncertain, wooden and, one is almost tempted to say, old-maidish; the large ring and the unnatural position of the little finger are interesting. Both pictures are in the National Portrait Gallery, London.*

or in his money. Her hands and the turn of her body reveal her real interest — children. She is reading a Bible, idly turning to the picture of the Virgin Mary with Jesus on her lap. She is wearing two simple rings on the little finger of her right hand, which is turned away from the money, and is resting on the biblical text. Her hands are of the delicate Sensitive type. The 'life aims' of this couple could hardly be further apart: the moneylender's predominance lies in the active and conscious spheres of money, whilst the wife's main feeling is for the less active and unconscious sphere. Their specific points of imbalance show no common meeting place. It is hardly surprising that the young woman, with a husband so obviously devoted to money, should have sex problems.

In our society a ring on the left hand finger of Apollo can have no significance other than the obvious one — it is the outward sign of marriage. Admittedly marriage in itself demands a radical change in attitudes relating to one's emotional life, and it is perhaps as a symbol of this change of attitude that the custom of wearing a ring on Apollo originated.

It is recorded that in earlier days the marriage was formally symbolised by the placing of the ring on all the fingers, one by one, starting at the thumb and finishing at Apollo, leaving only Mercury untouched. Perhaps this custom was a symbolic way of 'external-

ising' (making public) everything but sex which should be a private thing between husband and wife. The custom would, in these terms, be a sort of subconscious confessional — a therapeutic before the state of marriage.

A ring can do little more than hint at the type of imbalance in a subject's personality. Too much emphasis on the ring itself, without further palmistic enquiry into the hand, can lead only to inaccuracy of interpretation.

Much instruction can be gained by looking at the hands of famous people in paintings or sculpture and trying to relate their hand types to their life patterns.

When examining pictures or statuary for palmistic reasons one must take care to study only the greatest artists, for their works alone will yield valid conclusions. A comparison between the work of a truly great artist like Rembrandt or Holbein with one of the lesser renowned painters will quickly establish the gulf between genius and mediocrity. In portraiture at least the mark of the great artist is most plainly seen not in the representation of the face, but in the chirognomy and chirology of the hands. In this type of research one must try to be more careful than the nineteenth century chiromancer who wrote many pages of very delicate prose on the subject of the hands of classical statues in the British Museum without realising that almost all the extremities of these statues are modern restorations.

FINGER PATTERNS

The tracery of fine ridges on the fingers appears to have fascinated mankind from the very earliest times. It has been suggested that some of the Neolithic carvings found in certain dolmen, or burial passages, were inspired by such ridges: and one hypothesis goes so far as to claim that these carvings were hieroglyphic representations of the ridge formations found on the hand of dead chieftains, and served as a sort of magical identification. The Chinese have used finger-prints as a means of identification for hundreds of years, but only last century was the practice adopted by the West.

The medical and morphological study of these ridges, for which the word dermatoglyphics has been coined, was initiated in some respects by Grew, Bidloo and Malpighi towards the end of the seventeenth century, and since that time, particularly in the last sixty years, an enormous amount of research has been done in this field.

Anatomically speaking, the minute linear formations found on the epidermis of the hand serve a three-fold purpose: they act as secretion channels for sweat, they form a rough surface to aid gripping, and they form a corrugated texture which heightens the stimulation of the nerve endings beneath the epidermis and facilitates tactile sensitivity. Perhaps the most astonishing thing about these formations is their variety — not only does each pattern over the whole of the hand vary enormously, but even the patterns on very small areas vary sufficiently to enable accurate identification. No two patterns have ever been found to be exactly alike.

Epidermal ridges are developed in the foetus by the eighteenth week of pregnancy, and the individual pattern formation remains without natural change until death. As the hand grows in size, the ridges thicken, and towards old age they tend to become less sensitive, but at no time do they change their pattern in the smallest detail. This is, of course, not true of the so-called 'crease lines' of the hand which are in a constant state of flux. Both Herschel and Wicker made prints of their hands at different stages of their life, the first print being separated from the last by well over fifty years, but they were quite unable to perceive any change in the epidermal structure. I have in my own collection many prints of hands taken over a period of years which show no change in ridge formation, but considerable 'crease line' fluctuation.

There have been many attempts to destroy or alter the ridge patterns by means of acids, incisions and skin-graft operations, but on the whole such attempts have been bound for failure. There is one example of an American gangster who had skin from his side, which, of course, has no epidermal ridges, grafted onto his fingertips so as to evade identification in a crime. His painful operation, though successful in that it gave him ridgeless fingers, proved ineffectual, for he was identified by means of the patterns on the second phalange of his fingers!

However, it is not the morphological aspects of the study of ridge formations which interests us here, for the evaluation of character by means of these ridges, which might rightly be regarded as a sub-division of chiromancy, is an entirely different study called dactylomancy.

Dactylomancy appears to be a very ancient study in Japan and the Far East, but in Europe little attention has been paid to the significance of these individualistic markings. The earliest mention of these ridges in palmistic circles appears in a seventeenth century book *Chiromantia Harmonica* by Hoeping [123], but the text suggests that it was more the sensitive pads on the fingers rather than the pattern itself which was of chiromantical interest. If we read the cryptic comments as referring to the papillary ridges we must infer that the German palmist teaches that a person with circular whorls on all four fingers will be of a lecherous disposition! Whatever the reading should be, little else on the subject can be found until well into our present century. Most notably, Jacquin has paid a great deal of attention to the pattern formations in relation to character. He observed that the patterns on the fingers and emminences form a clue to the psychological disposition of the subject, whilst the malformations which sometimes appear on the minute palmar ridges were a sign of impending diseases of a physical and mental nature. Much of his medical diagnosis appears to be made by means of careful analysis of ridge malformations through microphotographs of palm prints.

My own findings in relation to the subject tend to support the ideas expressed in Japanese folk-lore, and in the work of Kojima which, unfortunately, I have only been able to study in European translations.

There are, fundamentally, three types of fingerprint patterns (though Mairs has identified thirty nine different types). These are the arch, the loop and the whorl. The percentage of hands in which patterns of the same types appear on all fingers is quite low, round about ten per cent, but all available statistics show marked variations in terms of racial groupings and different social levels. The graph at [124] is based on the statistics promulgated by Scotland Yard, and may be taken as relating to European types in general.

The simplest type of pattern is the Arch [128]. This is not a very common pattern monomorphically, and it individually occurs most frequently on the finger of Jupiter. The arch being the simplest formation, without any triadus, we would quite naturally expect it to belong to the most elementary type of person, and it is indeed found most commonly in the Earth hand. It is a regressive sign, indicative of a basic crudeness of approach to life and of a certain hard-heartedness which tends to insensitivity in relation to others. The tented arch is a little more complex in its construction than the

simple arch, and it has a corresponding effect on the energy it represents. The most persistent characteristic I have observed in relation to arches is stubborn defiance. People with arches on the majority of their fingers [132] are actively rebellious in most of their doings — they tend to rebel against society and are seemingly unable to accept many of even the simplest social conventions.

The loop pattern [129] is more commonly found. It has been divided into two types: the radial loop and the ulnar loop. The ulnar loop is by far the most common [133], whilst the radial loop is found occasionally on the finger of Apollo and only rarely on the finger of Saturn. Kojima came to the conclusion that 'a person with ulnar loops on all fingers is clear-spirited, mild-mannered, strong-willed, perhaps melancholy, and is likely to be cool in judgement and ruthless in business dealings'. Radial loops are regarded by the same authority as carrying a significance similar to the arch. The ulnar loop occurs too frequently for us to read anything extraordinary into it: one can infer from its presence a fairly conventional, unoriginal type of person. In monomorphic ulnar-looped hands it is best to establish significant character traits from other palmistic considerations.

The radial loop carries much the same significance as the whorl, and is essentially an indication of great individuality.

123 The earliest mention of finger patterns in a book is in Hoeping's Chiromantia Harmonica

124 Below right: A graph showing frequency of finger pattern occurrence on individual fingers, based on Scotland Yard data for 5,000 persons. Reproduced by courtesy of Dover Publications from Finger Prints, Palms and Soles *by Cummins and Midlo*

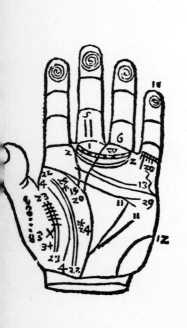

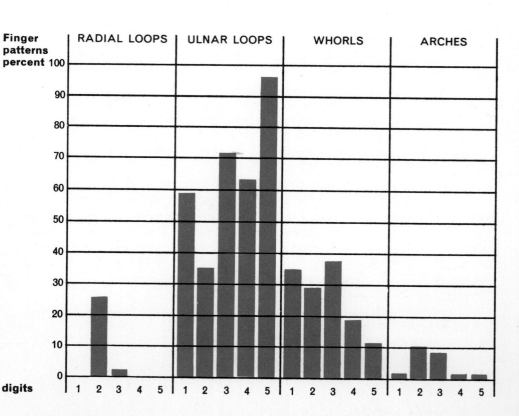

116

The whorl [130], [131] makes its concentric pattern around an epicentre which is usually in the middle of the finger-tip, and is united to the rest of the finger ridge by a sort of bridge supported on two triadi. It is certainly the most complex of the pattern groups, and we expect the possessor to be more 'complex' from a psychological point of view.

Jacquin observes that this type of whorl is a sign of an individualistic person who tends to be secretive by virtue of his disregard for others. Kojima examined the hands of over 200,000 criminals in order to ascertain the correlation between character, temperament and finger prints, and came to the conclusion that a person having whorls on all fingers would be restless, vacillating, sensitive, clever, eager for action and inclined to crime.

One whorl on a hand is a sign of individuality in terms of the particular significance of that finger. A whorl on the little finger, for example, in a hand which has only loops or arches, would suggest that the person was individualistic in his relationships with other people — he would tend to be unconventional in matters of sex or money. A whorl on the finger of Apollo would suggest a desire for originality of self-expression. The single-whorl pattern may be regarded as a sort of 'biological ring', for it performs much the same function as a ring in isolating one finger and investing it with a particular importance in relation to the person's life.

125 Below, left: The triadus; a triangular formation which is a useful aid for establishing the basic finger pattern type where it is not at first apparent. An arch has no triadus, a loop has one and a whorl has two

126 Below, centre: The earliest scientific record of an interest in dermatoglyphs, from Bidloo, 1685, British Museum

127 Below: The whorl finger patterm

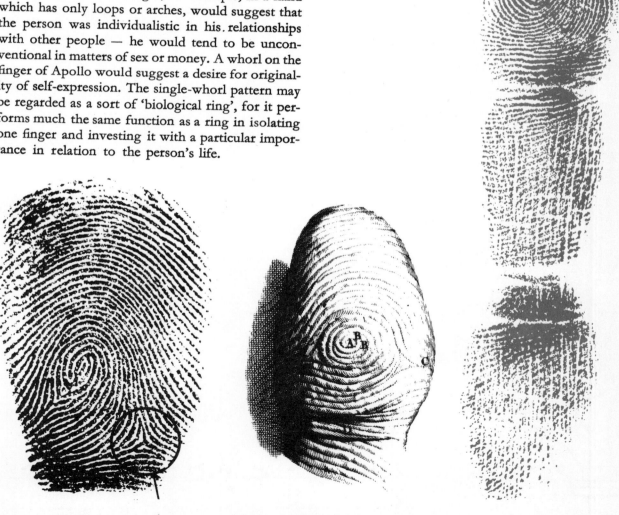

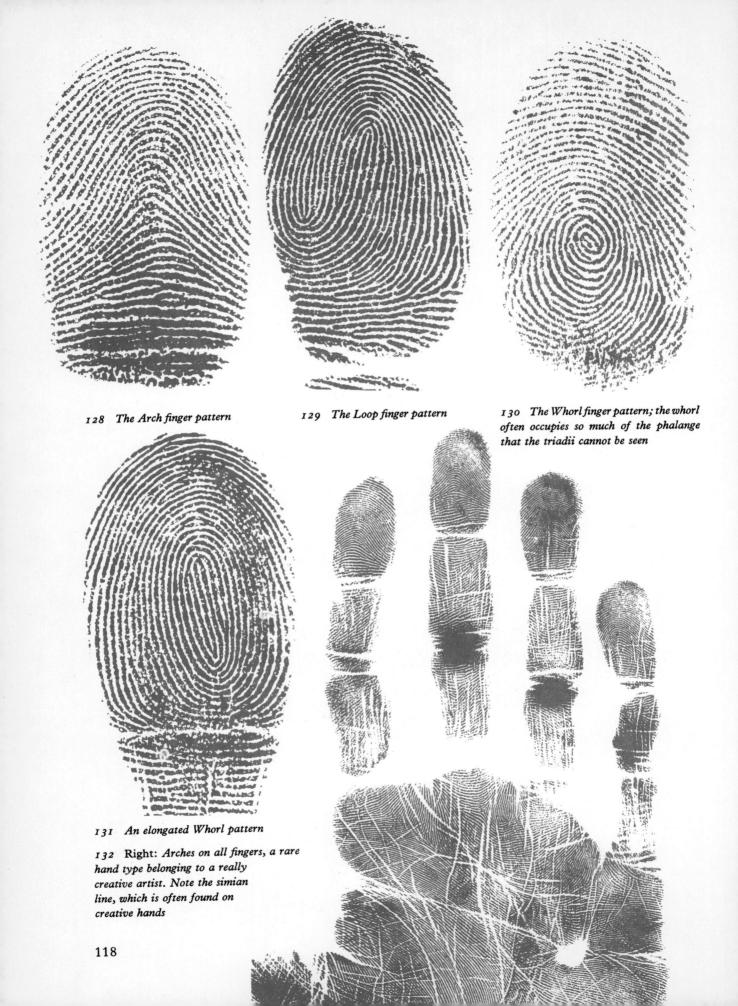

128   The Arch finger pattern

129   The Loop finger pattern

130   The Whorl finger pattern; the whorl often occupies so much of the phalange that the triadii cannot be seen

131   An elongated Whorl pattern

132 Right: *Arches on all fingers, a rare hand type belonging to a really creative artist. Note the simian line, which is often found on creative hands*

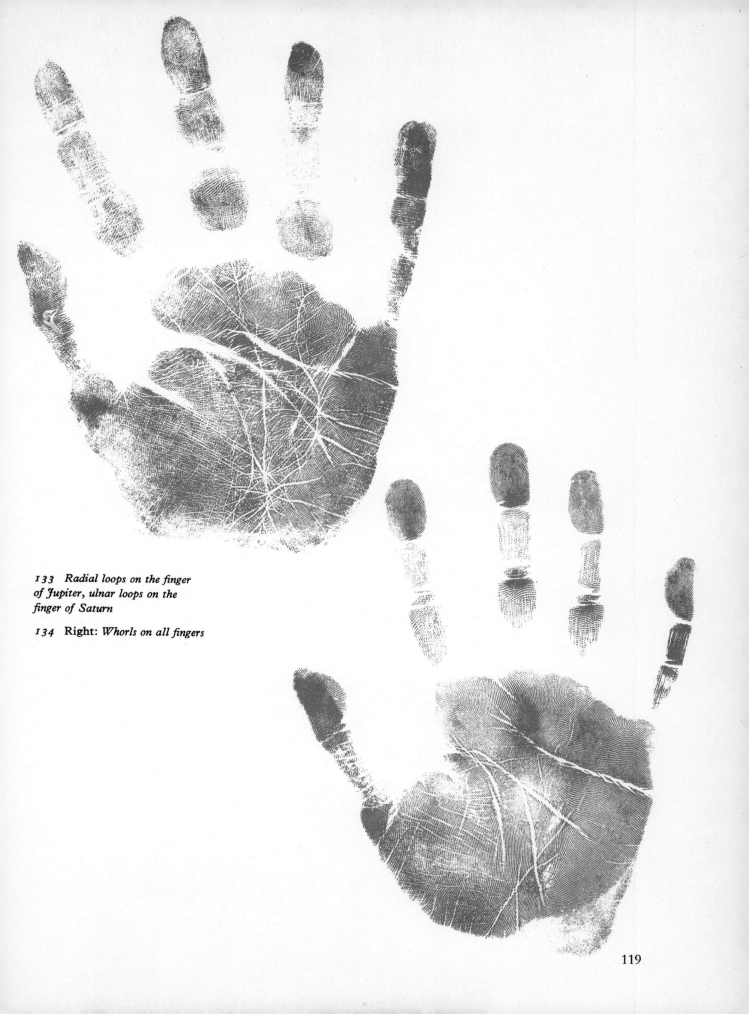

133 *Radial loops on the finger of Jupiter, ulnar loops on the finger of Saturn*

134 **Right:** *Whorls on all fingers*

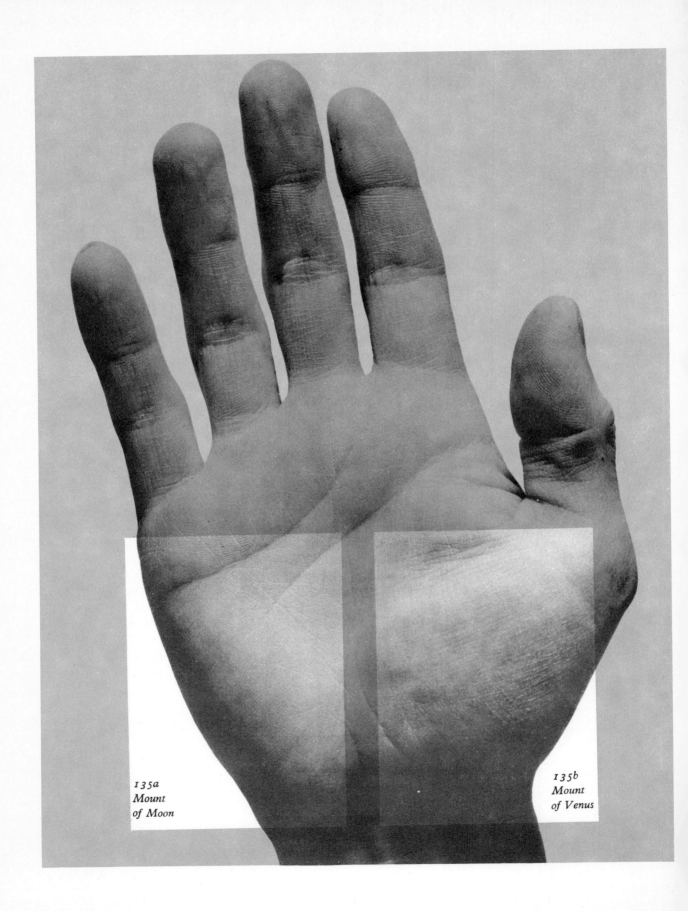

135a
Mount
of Moon

135b
Mount
of Venus

THE MOUNTS OF MOON AND VENUS

To the mount of Moon belongs the domain of Harmony in music as opposed to the melody, which is the special attribute of the mount of Venus.

Heron-Allen (*1892*)

These two mounts represent the active and the passive sides of the subconscious life of the individual. Their particular significance may be determined by their size (relative to the hand), shape, ridge patterns and linear formations.

The attributes of Moon [135] are rooted in the subconscious, and are always passive. Traditionally the Moon is female, and the controller of vegetative life on Earth. Because it has no light of its own, and is merely a reflector of light, it is sometimes equated astrologically with the personality of man.

Chirognomically the mount refers to the forms of imagination and the degree to which it plays a part in the person's attitude to life. A well-developed mount, or one with a strong whorled ridge pattern, indicates a highly imaginative make-up. The type of imagination, being of a passive nature, is rarely given external direction, and it usually takes the form of 'day-dreaming'.

A large and heavy mount of Moon [136] is rarely found on any type of hand other than the Practical hand. In such a hand it must be regarded as a sign of a strong creative potential, for although the mount in itself is only indirectly connected with creativity, its basic force of imagination may, when rooted in practicality, possibly be given external manifestation. A fairly large mount of Moon is to be expected on a Sensitive hand, but it mainly takes an elongated form, and often the bottom of the mount protrudes well down into the wrist [137]. This particular formation is, of course, one of the chief characteristics of a Sensitive hand, and it is seen most

clearly on prints of this hand type. Hypersensitivity is the result of such an extended mount.

In the Air hand a large mount is rare, but its significance is much the same as in the Water hand: it heightens the sensitivity and receptivity of the subject, and bestows on them a wider scope of imagination. The Fire hand is made more erratic by the presence of a large mount: this is only to be expected because the extroverted energies, so common to the type, though no doubt pure in origin, will very quickly become adulterated by imagination. Fire types with a large mount, or with an unusual ridge patterning on the mount, will find it difficult to be honest about things, for there will be a great confusion between the original perceptions and the subsequent alchemy of the imaginative faculty.

Whorl or loop patterns on this mount are always a sign of a strong tendency towards over-imagination [138]. They must be regarded primarily as atavistic markings, indicative of a basic instability. Such markings give undue predominance to the mount, separating the unconscious 'for special consideration' and the resulting instability is one in which the unconscious elements of the subject's life are not in tune with the conscious elements. From all available published statistics, there appears to be a very high occurrence of whorl patterns on the hands of mental patients. One must, however, be careful not to ascribe undue importance to this one sign without consideration of the hand type as a whole. It is not uncommon to find one or even two atavistic signs in the hands of normal people.

136 *A large mount of Moon on the palm of a 22-year-old Italian*

137 *An elongated mount of Moon on the Sensitive hand of a 23-year-old secretary*

The mount of Venus [135] is related to those energies which find a more positive and externalised direction than those of the previous mount. A large and heavy mount suggests a deep store of strong energies, and it is found most frequently on the Earth hand. In its position — as third phalange of the thumb — it may be regarded as the energy reservoir which is controlled by the phalanges of Will and Logic: these two give shape and direction to an energy which is in essence very primitive. The significance of this mount is thus intimately connected with the thumb as a whole.

'An excess of the mount,' writes Heron-Allen, 'will betray debauchery, effrontery, licence, inconstancy, vanity, flirtation and levity,' and although the observation is a little histrionic the idea behind it is based on truth. A large mount is a reservoir of high potential energy which constantly seeks immediate release. Unlike the subconscious energies contained in the mount of Moon, these energies must escape *via* the body — most suitably by way of strenuous energy. It is not surprising that the Practical type (which usually has a large mount of Venus) should take delight in physical activity, and that so many Practical types should like boxing and wrestling.

Some palmists, amongst them Spier, regard the mount of Venus as consisting of two halves — the

138 *A Whorl pattern on the mount of Moon*

upper part, which represents the sublimated force of the mount, and the lower part (the ball of the thumb) which represents the sensual and creative powers within the psyche. Certainly the lower half of the mount is connected with artistic ability, and I have observed that many creative people, particularly those who work under a continual internal pressure of activity, have a well-developed lower Venus. In excessively active types this part of the mount is much rayed with deep lines running across the mount, up from the line of Life and into the second phalange of the thumb. Such lines may be regarded as facilitating the passage of energies from the reservoir into external life. Although the lines help in this way they do suggest a certain superficiality in the passage of energy, and one must expect a manic state of activity — long periods of complete activity interspersed with short periods of utter inactivity. The hand at [139] is that of a well-known artist; he is intensely active and productive.

In traditional palmistry the lines on the mount are related to the 'humanity' of the subject. A much rayed mount of Venus is supposed to indicate warmth of temperament, whereas a mount completely without lines is supposed to indicate coldness and 'dullness in the matters of art'. It is easy to see how this interpretation is connected with the present one.

139 *The hand of an artist*

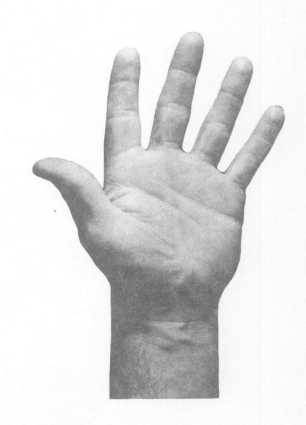

CHIROMANCY

As constant sorrow and grief leave their mark in the face in the form of wrinkles and lines, the hand reveals to an even higher degree the imprint of inner experiences because it cannot be influenced and controlled by the conscious mind and is thus capable of greater differentiation of expression.

Spier

The lines on the hand, 'the graffiti of the skies', as one Chinese commentator described them, have led to many extremely complicated systems of palmistry. It is not surprising that so much significance has been attributed to these line formations for they constitute one of life's most obvious mysteries. There is absolutely no rational explanation for their presence — they are certainly not solely the result of hand flexion, nor, one feels, are they merely the channels for 'astral fluids' as Desbarrolles and others have suggested. 'The movements of the hand have not the slightest effect upon its shape, expression and lines, as is often believed by the layman, for only the psyche, the mind, the psychological processes are the formative powers' is the comment of a modern psychologist.

There is a tendency nowadays to regard the lines as being of little value in character analysis, but this seems only an inevitable reaction against the undue interpretative significance placed on them in the past. Without doubt the lines do manifest a wealth of material regarding the character of a subject, and when 'read' in context, which is to say in relation to the hand as a whole, they are of the utmost importance to the palmist.

The idea that the lines of the hand are intimately connected with the psyche is, of course, as old as palmistry itself. Exactly how the relationship between the two was established no one has been able to determine, but there has been little doubt that the relationship is precise and full of significance. The chief difficulty, and this is the point on which

140 Detail from Gypsy Woman Telling a Fortune *by Gherardo delle Notti in the Uffizi Gallery, Florence*

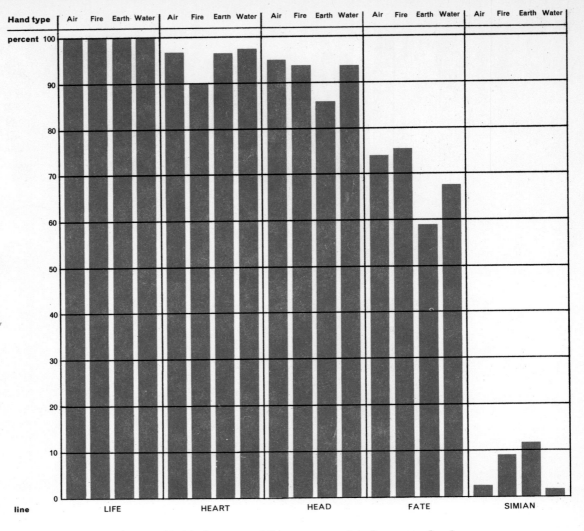

Hand type	Air	Fire	Earth	Water	Air	Fire	Earth	Water	Air	Fire	Earth	Water	Air	Fire	Earth	Water	Air	Fire	Earth	Water

141 Graph showing frequency of line occurrence, based on 1,000 hands

so many palmists disagree, is precisely *how* one is to interpret the lines in order to grasp their meaning.

Benham, working at the height of the Victorian era, regarded the lines as so many 'life maps', with each one as a sort of miniature plan of the past, present and future of a specific function. The system of interpretation he offered was, in theory at least, an exact science, and he suggested that reading a hand was little more difficult than reading a book once the language was mastered. Vaschide, who was also a doctor and research worker like Benham, called the lines 'motoric images', suggesting that their natures were largely determined by muscular action and memory, and he was, in spite of his strict scientific training, inclined to favour intuition as a satisfactory method of correlating their relationships with the psyche. Both these extreme points of view contain within them an element of truth: the whole of the truth can be found somewhere between the two, which are not, after all, mutually exclusive.

The lines, when interpreted properly, indicate the individual's psychological tendencies and, within certain limits, give some clue to his future. The 'future' so far as palmistry is concerned is not a hard and fast series of predetermined events in time; it is a loosely confined series of possibilities which are given actuality as the individual psyche reacts with the external world. In one sense the future is an extension of the present, 'seen from an aspect of time': but it can be changed and is therefore neither completely predetermined nor completely undetermined. Man's view of time in relation to temporal processes have lead him to this dualistic attitude which is so manifestly wrong: we are not completely free, nor are we completely enslaved. On a less theoretical level palmists have often changed the life patterns of certain subjects for the good — even to the extent of preventing suicides.

The lines indicate the highly individualistic state of flux between the person and the world: the flux which is described in psychological terms as 'the life pattern' of the person. In this respect, and in this

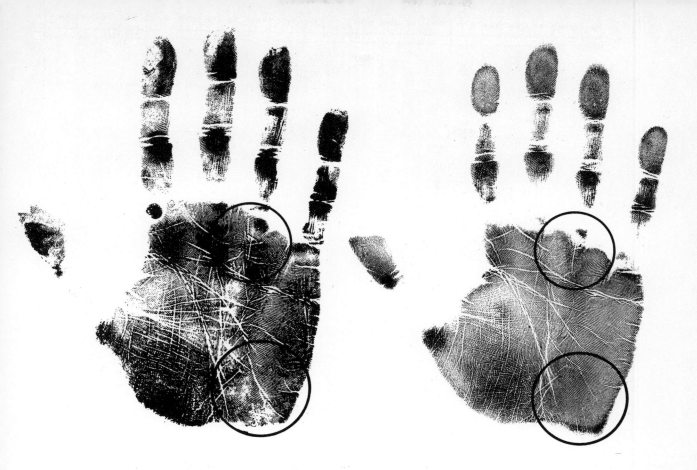

142 The hand print of an artist, and the same hand three years later. Observe how the strong line on Moon has almost disappeared, and how the many lines under Apollo have changed into one strong line. The first print was taken at a crucial point in the artist's life; he had suicidal tendencies, shown in the deep drop of the Head line towards Moon, and was completely lacking in artistic direction. Psychiatric treatment helped him resolve his problems to some extent, and he began to fit into society and to paint in the way most suitable to him. The change of lines under Apollo is significant.

respect alone, by virtue of indicating present directional trends in relation to temperament, the lines of the hand give a clue to the future.

From one point of view there is no great mystery as to why the lines should reveal 'the unknown'. The truth is that certain aspects of the future are not unknown. When Benham was casting around for some quotation to summarise his findings he chose Emerson's remark that 'the soul contains in itself the event that shall presently befall it'. He could equally as well have chosen something from Democritus, two thousand years earlier. We could quote with equal ease from Jung. In one part of himself the individual knows the future. The lines are merely the outward expression of this subconscious knowledge.

The number and complexity of the lines vary to an enormous extent. As we have already seen, an Earth hand may exhibit only three or four lines, whereas a Sensitive hand may be completely covered with a fine mesh of lines. Only very rarely does a palm contain fewer than the three main lines of Heart, Head and Life. I have never seen a hand without a Life line, but I have on one or two occasions seen a palm which appeared to have no Heart or Head lines. The Fate line is more often absent. The chart at [141] which is based on 1,000 prints from my own collection, gives some idea of the frequency of occurrence to be expected from the major lines.

In addition to the main lines there are often to be found numerous smaller ones which have been given names by certain chiromancers. Mangoldt calls these 'subsidiary lines'. It is quite a common thing for the subsidiary lines to change as the inner attitude of the subject changes, but the main lines change less often. [142] is two prints of the same subject taken with an intervening period of three years. The obvious changes in the line formations are not, as the subject's case history demonstrates, haphazard or lacking in significance.

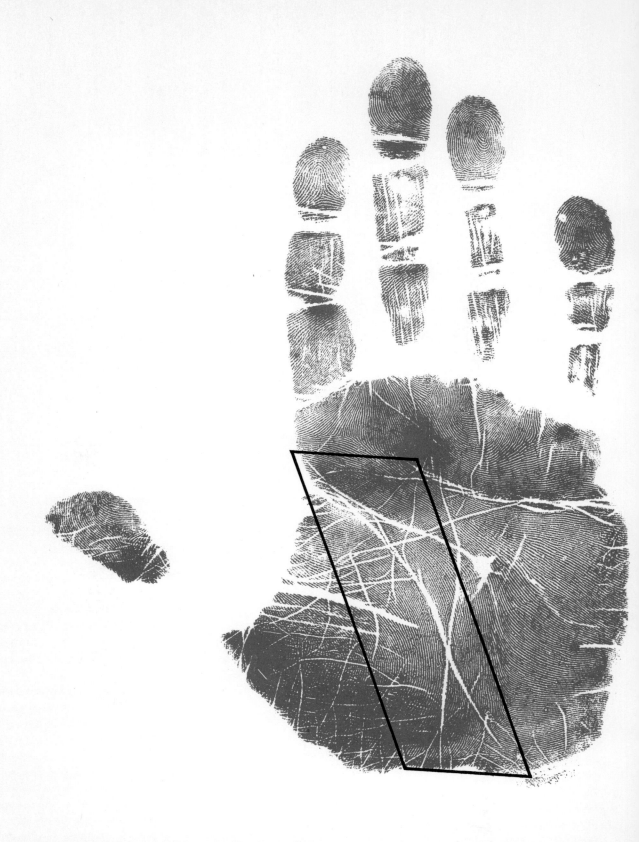

143 *The Life line on the hand of a 60-year-old nightwatchman*

148 *A trauma recorded on the three major lines of the hand,
the effect of a serious accident*

149 *Weak Heart and Life lines; the subject has a hole in the
heart*

150 *A break in the Life line*

151 *A trauma recorded on the Life line*

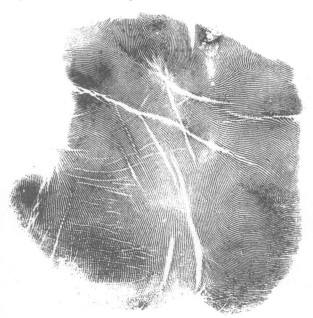

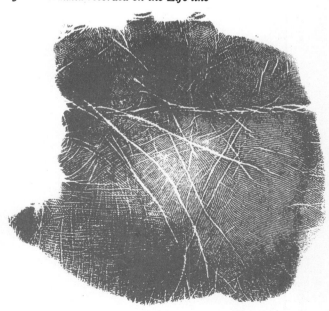

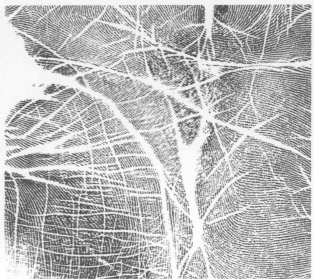

152 *Life line rising from mount of Jupiter*

154 *Life line rising from Jupiter on the hand of a theatrical producer*

153 *Chained Head line*

The only observation which Spier makes about this particular line is that it indicates a hypersensitive person who is 'easily hurt'. Since extroverted and ambitious people tend to be more than usually egotistical they are the more easily hurt when their egos are pricked. It appears, therefore, that Spier's interpretation indirectly confirms my own.

When the line of Life springs from the Head line the physical energies are controlled to some extent by the mind, and this leads to a certain degree of shrewdness. A clear and unchained fork between Life and Head is always indicative of a certain calculating shrewdness of character which tends to put emotional considerations in second place to 'hard-headed' considerations. It is the typical marking of the businessman. Such a restricting influence of the head over the energies can, of course, in extreme cases, lead to disharmony. Shrewdness is an excellent characteristic up to a certain point, but beyond that level it leads to a 'coldness' and emotionally inhibited state which, like all imbalance, can be disruptive to normal life relationships. Benham calls an excessive displacement of the Head down the Life line 'a typical criminal marking'. The example print at [155] is from the hand of an extremely competent and very shrewd businessman.

Certain palmists suggest that the point where the line of Life leaves the line of Head gives the time of life at which the subject is freed from the influence of the home. This interpretation is not tenable, for it leads one to suppose that about forty-five per cent

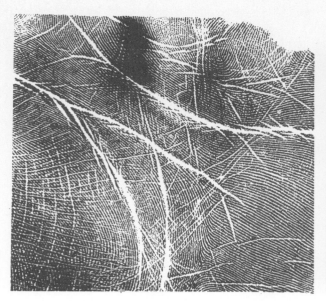

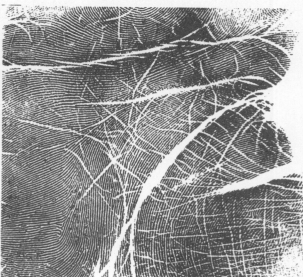

155 Life line and Head line coming together on the hand of a businessman

156 Impulsive open commencement of the Life line

of the population have had no family life of any description. I have observed something which could explain the origin of this reading, however; a person whose Life line leaves the Head line deep down in the hand often feels, by virtue of his natural shrewdness, that it is a better financial proposition to live at home whilst establishing himself in the world. He thus tends to leave home quite late in life, and this fact alone may have given rise to the old teaching.

When the line of Life takes its point of origin below the Head line, and independently of it [158] we must expect a less restricted use of life energy than in the former case. The fact that the Life line is divorced from the Head indicates that action is less inhibited, but that at the same time it is inclined to be impulsive, less controlled by reasoning. Reasoning, in this context, must be taken as rationalisation of inhibitions. The space between Life and Head, taken in relation with the chirognomy of the thumb and the length of Jupiter, will give a fairly precise picture of how a person is likely to act in terms of his hand type.

When Life and Head form between them a reasonably short-chained link [153] one must infer that the activity of the person is vacillatory in quality and characterised by a more or less rapid oscillation between extroverted and introverted states. The generation of energy is uneven and its application variable.

The course of the Life line is related to the quality of the mount which it encloses. In general, as we

have already seen, we must take a large mount of Venus, with a correspondingly large sweep of Life line enclosing it, as significant of a high and powerful reservoir of energy which readily participates in the subject's life. When the Life line is pressed in towards the second phalange of the thumb, and there is a consequent restriction of the mount, we must expect a low reservoir of energy and a corresponding lack of warmth and vitality.

We must relate the insertion of the Life line to the four-fold division of the hand which we discussed in the chapters on chirognomy. One can easily imagine the significance of a Life line, the representative of vital energy, which passes its force into that quarter of the hand which relates to imagination, passivity and inaction. Such a line would suggest that vital energies are unstable, uneven and badly directed. The conflict between the active life force and the passive life force, represented by such a line, would build up to high peaks of tension which must be released explosively at unexpected intervals. This conflict produces a highly strung individual, moody in disposition and with a marked tendency towards depression.

In the ancient traditional forms of palmistry the line which separated from the Life line and ran in an outward sweep towards the mount of Moon was supposed to indicate travel. In fact, as Jacquin has observed, the line merely indicates a restless disposition, which in itself often gives rise to a desire to travel.

135

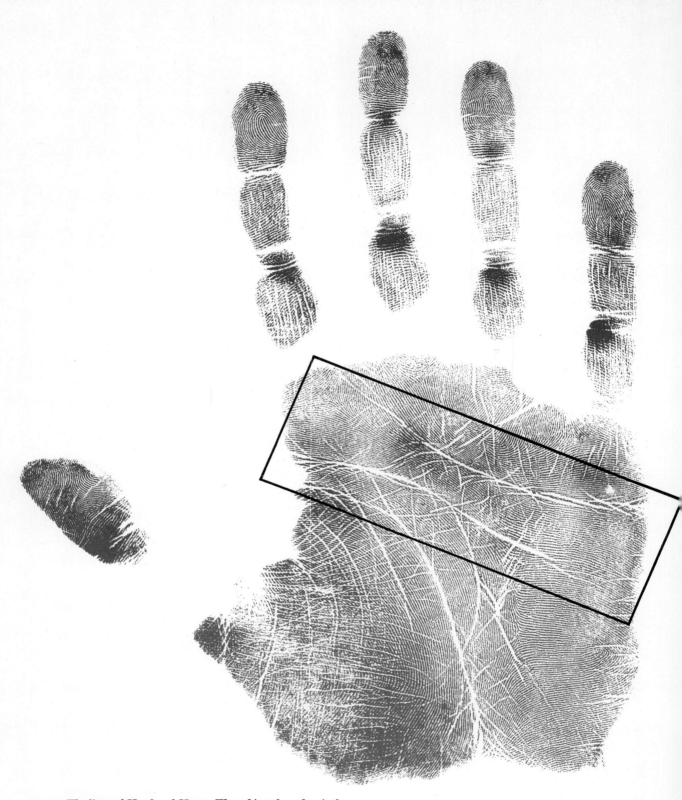

157   The lines of Head and Heart. The subject does chemical research at Oxford; the chain about one-third the way down the length of the Head line indicates a particularly difficult period of Head activity

THE LINES OF HEAD AND HEART

Although it is customary to discuss the Head and Heart lines separately I have found it more realistic to consider them as a unity. This is necessary not merely because in some hands the two do in fact join together and form one line, but because the two have significance only in relation to each other. Mentality and emotion, which are represented by the Head and the Heart lines respectively, should work together in harmony, for they represent between them, like two scales on a balance, two different sides of human understanding. The intimate relationship between them is such that it is impossible to use one without involving the other. Unfortunately the natural balance between the two is very easily disturbed and is rarely appreciated. Modern educational methods, which place so much emphasis on mental training and no emphasis on emotional training are, I feel, largely instrumental in leading to the severe emotional problems of our day. Little can be done to restore a balance and harmony in the adult and preserve them in the child until the nature of this balance between mind and emotions is properly understood.

The state of balance between these two functions can be determined by a detailed analysis of the Head and Heart lines. At this point, for the sake of simple description, and out of deference to certain traditional teachings which appear to be based on fact, we shall examine these two lines separately and then proceed to evaluate their significance as a unity.

The Head line usually arises from beneath the mount of Jupiter and runs outward towards the percussion of the hand. It may be regarded as a sort of canal transporting energies from the conscious sphere of the hand to the subconscious sphere. This analogy can best be understood when one grasps how deeply so-called intellectual decisions are rooted in our subconscious mind. The course and insertion of the Head line varies enormously. It may be quite short, ending abruptly under the finger of Saturn, or it may be very long, running in a gentle curve towards the mount of Moon and even ending up at the racettes.

The characteristics of the Head line reflect the characteristics of the individual's mentality — his powers of rationalisation, concentration and ability to comprehend. It is, therefore, intimately connected with the emotional life of the individual. I have not found the traditional teaching (that the length of the line indicates the depth and power of the intellect) to be accurate: the length of the line, taken in relation to its quality and point of insertion, relates to the subject's breadth of understanding. We find accordingly that a long line of Head indicates a wide field of understanding, and that the nature of this understanding is determined by the area on which the line terminates. If the line runs in a more or less level course towards the percussion and ends above the mount of Moon [160] the understanding, though wide in scope, will be limited by a practicality which tends to eschew imagination. If the line runs in a deep curve towards Moon [163] the understanding will be equally wide in scope but limited by an imagination which repels 'mere practicality'. A Head line which echoes the line of Life, running in a deep curve towards the centre of the wrists, has always been taken as a strong indication of suicidal tendencies. Certainly such a line would only be found on a person so utterly dominated by imagination as to be completely out of touch with reality, with a tendency to depression, and a strong desire to escape from life. The two suicide cases reproduced in this book have Head lines of this nature.

The 'ideal' Head line is one which strikes a balance between these two extremes. If it is of good length, even quality and proceeds in a gentle curve to end on the upper part of Moon, one can expect a first-class mentality. One of the finest Head lines of this description belongs to a world-famous biologist and writer [159].

A shorter line of Head usually indicates a more limited mental range, but does not reflect the depth of the subject's understanding, which can only be gauged by considering the length in relation to quality.

The quality of the line is of paramount importance for it shows the degree of concentration at the command of the subject. The highest degree of concentration would be found in a single, strong and even-running line. A chained line of Head indicates that the subject has fluctuating attention — that he has periods of relatively good concentration accompanied by periods (of more or less length depending on the length of the chain) during which he is quite incapable of concentrating. A double Head line, with two lines running parallel, indicates very bad concentration. This type of line has been taken by some palmists (notably Cheiro, who wrote a very

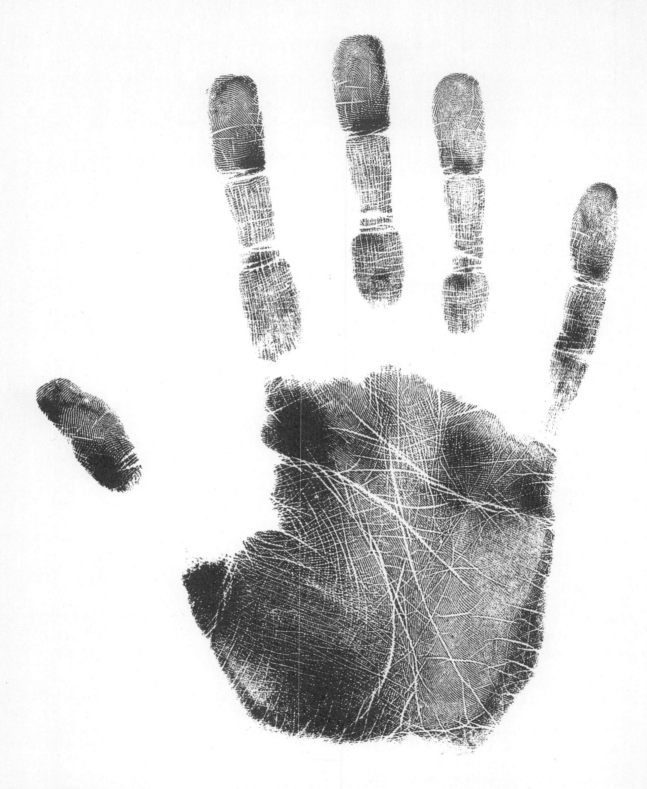

158 An imaginative Head line, usually found, as in this case, on the hand of a Sensitive type

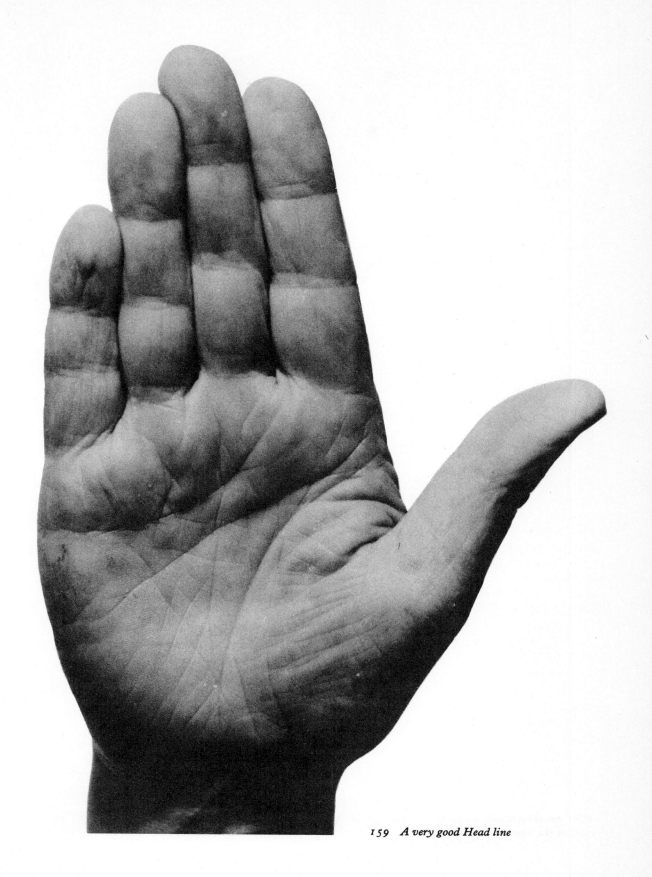

159   A very good Head line

involved account of a man with a double Head line) as a sign of schizophrenia, but I am quite unable to support such claims. Bad concentration, allied with a bad memory, can often lead to a certain inconsistency of personality, however.

Clear breaks in the Head line are indicative of some mental trauma. The very noticeable break in the line of Head at [161] was the record of electro-convulsive treatment given to a mental patient at the age of seventeen. As in the case of the Life line, one must be careful to distinguish between what are evidently breaks in the line and what are merely 'shearings'. Shearings in the line indicate either a change in mental occupation or change of situation where mental impressions are given a new lease of life.

The Heart line arises at the percussion of the hand just below the mount of Mercury and runs across the hand below the finger mounts, and usually terminates near the mount of Jupiter. It may be regarded as a canal transporting energies from the unconscious half of the hand to the conscious half. This analogy is given extra significance when we see that emotional energies, which are represented by the Heart line, spring from the subconscious and are directed towards the survival of the individual ego: Jupiter is the finger most clearly connected with this ego.

Although the course of the Heart line is fairly steady in normal people, its point of insertion can vary as much as that of the Head line. It may end right up between the fingers of Jupiter and Saturn [162] or it may branch down towards the beginning of the Life line. It may even end in a fork on both these areas.

As we have observed, the characteristics of the Heart line reflect the characteristics of the individual's emotionality — his emotional depth, quality and direction. The line is thus intimately connected with the sexual type of the subject. A most curious fact is that although the connection between this line and sex was established beyond doubt only in the early part of this century, one of the earliest writers on palmistry was quite obviously aware of the connection.

> . . . *yef this lyne contynue and be depe and brode, it signifieth good dysposcicion of those partes that longe to the begetyng of chylder.*

The type of sexuality may be determined by the strength of the line and by the point of insertion.

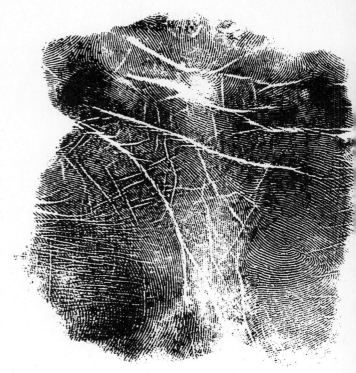

160   *A Practical Head line*

161   *A trauma recorded on the hand of a young woman*

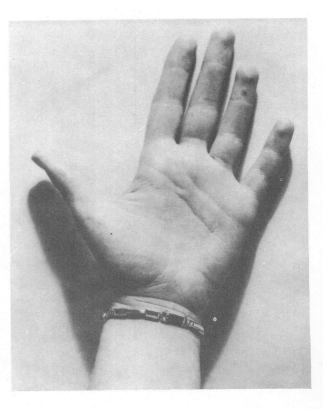

140

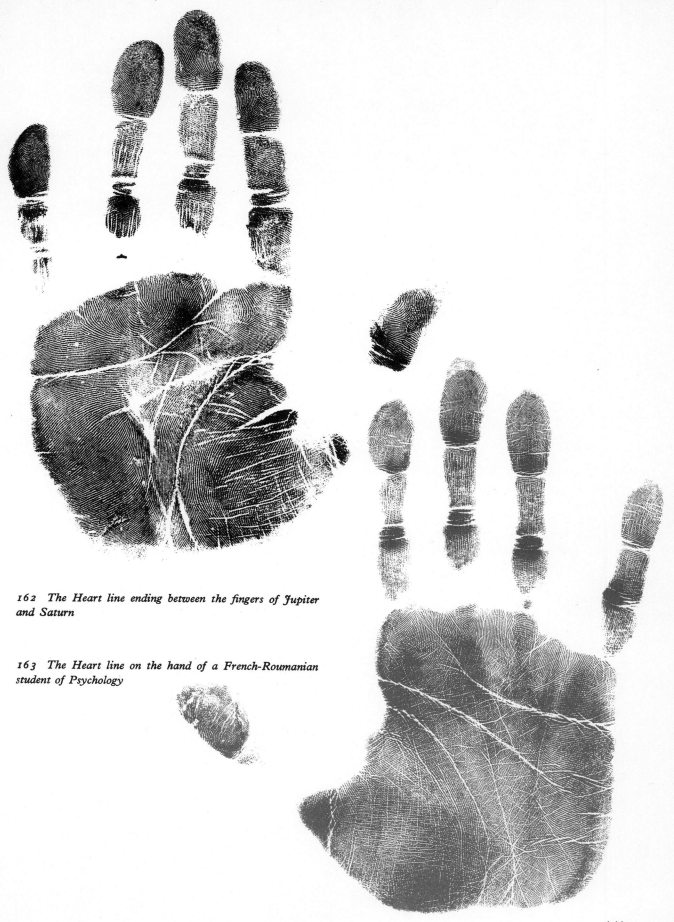

162 *The Heart line ending between the fingers of Jupiter and Saturn*

163 *The Heart line on the hand of a French-Roumanian student of Psychology*

Should the line run clearly and strongly between the fingers of Jupiter and Saturn a healthy, physical enjoyment of sex can be expected. The line must, to a certain extent, add something of the sensuality normally found in a developed girdle of Venus (see page 151) and from one point of view this line could be regarded as consisting of a girdle running into the Heart line. The craving for changing experiences must be interpreted in terms of the hand as a whole, but one can be assured that physical sex will be a great demand. As the line insertion drops further down the hand towards the Head line, there is a corresponding coldness in the approach to sex. When the line of Heart ends very low down in the hand, below Jupiter, one can expect a more inhibited and less physical approach. This type of sexuality has been described, somewhat misguidedly, as 'idealistic'. Certainly physical sex is not the chief aim of this type. The qualities carried by the line are restrained by the influence of the head. The resultant 'idealism' requires a deeper relationship with a partner than mere physical contact affords. Love, to this type, is only partially physical: 'So must pure

lovers' souls descend to affections, and to faculties, which sense may reach and apprehend.' (Donne)

One must of course constantly refer the Heart line to the finger of Mercury and to the mount of Venus when attempting to determine its significance. When either of these two aspects of the hand suggests sexual difficulties, the insertion of the Heart line may lend a further clue to diagnosis of the real problem. In general I have observed that when in a male hand the line of the Heart curves down at its termination to the base of the mount of Jupiter [165] there is a strong element of femininity present in the sexuality of the subject. Equally, when the line curves down in a similar fashion in a female hand, there is a strong element of masculinity present. These tendencies may not *per se* go so far as homosexuality, but there is sufficient ambivalence to warrant a thorough check on other aspects of the person's sexuality.

A chained Heart line is very common. Its significance, according to Spier, is physical deficiency in connection with the circulation, but I am more inclined to regard it as relating to the emotional

164 An extremely broken Heart line on the hand of a young boy with heart trouble

165 Below: An 'idealistic' Heart line

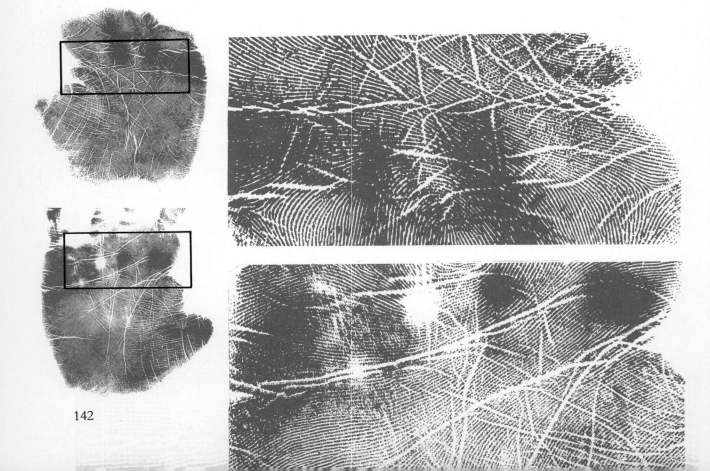

166   *The beginning of a simian line*   167   *A full simian line*

168   *Hair-like lines dropping from the Head line; this is the commonest form of incipient simian line*

169   Below: *A chained simian line on the hand of an artist*

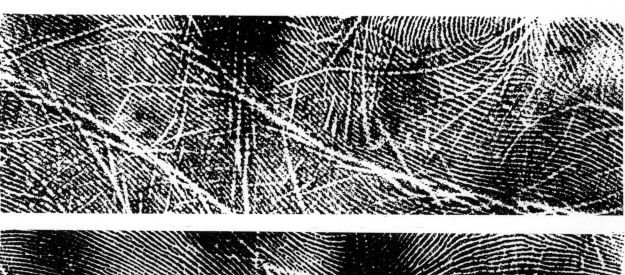

calibre of the individual. A richly chained Heart line signifies an emotional calibre with problems and difficulties. A line which is not chained, but accompanied by many islands and branch lines, suggests that although the emotional life of the individual is characterised by 'ups and downs' there is an underlying steady level of emotions, which gives the person a degree of emotional stability.

Breaks in the Heart line are more frequent than in any other major line. Single breaks have a traumatic origin, whereas a badly broken line points either to some form of Heart difficulty, physiologically speaking, or to some emotional unevenness, psychologically speaking. The extremely ragged Heart line shown at [164] is from the hand of the young boy with a hole in his heart which we examined in connection with the Life line.

We have already commented on the deep connection between the emotional and mental aspects of a person's life. A little experience of the Head and Heart lines will convince the student of the need to interpret the two lines as a unity, for together they show in a particularly vivid way the type of balance or imbalance in a subject. From a comparison between the two lines it is relatively easy to see which particular sphere of intellectuality or emotionality will be used by the person in his attempts to adapt to life. A careful analysis of the two possible spheres will give a clear picture of how the person will adapt, whether it be with a predominance to the emotions or with a bias to the intellect.

In some people the two processes represented by the Head and Heart lines are so undifferentiated that they are never able to use them separately. Chiromantically this struggle between the emotions and the mind is represented by a line or series of lines emerging from the ending of the Heart line and falling in towards the Head line [168]. This line is the early beginning of the so called Simian line, which is of great importance to palmists, psychologists, anthropologists and to the medical profession.

The true simian line is, technically, a running together of the Head and Heart lines [167]. Its name is derived from the fact that it occurs so frequently on the hands of monkeys and gorillas. In general it is regarded as an atavistic sign of degeneracy.

The simian line has many forms and many degrees; the illustrations [166]—[169] show something of its most usual forms. In all cases it is composed of elements common to the line of Heart and the line of Head, and it may be understood from one point of view as representing a conflict between these two. We must remember that the Head line moves from the conscious sphere to the subconscious — these two natural tendencies are restricted in the simian line, and the result is an enormous inner conflict.

One very strange fact which my observations have pressed home to me is that this conflict is found in two apparently different types of person. In cold statistics the simian line in its pure form is not common, and although figures vary, about six per cent of all hand types appears to be a fair estimate. However, I have observed that the simian line occurs in a high proportion of criminal types. So often does this line appear in the criminal class that it has been taken as a sign of criminality. The only criminal hand reproduced by Cheiro (a print of Dr. Meyer, convicted of murder in 1894) shows a marked simian line, whilst earlier references in palmistry books give savage pictures of violence and brutality in connection with the line. The high frequency of simian line occurrence in mongoloid idiots has been remarked upon by every research worker on the hand since Vaschide, and it is now one of the signs of a mongoloid tendency in a baby.

It is to be expected that inner conflict should give rise to the criminal type — and in fact it is quite possible to define the criminal in terms of conflict — but to consider the simian line purely from this angle is to miss its true significance.

The second class of people in which I have observed a very high incidence of simian lines is composed of two types who appear at first glance to be distinctly different. One type may be defined as 'religious' and the other as 'creative'. Both these types have been largely ignored by research workers who, by virtue of the present state of psychiatric studies, are disposed to work only on abnormal people, and this in itself has led to a misunderstanding of the line's meaning.

The connotation attached to the words 'religious' and 'creative' is unfortunate, for 'religious' does not give a very accurate picture of these types, and at the same time it is slightly misleading. The type I am trying to describe is not the quasi-sentimental Christian who believes in 'doing good' but rather the earnest seeker after some form of inner meaning. Equally, when I speak of the 'creative' type I do not necessarily mean the type who paints pictures or sculpts to gain the approbation of his own social clique, but artists or musicians who create in a sort of agony 'to relieve themselves of an intolerable burden' as Michaux puts it. Like the criminal class, the lives of these people are characterised by a strong internal struggle: on the one hand racked between the devil and the saints, 'broken and dashed to pieces in my religion', and on the other hand standing mid-point between two similar forces of destruction and construction so familiar to the artist.

Perhaps a better term to include both these types would be 'evolving' — those who are consciously or unconsciously trying to free themselves from the human condition, those who are subtle alchemists searching to transform dross into gold. Such people who seek after self-improvement, either within the framework of a philosophical credo or within the framework of a search for beauty, may be said to be evolving types. I found that in one religious group of people in the Midlands, of the thirty-five

whilst the religious class may be regarded as the *evolving* types. In this type of cosmo-conception humanity must be pictured against a background of Jacob's ladder — some ascending, some descending, and none able to remain still for ever.

I have not been able to find any definite method of determining exactly whether or not certain types of simian hands are on the ascending or descending scale. On a Practical hand, with other atavistic signs such as a deficient third phalange of Mercury, high mount of Moon or low-set thumb, one would expect a degenerate criminal. This is not always true, however, for as Jonson says in *The Alcymist*, 'The children of perdition are oftimes made instrument even of the greatest works' and the forces for evil may eventually, by some forces unknown to us, give way to the good. This appears to be one reason why so many moral degenerates create such fine works of art: it is not only in the Far East that artistic striving is intimately bound up with the religious experience, and divorced from moral considerations.

On a Fire hand, with fine sensitive whorls, good

170 A hand with a strong simian line

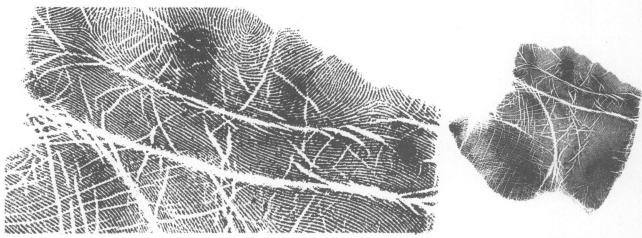

people at the meeting eleven had strong simian lines and six had weak ones. A much higher proportion of simian lines occurs in the hands of creative people.

The very idea of evolution carries with it the opposite idea of involution, and it appears to me that the simian line is the external manifestation of the inner struggle between these two forces. The criminal class may be regarded as the *involving* types,

finger balance, well-proportioned thumb and few signs of degeneracy, one would expect an evolving type, but one cannot be absolutely certain without a detailed analysis of all hand factors. It would appear that both the force for good and the force for bad are in both types of people, that they are both potentially devils and saints at the same time. How the struggle between these forces will end cannot, in the last analysis, be determined.

145

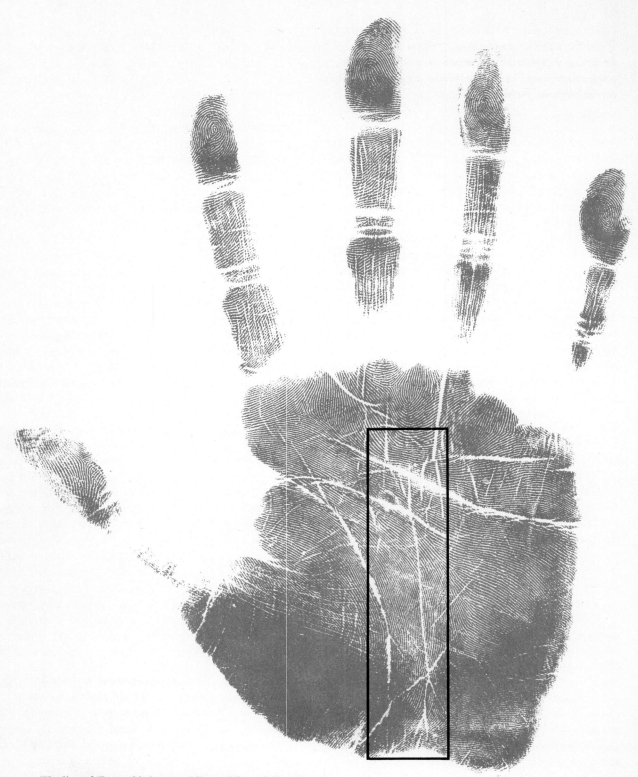

171 The line of Fate; this is a good line, without deflections or breaks, belonging to the editor of one of Britain's largest newspapers

THE LINE OF FATE

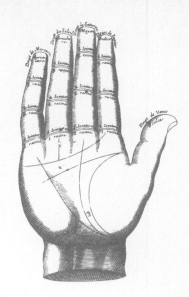

If the Fate line is simply absent from a hand, it denotes an insignificant life, which takes things as they come, meeting with neither particularly good nor particularly bad fortune.

Heron-Allen

Alternatively called the line of Destiny, the line of Fortune, and the line of Fate (the *long longitudinal line* of medicine), this line begins in the lower part of the hand near to the wrist and runs upwards towards the finger of Saturn. Its course is often erratic and its point of origin may vary enormously. The fact that its length may vary anything from one to ten centimetres makes it the most unstable of all the main lines. It is absent in about twenty per cent of hands.

The meanings ascribed to the Fate line have varied almost as much as the line itself. The traditional viewpoint that it is related to destiny has not been entirely discredited by modern research, but its interpretative importance has been mitigated somewhat. There can be no doubt that the line is related to the inner adaptability of the subject; more precisely, the quality of the line indicates the quality of 'inner freedom'.

Adaptability has been defined by more than one authority as the measure of intelligence, and consequently the correct interpretation of the line of Fate must bear in mind the nature of the other main lines.

It is quite logical that the line which separates the active and passive sides of the hand, and at the same time links the conscious and the unconscious, should be connected with the problems of adaptability. Our whole life, the state of our mind, and our aspirations may be defined in terms of adaptation. Every moment of our lives demands a change in equilibrium — each moment is 'a new and shocking evaluation of the past', and if we are unable to adapt to the changing world we are left behind and our survival is threatened. It is to this adaptability which the line refers, and it is not lacking in significance that the Fate line was at one time called the line of Saturn, no doubt in reference to the mediating power of that god.

The presence of the line must in itself be taken as a sign of a reasonable adaptability, but the nature of this adaptability might be determined by reference to the nature of the line. A long line is a good indication that the inner attitudes of the subject are relatively free — that there is, in other words, a high degree of adaptability present. The strength of the line can only be judged by comparison with the other lines in the hand. A Sensitive hand usually contains quite delicate main lines, whilst the Earth hand contains very strong and deep ones. A weak line of Fate is a sign of poor adaptability, whilst a chained line of Fate suggests that the adaptability of the person is uneven — the individual will find little harmony in himself, and this will lead inevitably to uncertainty of action.

The Fate line does not in any way refer to the individual's position in life, but from it one can estimate the degree of 'inner harmony' within the subject in relation to his environment. Print [172] shows the hand of a millionaire: his Fate line is relatively weak and broken, and is therefore significant of a general feeling of insufficiency and uncertainty. The marked line of creativity which runs from the Fate line, perhaps a little vacillating in course, across the lower half of Moon indicates the reason for this feeling: although the subject is pre-eminently successful in life so far as material possessions are concerned, he has a strong creative urge which has little or no outlet. The man's re-creation (in what little time business will allow) is in fact painting.

The forceful hand at [173] shows a very strong line of Fate. This man, a painter, though in a considerably less secure and established position than the previous case, is very happy in his pursuits. His sense of adaptability is very good, and he is full of confidence about his work (if not about his internal life — note the short finger of Jupiter). In this hand the abrupt turn of the Fate line at the top towards Jupiter is a sign of a strong ambition. The length and strength of the line itself indicates that these aspirations are being achieved.

A double line of Fate (which occurs with surprising frequency) must be regarded as an extended island. Adaptability — the relating of outer demands to inner demands — is the chief conscious problem of such hands.

As Spier points out, the Fate line changes quite considerably in some hands during childhood. Some babies who are born without the line [174] may develop one, even quite abruptly. The line appears to change very little after the age of twenty, however, by which time some rigid attitude which governs adaptability is already well established. The line is obviously more dependent on environmental factors than the other three main lines.

172 The hand of a millionaire showing a weak Fate line

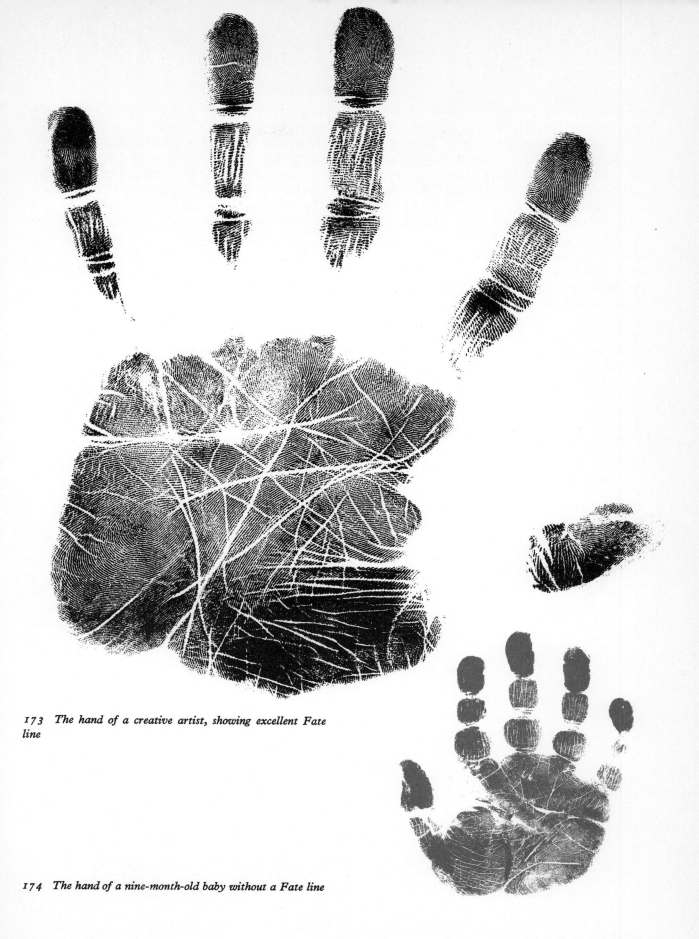

173 *The hand of a creative artist, showing excellent Fate line*

174 *The hand of a nine-month-old baby without a Fate line*

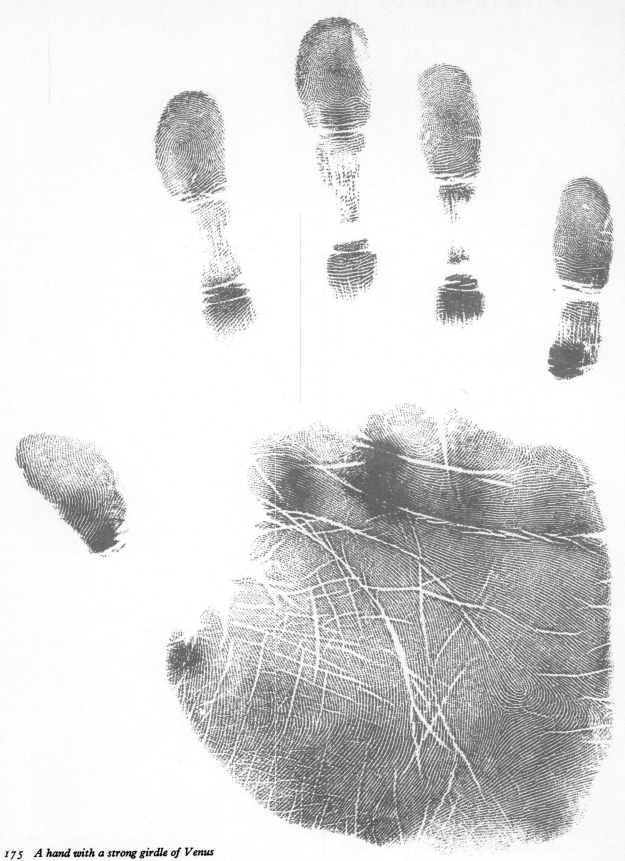

175 A hand with a strong girdle of Venus

SUBSIDIARY LINES

The significance of the subsidiary lines is completely overshadowed by the importance of the four main ones. They are more changeable in structure, more difficult to locate and only significant in relation to the hand type as a whole. In order to understand their meanings one must bear in mind the old analogy of lines as energy conductors. Each line may be imagined as passing energy in a more or less nervous state from one part of the hand to the other. The direction of the energy will give some clue to the undercurrents of the subject's temperament and behaviour.

It follows from this analogy that, speaking in general, hands with many lines belong to people of a nervous and sensitive disposition, whereas hands with few lines suggest less nervous, more vital 'down to earth' types.

The girdle of Venus starts between the fingers of Jupiter and Saturn and runs across the finger mounts [175]. It may be regarded as an adjunct to the line of Heart, and in some cases this is precisely what it is. In itself the line adds a degree of emotional sensitivity to the hand. Chiromantically the line acts as a connection between the external conscious and the inner conscious quality of the personality. It links the self-assertive elements with the emotions, and therefore tends to be a dangerous marking. People with marked girdles are in constant need of excitement and variety; I have seen the line very strongly marked in the hands of drug addicts, and others in continual need of artificial emotional stimulation. A short girdle is itself a good sign of emotional alertness, but when it extends across the palm in a series of broken and chaotic lines [177] the sensitivity of the individual is so high and erratic as to be dangerous. A craving for variety and excitement results in an inner restlessness which can be quite disruptive. One can easily understand why tradition links this line with a strong sexual appetite.

The line of Apollo [176] usually runs from a point near the line of Fate towards the third finger. It is often referred to as the line of intuition, and is associated with the creativity of the person. The presence of a strong line is no certain showing in itself of creativity. As its localisation (under the finger of Apollo — the finger of distant emotional relationships) would suggest, the line relates to the subject's emotional direction, and is thus indirectly connected with creativity in the widest sense. It is significant that when the subject at [142] found an emotional direction after treatment, the many lines under Apollo gradually merged into one. The usual interpretation of many small vertical lines under Apollo is 'jack of all trades — master of none' and there is an element of truth in this belief, because a diversity of emotional directions and interest can lead only to a dispersion of energies quite foreign to the mastering of one trade or creative activity.

Quite often the line of Apollo is very short, starting just above the line of Heart. If it is longer than this its significance will change in accordance with the area from which it is conducting energy.

The line of Mercury usually arises from the lower part of the Fate line, and ends on the mount of Mercury. Its presence confirms a degree of 'subconscious vision' — an ability to emotionally comprehend something more deeply than by ordinary means. Mercury was the messenger of the gods, and it is in these terms a fine representative of the intuitive faculty. Mediums, clairvoyants [178] and highly intuitive people always have this line. It is only rarely a single line, and more often is composed of numerous small, hair-like lines which suggest a certain unevenness of application.

There are many lines of the hand to which significance has been attributed. In particular Spier mentions 'the line of milieu' and the 'poison line', but a thorough discussion of these lines, though interesting, would be sadly unproductive. Much more systematic research is required before we can pronounce with any certainty on the majority of subsidiary lines. It is apparent, for example, that the line which is often seen to run across the base of the hand on the mount of Moon is connected both with the reproductory system and with creativity, but until medical histories are correlated with hand formations in a much more systematic and thorough way, little of further certainty can be claimed.

176 *The line of Apollo*

177 *The girdle of Venus*

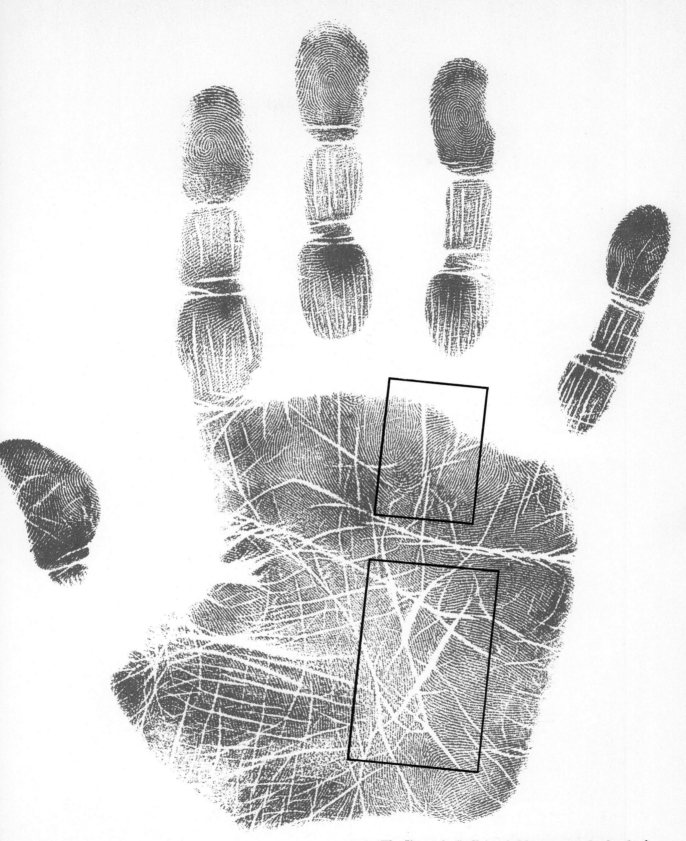

178 The lines of Apollo and Mercury on the hand of a clairvoyant

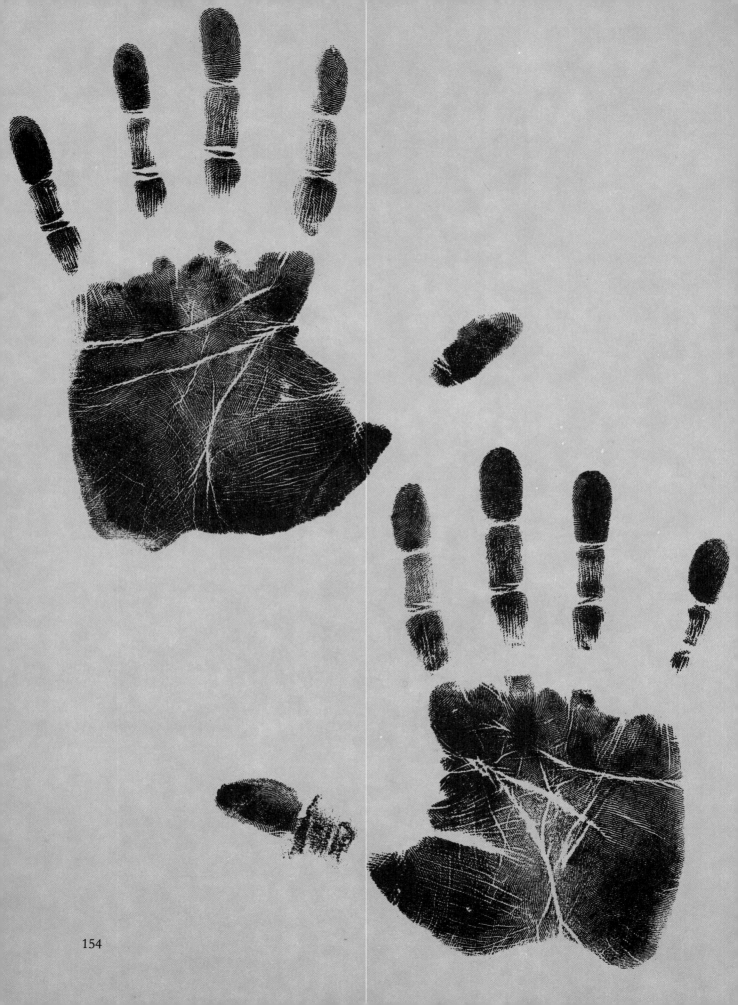

CONCLUSION

In spite of all the words, explanations and illustrations we have succeeded only in touching the surface of palmistry. The ancient art is almost lost, and what remains of it is really too foreign for our understanding. For this reason we must regard palmistry as a very youthful study and seek to learn more about the hand and its secrets. Unlike the vast complexities of technology and specialised science, palmistry is still young enough for laymen with sufficient real interest to make discoveries for themselves.

The strong force of superstition is, with this age as with any other, the chief obstacle to a systematically conducted study of the art. It is almost ironical that we should, in this day and age with so much intellectual freedom, stigmatise as superstitious a study so full of potential significance and utility. In regard to these superstitions about palmistry — those which, for example, keep palmists on the wrong side of the law or which condemn the art as unscientific as if that label in itself was an anathema — I can do no better than quote the words of S. T. Cargill, which sum up the matter perfectly:

> *It must be freely conceded at the outset that every subject upon which millions of human beings have expended vast outputs of thought for innumerable generations must be worth systematic study, and any effort to discriminate unfairly in a spirit of sectarian conceit against one or other branch of knowledge, whether in space or time, can only serve to warp the judgement and narrow the outlook.*

I have tried to emphasise that palmistry is essentially the art of combination. Anyone who seeks to interpret the hand in terms of only one or two specific qualities has not understood the first axiom about palmistry, and his efforts are bound for failure. Palmistry is a practical thing — it can no more be studied abstractly and without reference to living hands than medicine can be studied without reference to human bodies. Consequently, because the art is essentially one of combination, and because it is a practical affair, a book such as this, which deals with simplified theory, can only have a true meaning in relation to a wide experience of different hand types. A person who wishes to master this art, which, like any other worthwhile pursuit, may take a life-time in the mastering, must look at hands for himself in order to establish his own truths. He is advised to regard these theories only as a scaffold.

Palmistry, being an art and therefore intensely personal, will be based on different theories; one might almost say as many theories as palmists, because different experiences, different interests, and above all different hands, must give rise to a diversity of teachings. One should no more expect two palmists to hold the same beliefs than one can expect two painters to paint the same way.

179 Left and right hands of a past world champion speedway rider

THE HISTORY OF PALMISTRY

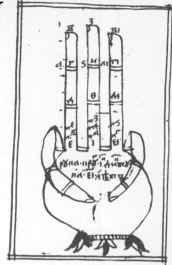

To be merely modern is to condemn oneself to an ultimate narrowness

G. K. Chesterton

The history of palmistry is almost entirely the history of certain superstitions. In reality there is no such thing as palmistry, there are only palmists. No deep accumulation of systematised knowledge has survived which might be described as a palmistic tradition, though many definite features have been preserved and have been repeated through the ages so that they now constitute a body of teaching often referred to as 'traditional palmistry'.

Palmistry has never been a strong force in the eddies which have shaped our history in the West, but the fact that it is an art which has occupied so many minds for so many centuries demands that some account be made of its development. So far as I am aware this is the first serious attempt to write a history of Western palmistry. The perfunctory 'histories' found in most books on the subject are too wildly inaccurate to be worth much attention, and my chief hope is that this text will remedy the position by replacing the old imaginative guesswork with a new and reliable account of this very ancient art.

The very nature of palmistry limits any history to a record of what has been written about the subject. This is so because the true practice of palmistry has always been intuitive in character and has therefore been difficult to record in words. We are thus faced with the fact that although there are literally thousands of records dealing with its outward forms, there are virtually no records which deal with its inner form. This history is therefore concerned mainly with the outward form of palmistry — with the art as it has been preserved in books and manuscripts. I can best sum up the matter by misquoting Carlyle in saying that the history of palmistry is just the biography of its leading individuals.

It is very difficult to assess the accuracy of early palmists in foretelling the future. A palmist can deal with only one person (or rather with one hand) at a time and any prediction he makes is usually a personal affair in which the outcome of the prophecy is often kept secret or is merely forgotten with the passing of time. This is not so with other forms of prophecy, in which the future of whole races, cities and even civilisations may be foretold. Such prophecies are usually intended for wide publication and are consequently not easily forgotten — on the contrary they are often carefully preserved and embroidered upon by later generations. Thus we find the world prophecies of St. Malachai, Nostradamus, Savonarola, Tycho Brahe and other seers are still with us, whereas the personal prophecies of Cocles, Achillinus, and other great palmists who were much consulted in their day, have been almost forgotten. Those prophecies which are still remembered have an almost universal interest in that they were predictions concerning great men and princes. On the whole, however, the predictions made by palmists were private and personal matters concerning people and events which no longer interest us.

Limitations of space have compelled me to be selective in the names and achievements of all those palmists who are known to us. Only the most famous or infamous are included, whilst the lesser known and less important chiromancers like Del Rio, Laigneau, Corvaeus, Kemker, della Porta (a list which could be extended infinitely) have been left out. I have found it very difficult to be impressed with modern palmists. Of the three hundred and fifty or so books which have appeared on palmistry in the past twenty years perhaps five or six are worth serious attention.

180 The 17th century Dutch genre painter David Teniers and his wife consulting a gypsy palmist; detail from an engraving by Surugue after Teniers, British Museum

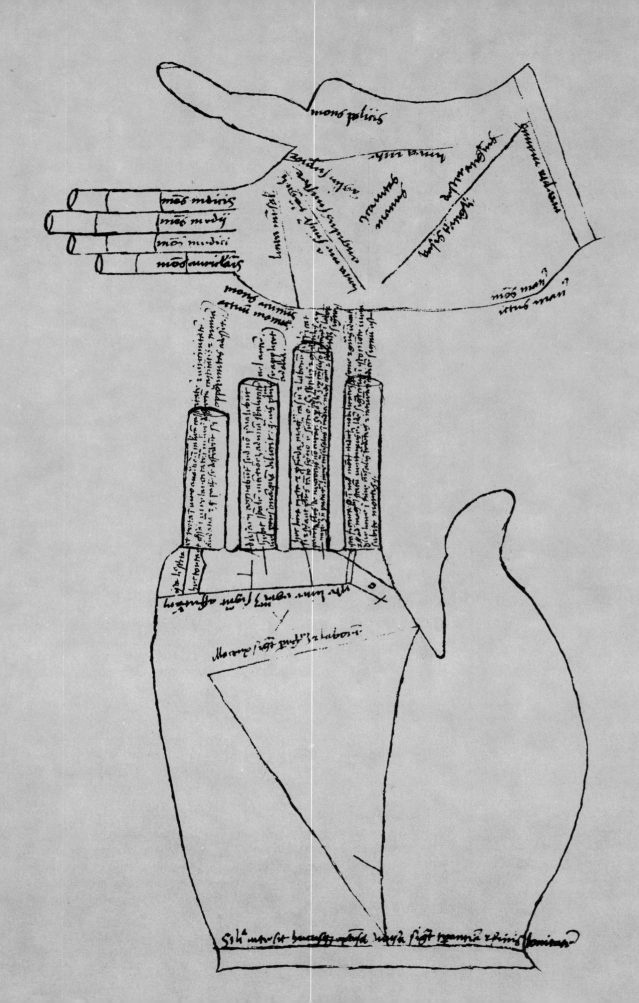

EARLY PALMISTRY

There is no remembered beginning to an art already old before Aristotle was born. The origin of palmistry is for ever lost in the silence of unrecorded antiquity, whilst the poor fragments of the art which have survived stand as tantalising evidence of some long-past Golden Age of chiromantic knowledge.

Baron von Humboldt records a story of a parrot which, having at one time lived among a tribe of Indians, had learned a little of their language. The tribe died out, and the long-lived parrot alone remained, babbling words in a language quite unknown to men. The language of palmistry in its earliest form might be likened to the parrot's chatter, for on the whole it consists of words and symbols which are but poor reminders of what might well have been a comprehensive system of knowledge.

Even by Aristotle's day, from which date the first certain references to palmistry in the West, the art was in what can only be taken as a degenerate and fragmentary form consisting of little more than a series of physiological notes. One or two centuries later it had become merely the subject for satire, and was already classified as a 'foolish, false, vain, scandalous, futile, superstitious practice'.

In fact, there is a surprising scarcity of reference to the art of chiromancy before mediaeval times. Ancient comment on the subject is scanty, which makes it all the more surprising to have *La Grande Encyclopédie* claim that palmistry was 'highly esteemed in Rome' and that 'the most learned minds of antiquity valued it highly'. The actual documented truth is not so sweeping. The earliest references are found in the works of Aristotle, the one most often cited being found in *De Historia Animalium* (i. 15).

Besides Aristotle, we have a couple of references by Pliny in his Natural History; Suidas makes mention of a treatise by Artemidorus dating from about 240 B.C. which has since been lost; and there is a not very pleasant comment by Juvenal on 'the cheap chiromancer's art'. This is the complete list of certainties — incredibly restricted in scope when compared with the traditional list of 'authorities': Anaxagoras, Hippocrates, Plato, Ptolemy, Galen, Paulus Aegineta, Avicenna and Averroes — all authorities by repute only. None of their chiromantical works has survived, though it is quite probable that each of these writers did mention palmistry, if only *in passing*, in more general books on physiognomy, astrology or medicine.

But if there is a shortage of evidence, there is no shortage of guesswork about the origin of palmistry. One of the earliest known accounts of its inception, found in a fifteenth century manuscript, claims that:

Tales Milesias, the wyche was the fyrst phylosophyre in the citee of Atene, by the answere of god Apollo, fyrst dede wryte the syence of cyromancie in the longgage of Parce; and mayster Arystotyll translatyd it owt of Parce into Grece.

But unfortunately this is probably little more than mediaeval *argumentum ad vericundiam*, for the same manuscript refers later on to the chiromancy of Albertus Magnus, whose works have been fairly well preserved, and show no knowledge of the art.

A much more interesting legend is quoted as authentic by Heron-Allen, the famous chiromant, usually more accurate in matters of scholarship:

It is said that Aristotle, when travelling in Aegypt, found an Arabic treatise on this science of the hand, graven in letters of gold, upon an altar dedicated to Hermes, and that he sent it to Alexander, as being worth the attention of the highest savants, where it was translated into Latin by one Hispanus.

In a later book, Heron-Allen writes about this legend, 'I do not know where this statement originated: probably among the vaticinations and literary irresponsibilities of some of the older chiromants... I presume that the account arose in this way: there is no doubt that when Aristotle — subsidised by Alexander — made his expedition into Asia for the purpose of compiling his "History" he was in the habit of sending the results of his investigations to Alexander as they were completed, and in the course of this journey visiting Egypt, he picked up a quantity of the occult knowledge of the Egyptian magi.'

Taisnier, writing in 1562, mentions that Aristotle wrote a book on the subject of chiromancy for the instruction of Alexander, but he makes no reference to the legend. We can, therefore, assume that the story was invented after this date, for it is the sort of thing which Taisnier would have delighted to record.

There can be little doubt that in fact the story was fabricated by Praetorius of Zeitlingen, who confuses it with the legend concerning the introduction of Hermetic philosophy, the *secreta secretorum*, into Greece. It is a confusion not without real

181   A page of very beautiful drawings from the manuscript by Rodericus de Majoricus in the British Museum

182 Siva, *South India, with detail of right hand showing palmar markings*

significance, for it demonstrates clearly the desire to attribute an esoteric origin to palmistry. Such a source is highly probable, and would account for the paucity of written teaching, for the essence of hermetic thought is a guarded conservation of knowledge rather than dissemination, and it tends, therefore, to be oral in character. Alchemy, with which palmistry was doubtless associated in the earlier days, had both an esoteric and an exoteric face, the latter serving to hide the real nature of the esoteric search. Palmistry could have had this dual nature, though there is no supporting evidence for such an argument.

It is most usual for writers on palmistry to quote sacred writ as referring specifically to chiromancy: *Job xxxvii 7* is particularly favoured, with *Proverbs iii 16* a close second. Extensive literature on the subject has been admirably discussed by Heron-Allen in *A Manual of Cheirosophy*, 1892 (pp. 55—59). Sir Walter Scott summed the matter up in his *Letters on Demonology and Witchcraft* when he referred to 'those who claim the support of the Scripture for their own individual theories without regard for the niceties of translation which would be of the utmost importance in such cases'.

Despite the losses, confusions and silence of the past, palmistry is of very great antiquity. Spier refers to the 'chirological writing of the literature of India, dating from the Vedic period, that is to say about 2000 B.C , whilst the art, in a form remarkably similar to our own, has a written tradition in China which goes beyond the Fourth Century before Christ'.

The earliest reference to palmistry in Indian literature is found in the *Vasishtha* Rule 21 where an ascetic is forbidden to earn his living either 'by explaining prodigies and omens, or by skill in astrology and palmistry, or by casuistry and expositions of the *Sastras*'. This ruling is also contained in the ancient code of *Manu* (vi, 50). Both these texts are of Vedic origin.

In later times, palmistry became so important and was so highly regarded as an art in India, that the hands of gods in statuary and paintings were carefully marked with lines and symbols which intentionally bore no resemblance to the lines found in real-life palms. The reason for this was undoubtedly that the Indians intentionally avoided stigmatising their gods with any mere human characteristic. Indian gods, and the representatives of gods, free from the effects of *Karma*, could hardly be expected to have markings which revealed their fate.

The road to India was open to the Greeks, for there was an established trade route which had been used by the Arabs for centuries — we must also remember that Alexander the Great was a pupil of Aristotle, and had himself reached India. It is very likely that Desbarrolles, the famous French palmist of the last century, was right in claiming that Western palmistry originated in India.

Craig reports that the science, in its primitive form, is recorded as having a place amongst the ancient Egyptians, but there is little evidence for his statement. Nor does there appear to be any foundation in Katherine Saint-Hill's claim that 'the oldest manuscript the world knows of, found among the most venerable papyri of Egypt, is a prescription for the composition of women's face-paint, or "make-up", and the second is a treatise on hand-reading'.

Ancient Egyptians, Chaldeans, Sumerians and Babylonians have at one time or another been hailed as the originators of the art, but this again can be nothing more than elaborate guesswork, for no records remain, and the form, extent and origin of early palmistry is quite unknown. We can be certain of only one thing — that when Aristotle wrote his few words about the hand, palmistry was already an old science with at least an oral tradition of very long standing.

Unfortunately most 'histories' of palmistry have done more to obscure the real truths than to clarify them. A fairly typical sample of the sort of irresponsible guesswork which went into early 'histories' can be found in Richard Saunders' *Physiognomie and Chiromancie*, published in 1653:

> *We find in the truths of Antiquity, the Hebrews, Chaldeans, Arabians, Indians, Greeks, Latines, and Italians great students in, and promoters of, this high part philosophy; who with no small pains have in their*

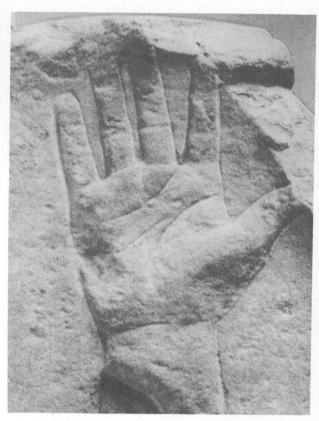

183 A hand from a 5th century Greek Island sculpture, showing the lines of the hand. Detail from the metrological figure in the Ashmolean Museum, Oxford

> *several Tongues written large volumes thereof, as Aristotle,* princeps philosophorum, *Virgil, Plautus and Juvenal have copiously observed. Great magistrates have loved, used amd honoured this Science, amongst whom were Lucius Scylla, and Julius Ceasar, as Suetonius and Josephus report; who affirm that by the hand the said Ceasar discovered the false Alexander who said he was son of Herod. Infinite copious might I be in this Subject should I run through the whole classis of those famous Noble Heroes who have spent (to their eternal fame) their pains in this Science, but lest I should be too prolix I have alphabetically recorded in the following page, the names of all those whom I have had the happiness to consult with in this work.*

Saunders in fact furnishes us with a list of some 150 'Noble Heroes', ranging from the old stand-bys like Albertus Magnus and Aristotle to Cocles and Taisnier, who were reputable chiromancers. Such errors as Saunders makes he had on 'good authority', and in terms of the scholarship of his day his errors are not too disturbing. What is disturbing, however, is that his errors have persisted well into our present century, and can be found in most modern books on palmistry.

Fortunately for us it is not merely a string of erroneous superstitions which have been handed down to us. The nomenclature of chiromancy — which we can assume to have been in use before the birth of Christ — is particularly interesting, and is another pointer to a Golden Age of knowledge; for the particular qualities attributed to the different parts of the hand so many centuries ago are still used, and are still valid today. In other words, the fragmentary palmistry which has survived from ancient times, suffering as it does from the misrepresentation and accidents of centuries of scorn and scholarship, suggests a teaching which might well have been comparable to many palmistic teachings of modern times.

Heron-Allen, touching upon the meeting between the *gitana* and D'Arpentigny which gave rise to modern palmistry, writes:

Running through the chaotic nonsense which the gipsy recited, the listener [D'Arpentigny] *had been struck by the recurrence of certain expressions which seemed to him to be echoes of a forgotten language — of a language whereof the essential character retained much of its ancient force.*

In a similar vein, Professor Craig, commenting on the palmistic teaching of some old English texts of the fourteenth century, writes:

What surprises one is that the subject has remained practically unchanged. The sum and substance of the large majority of books on palmistry which appear annually is the traditional system of lines and divisions (presented in these manuscripts).

The teachings which Craig mentions readily admit their indebtedness to a much older tradition, and his comments may in a general way be taken to stand for the whole system of palmistry known to us. It will be interesting at this point to compare two paragraphs taken from different palmistic writings to show the degree to which traditional formulae have persisted. The following quotations are separated in time by about five hundred years: the first comes from the early fifteenth century manuscript known as the *Digby Roll*, and the second is taken from *La Grande Encyclopédie*. They are both discussing the significance of the area between the Heart line and the Head line.

184 A Roman symbolic hand about 5¾ inches high, cast in bronze; the significance of the symbols is unknown. British Museum, 1929

> *If the table, between the line of the heart and the line of the head, is large and broad in appearance, it tokens open-handedness and free heart in all a man's life. If it is narrow in appearance it betokens niggardliness all a man's life. If it is in some places narrow and in some places broad, sometimes he will, in his old age, be open-handed, and sometimes close-fisted. The same table, if it is broad and large, it tokens kindness and friendliness of manner. If it is straight and narrow it betokens avarice, discord and enmity.*

> *When the quadrangle* [the table] *is large and the line of heart and the line of head parallel along the most of their course, it indicates a spirit of wide ideas and is healthy in outlook, and of well balanced nature. The subject is loyal and faithful to his friends: it is also a good sign from the point of view of physiology, for there is a natural resource against illness. If the*

opposite be the case, if the two lines run towards each other [and the table is narrow] *they affirm that the ideas lack wideness of vision. The subject does not hold his word, or he will go back on it. One cannot depend on such a person, for he is probably a liar.*

However, beyond such indications as these of an early established tradition, little else has survived. A search into the past for the origin of the art brings only disappointment, for the few conclusions drawn belie the work involved. An ancient teaching there certainly was, but its origin and scope are as lost to us as only the past can be: it is as far away as the *Vedic* hymns, and as obscure as the chatter of Humboldt's parrot.

From half-guesses and probability, from obscure reference and wild documentation, we suddenly find ourselves plunged into certainty in the thirteenth century. It is from the early part of this century, possibly from the late twelfth, that we have inherited several chiromantical manuscripts. With varying degrees of thoroughness they all deal with the subject in complete confidence of its antiquity, and are delightfully saturated with the mediaevalist reverence for symbols. The main body of extant chiromantical manuscripts is to be found in the British Museum and the Bodleian Library. They have been classified, in terms of form and quality, into five main groups.

The simplest treatise deals only with main lines of the hand, the formal introduction and argument being very slight, in some cases non-existent. This type of treatise has been described by Craig as 'hardly more than a series of notes accompanying drawings of hands', but in at least one manuscript there are no drawings at all. Naturally the text is written in scribe's mediaeval Latin, and all the drawings are clumsy. The main divergence from modern terminology is in the use of the word *mensal* for what we now call the Heart line: this was eventually translated into *table*, and for a long time the word persisted in English palmistries.

Curiously enough, this sort of treatise deals only with three main lines: the line of Fate, the Head line and the life Line, which were regarded as invariably forming a triangle. The treatise appears to brush aside the fact that there are four main lines in the hand, and that when only three appear they are not the ones which form the triangle. This curious attitude to the lines on the hand was probably a result of the strange mentality of the mediaevalists — much

185 A page from a 14th century manuscript on palmistry in the British Museum

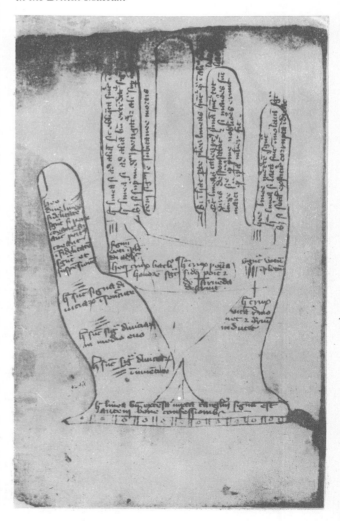

163

too steeped in symbols to care about what we call truth. On the whole pragmatism held little sway in mediaeval thought, and strict symbols were preferred because they were felt to be somehow more true than truth itself, touching upon a deeper, emotional level of understanding. There can be no doubt that in choosing to favour three lines they were thinking in terms of the Godhead — they saw manifested in the palm of Everyman the living symbol of the Trinity, each line of which reflected perfectly the qualities of the Holy Triad. The interpretation of these three lines appears to have been linked up with the three principles of Aristotelian origin: *Vegetabilis*, concerning unthinking, vegetable life, *Sensibilis*, relating to animal emotions, and *Racionabilis*, exclusive to mental activity. These three, in different admixtures, were supposed to account for all degrees of life in the Universe. It is the age-old, seemingly universal, Trinity. The rigid system of interpretation of these three lines and of the special signs which were supposed to be found on the hand appears to have been as inflexible as the mediaeval social hierarchy.

No planets or mounts are dealt with in this simple form of manuscript, but the 'meanings' of many special signs are revealed. The text, always quite short (sometimes filling only one folio), consists largely of notes which might serve as reminders in a teaching which is mainly oral. Judging from the character of those manuscripts which have survived, we can assume that this simple form of chiromancy was very popular in the twelfth and thirteenth centuries. As late as 1541 a treatise of this type, with almost the same contents, was set in print as *An Anonymous Book on Chiromancy*, but it did not seem to appeal to the sixteenth-century attitude of mind, which demanded a greater prolixity of argument, and a more accurate appraisal of the actual nature of the human hand.

The second type of manuscript, called the *Summa Chiromantia*, is the fundamental treatise on palmistry, and has endured in its essential features until the present day. The British Museum possesses the earliest known manuscript of this kind, which is attributed to one Johannes, who flourished towards the end of the fourteenth century. Another, 'one of the most elaborate of its time', is attributed to Ricardus Dore, a monk of Buckfastleigh, and comes from the following century. It is idle to speculate

whether or not the Johannes manuscript is that supposedly written by John Gaddesden, a doctor of physic who studied at Merton in that century. According to Freind, Gaddesden was 'greatly skilled in physiognomy and did design, if God would give him life and leisure, to write a treatise on chiromancy; but to our unspeakable grief, this excellent comment upon fortune telling is lost'.

In essence the manuscripts consist of a thorough chiromantical description of the hand: they mention the four principal lines, the planets, mounts, special markings, sister lines, triangles, quadrangles and the proportions of the hand in general, whilst there is special reference to nails, joints and chiromantic theory. The sum and content of these manuscripts can be studied in almost any modern fortune-teller's 'palmistry'. It is precisely this kind of manuscript which shows something of the antiquity of palmistry, for, old as his documentation is, Johannes quite readily admits it to be merely a collection, 'a little bouquet', made from the writings of older authorities, whilst Ricardus refers, in the mediaeval formula, to Avicenna, Rasis and Albertus.

There are ten complete manuscript copies of this treatise in England, and a further six which are closely related to them in form and extent: these may be termed the third kind of manuscript in the present classification. This last type is in fact an amplified treatise on the style of *Summa Chiromantia*, but it generally contains more drawings of hands. Like their prototype, these stem largely from the fourteenth and fifteenth centuries. However, one copy in the Ashmole collection at the Bodleian was certainly produced in the thirteenth century. It shows two delicately inscribed hands on an illuminated chequered background — one of the loveliest illustrations of the whole mediaeval series. On the whole, considering the extent of chiromancy these manuscripts cover, they are very short, some of them extending to little more than two folios. In several instances the chiromantical text forms part of a larger work on Physiognomy: one in particular, again in the Bodleian, is a copy of a physician's text allegedly by Avicenna, and might well be the ground for the tradition of Avicenna as a palmist.

The so-called *Aristotle Treatise* is the fourth manuscript classified. It differs in arrangement from the last two kinds, and does not refer to planets, special lines and joints, whilst the triangle is given priority

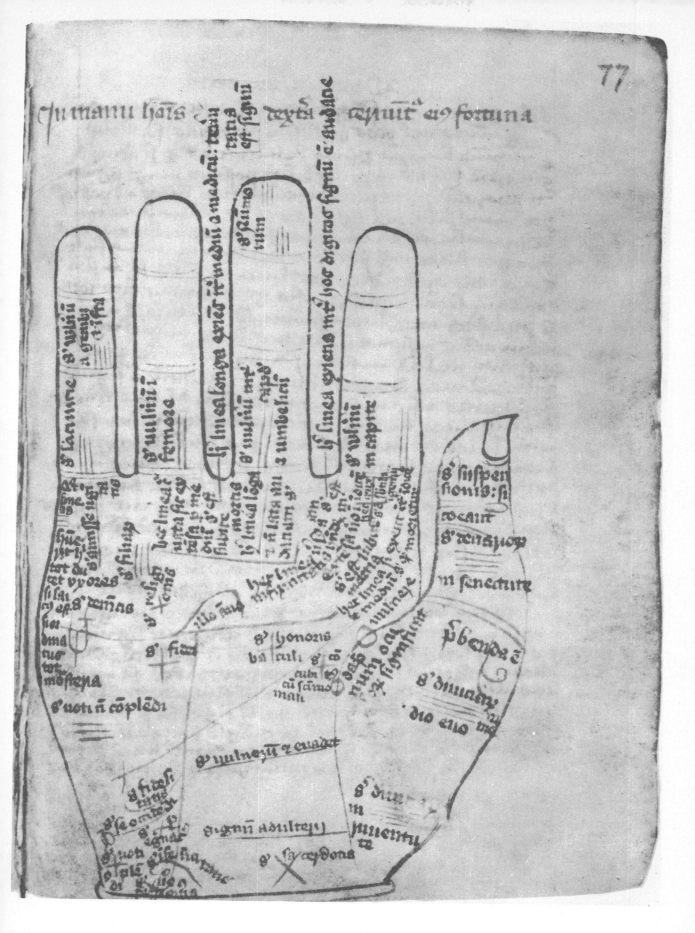

186 *A manuscript of the* Summa Chiromantia *type in the Bodleian Library*

over the four principal lines. It is an altogether longer treatise — almost a book — and contains many drawings of hands. A companion treatise, the fifth in the classification, was compiled by Rodericus de Majoricus at Oxford University in the fifteenth century, but there are only three extant copies of this manuscript, two of which are in the British Museum, and one in the Bodleian.

Both these last two kinds of manuscript are supposed to be copies of a work written by Aristotle, but in fact there is no evidence for such belief. The anonymous *Cyromancia Aristotelis cum Figuris*, which was published at Ulm in 1491, argues closely with the manuscript of *Aristotle Treatise*, but it quotes Aristotle's *De Historia Animalium* in support of its argument, and makes no claim to his authorship. The British Museum catalogue quite sensibly relegates it to the many 'questionable and suppositious works'. It has been suggested that the book was compiled by some commentator from Aristotle's many references to the hand and chiromancy, but this is hardly likely, for it does not parallel any of Aristotle's comments on the hand. The functional importance of this book has been missed by all commentators. It presents an argument for the art of chiromancy by showing that it cannot possibly savour of witchcraft, since it was practised by Aristotle and other savants. Such an argument, which is of course technically invalid, was, when related to the background of its time, vital to the survival of chiromancy. The psychotic *Malleus Maleficarum* was already published by 1491, witchmania was rampant, and it is incredible that chiromancers escaped the wrath of its authors.

A second treatise, entirely different in conception and also attributed to Aristotle, was incorporated in *Aristotle's Masterpiece*, published in London during 1738, but again the authenticity is more than questionable. Benham appends this section on palmistry in his own excellent book of 1900, and appears to have no doubt that the text was 'written by Aristotle about 350 B.C.' being 'the oldest treatise on the subject known'. There is, however, no evidence that either of these two printed books, or indeed any of the six manuscripts claimed to be after Aristotle, are authentic, even as compilations.

188 Opening page of an early treatise on palmistry in the British Museum

187 The first page from Cyromancia Aristotelis cum Figuris, *published at Ulm in 1491*

Since so many different people have written so many different things about this art of chiromancy, I wish to establish an element of certainty amidst all the confusion and doubt which has arisen, and to rid the art of all its false teachings. With this aim in mind I have compiled the following treatise on chiromancy in as intelligible and clear a form as I am able, with the intention of creating some sort of order from all the various claims made concerning the art, and presenting them in a more easily understandable form.

The author then goes on to discuss whether or not 'the practice of this art is lawful in the eyes of God'. In support of the art he quotes De Anima and De Historia Animalium by Aristotle.

Um diuersa diuersi de arte ci
romancie scripserunt·Ego vo
lēs ad certitudinē reducere cō
fusa z dubia seu falsa relinque
re·tractatū presentē compila=
ui in quo ita plane z lucide sic
potero artē pdictam ptracta=
bo z vt oīa que de ipa dicenf
ad certū ordinē reducanf z fa
cilius inueniant . Tractatū hūc sub vndeci capitulis ter
minabo. Primo videndū est vtrū ista ars sit licita scōm
legē dei. Dicendū ē quidē dicūt ipsam esse illicitā hac ra
tione:qz oīs diuinatio ē illicita scōm legē dei Unde in le
ge pceptū fuit a deo maleficos et diuinos nó pacieris vi
uere sup terrā.Tales aūt esse videnf qui de futuris se in
tromittunt pdicendo p signa reperta in manib9 vnde vi
detur esse illicita. Sicut piromancia que ē de diuinatióe
que fit in igne:et sicut geomantia que fit p pūctuationes
factas in terra vel in aliquo alio loco sicut in tabula vel
pgameno et sic de alijs multis sciētijs p quas sit diuina=
tio:quas ptēt p ecclesiam esse repzobatas z cōdemnatas
Alij dicunt eā non esse illicitā qz aristotiles tradidit artē
phisonomie p quā docet iudicare de hoīe vel muliere ģ
lis sit in mozibus p liniamēta in facie reperta et figuram
faciei.Cū igif illa sit sine pctó quare ista p quā daf iudi
ciū p signa manus nó poterit esse sine pctó. Manus enī
post faciē est ps delicatioz et organū organoz scōm phm
tertio de anima circa finē:p quā melius potest dare iudi
ciū vt videf · Item phus in·iii·libzo de aīalibus de hac
arte facit mentionē dicēs Si linee manus sunt longe vel
tres scindentes concauū manū vel palmā significanf lō
gitudinē vite Breues vero paucitatē vite significāt Itē
a ii

An dich die lini des lebens zwischen dem dā vnd dem zaiger groß ist das beteüt künstige mā schlacht an mannen vnd an frowen vindu der vn der am rütz oder stein das beteüt armüt vnd hät leben / in dem alter ist die selb lini oben an dem dā gantz das bezaichnet erhangen werden Ist aber die selb lini vnden gantz on all stoebung das beteüt ain vnseligī menschen Ist sie aber zerstrewt hin vnd her des selben reichtum vnd gūt wirt zerstrewt es sey dann das er dem wider stannd mit grosser weißhait Ist die lini des leben gantz von der raaß bis auff die vndber das ist ain zaichen lanck lebens künhait vnd keckhait Ist sie aber zu kurtz die sach kompt selten zu gūtt Wan aber sie gewalt wirt in zwaitail das beteüt reichtum vnd erfinsu an dem graff ain. O. der mensch verlürt ain aug sind aber der O zwaij er verlürt baide augen ist die lini des haupts wol auff gerockt vnd ist gantz das bezaichnet ain gūt gplexion wan sie aber graut durch den berg der hand das be teüt lang leben ist aber die lini zū kurtz vnd gat durch den triangel das beteüt ain vnrewen hessigen menschen ist die lini des haupts gantz das bezaichnet ainen bösen tod So vindu geschribn in der ersten hannd vnd zaiger wie ietzliche lini vnd berg vnd ballen in der hand vnd an den finger sey genant

THE FIFTEENTH CENTURY

The oldest known palmistry manuscript in English is the *Digby Roll IV* in the Bodleian, which consists of three strips of vellum sewn together to form a roll approximately seven inches wide and eighty-seven inches long. It is of the *summa chiromantia* type, though written in Middle English in a hand which dates it before 1440. Certain omissions and mistakes in the text point to its being a manuscript copy made by a scribe, but the original is lost.

Two further manuscripts of a unique kind exist: one is in the Garret collection in the Library of Princeton University, and the other is in the collection of All Souls College. They are both from the hand of John Metham, 'a sympyl scoler of phylosophye', who worked under the patronage of Sir Miles and Lady Stapleton at Ingham, in Norfolk. The manuscripts are written in early English and were, on the testimony of Metham himself, 'rudely translated from the latin of one Doctor Aurelyan in the year 1448'. Nothing is known of this Aurelyan, and little more of Metham except that he was 'a scolere of Camryg' and that he wrote these tracts in the twenty-fifth year of his life. Each of these two manuscripts was published in 1916 by the Early English Text Society in a form which facilitates line by line comparison. Except for spelling, and except for two accidental omissions, they are identical, though the Garret Manuscript appears to be later than the All Souls version.

The texts form a fair sample of the more thorough mediaeval writings on palmistry. They are of the *summa chiromantia* type; mention being made of the four principal lines, the fingers, planets and triangles. The whole text is a most curious mixture of fact and fantasy; observations of a definite pragmatic kind jostle the most incredible imaginings:

Smale nayles, long and rede, betoken goodness of wytte and sotylness. Shorte nayles, naroth and small, betoken vyciousness, evell teached, foltishness and a nygart.

And yef this token appeare in any parte of the triangle W, it signifieth that a man shuld be hanged by the nekke; and yef a woman have this token, she shuld dye myshevously in fyre or water.

Why, after so long a silence, we should suddenly inherit these thirty or so fascinating documents of the thirteenth and fourteenth centuries is hard to answer, for no history can give an accurate picture of the maelstrom of activity which bridged the ancient and modern worlds. The compendious and fanatical scholarship which followed Alcuin and culminated in Petrarch dredged up much classical mud, and with it many treasures. These documents may be counted among the treasures, but how long they had remained hidden, and who had created them originally, it is impossible to say. Their survival is due chiefly to the organised scholarship of our universities, and to the fact that the secular power, already emerging in art at this time, was strong enough to deal openly with an art which might have been deprecated by the Church.

Thomas Aquinas, in giving ecclesiastical blessing to Aristotelian thought, created an official secular culture which ran parallel to but independently of the established dogma. This must have contributed to the study of palmistry which, after all, with or without justification, was supposed to have come directly from Aristotle, and seems to have developed along with this secular culture which, it is interesting to note, was of a distinctly Arabic origin.

Averroes, who was largely instrumental in reintroducing the Philosopher to the West, and who is in fact the one most likely to have brought palmistry to Europe, is not mentioned in connection with palmistry as often as would be expected. Of course, this could be due to the later reluctance to use his name which was associated with heresy at one point. Perhaps fear of an Arabic invasion also played a part.

Avicenna, Prince of Physicians, was a century earlier, and is constantly quoted as having written on palmistry; he was too firmly established in the medical tradition to be relegated to obscurity. It would be very surprising if a man so much in advance of his time, so erudite and wide ranging, who contributed so much to mediaeval medicine, alchemy, musical theory and physics, should not be at least interested in palmistry. Perhaps ancient writings correctly ascribe a chiromantical treatise to Avicenna, and it quite possibly could be that he first introduced palmistry to the West by way of his Aristotelian commentaries: palmistry almost certainly entered the West as a subdivision of medicine and astrology. If Avicenna was responsible for its introduction to Europe, we would expect to find documents earlier than the twelfth century dealing with or alluding to the art. Although there is some doubt as to which of the two Arabic philosophers was responsible for the introduction of chiromancy to Europe, there can be no doubt of its Arabic source.

Right noble and high-born lady, as the songs of the poets relate, the request of an important person is to be taken as a most strict commandment which it is not befitting for a subject to disobey in the least. I was caused by your own ardent request to waken as from a long and sober sleep when I gathered from your words that you would like me to direct my studies for a while towards making you a treatise on palmistry, and this in a simple rendering of our English language. But since it is many years since I occupied myself in such youthful occupation, my understanding of them is the fainter, and my mind more barren, and my willingness the more unready. But since it is not befitting that such a kind Lady as yourself be disobeyed by her servant, I have respectfully constructed a small treatise upon a few principles of palmistry which may be understood and used without any possibility of evil, by every person. I trust you will not in any way harm your own adult mentality by placing too much faith in the childish fancies of this immature science

Whatever the origin and purpose of these manuscripts we can be sure that they mark a strong current of interest in palmistry, and on their testimony alone we can be certain that there was a lively, if slightly inhibited, practice of the art during mediaeval times.

There is a tradition, but no certain showing, that the Church was opposed to palmistry. Chiromantical manuscripts were obviously written in monasteries, and occasionally writers significantly argue about the 'morality' of palmistry, but the only certain ecclesiastic reference, a deprecation, is from John of Salisbury's pen. Some opposition to the art there probably was, for with the degeneration of ecclesiastic power, palmistry blossomed out into flowers more remarkable for their numbers than their beauty.

In the same decade as Gutenberg was experimenting with movable type, a book on palmistry was being circulated in the Humanist circles of Southern Germany. This was *Die Kunst Ciromantia* which had been written by Johann Hartlieb about 1448, but not published until several years after his death. It has survived as a blockbook, with each page of text illustration cut from one single block of wood, and printed, possibly by one Jorg Schapff, in Augsburg round about 1475. Quite certainly it is the first published book on palmistry.

Nothing much is known about Hartlieb, except that he studied in Vienna and that his authorship of an *Art of Love* — nothing to do with Ovid — gave him some sort of diplomatic position in the Munich court of Albrecht III of Bavaria. He was dead by 1469, and because he did not live to see the publication of *Die Kunst Ciromantia*, several authorities believe that he was reluctant to publish for fear of ecclesiastical persecution. This, of course, is possible but very unlikely, for the intellectual atmosphere in the Humanist courts was not greatly inhibited by such fears. In addition we have the

fact that Hartlieb quite openly dedicates his book to Duchess Anna, the wife of Albrecht III, an event celebrated by a whole-page woodcut in the printed version. The truth is more likely that Hartlieb did not intend to publish the book at all, and that after his death some enterprising printer saw latent commercial possibilities in a cheap publication of a popular manuscript book.

Whatever the story behind the authorship and printing, we are left with a rare but disappointing book; its interest and value is purely historical in that it represents the earliest printed book on chiromancy, for its contents are fairly useless. The text consists of little more than a series of short notes explanatory of rather obscure signs to be found in the hand; there is little preparatory matter, and on each page we find a massive hand interspersed with pithy sentences in old German. The relative subtlety of the mediaevalist who warned us 'not to deme of oon lyne a-lone but of many accordyng' is completely lacking in the series of unequivocal interpretations of special symbols:

This is the sign of a woman who will sacrifice her life for a son who will be executed for brigandry.
This sign means that a man must be on his guard with nuns, if he does not wish to die as a result of their love.
This is the sign of a girl who will be seduced by a student.
This is the sign of a woman who will be interred alive.

One is left with a strange picture of fifteenth-century Germany if such interpretations are to be taken seriously. The truthful picture was even more strange, 'to such an extent had the horrible become familiar'.

In his preface, Hartlieb explains that the destiny of a man can be told from the right hand, whilst that of a woman can be seen in the left hand; consequently, each of the forty-four plates are presented as a double spread with the hand of a man on the right, and the hand of a woman on the left. The interspersed notes scarcely give the basic elements of chiromancy, showing little understanding of the principles involved. We can only presume that Sotherby was being drily humorous when, in his commentary to this book, he wrote of 'the mysteries of the designs,

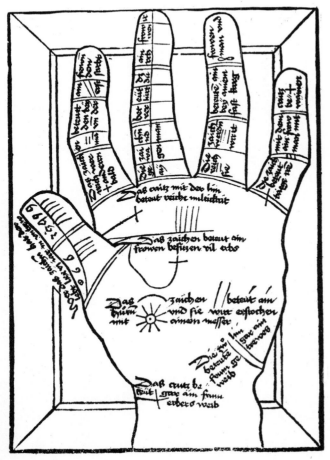

191 A hand from a page from the blockbook Die Kunst Ciromantia; *the text deals exclusively with special signs*

wherein are contained all the secrets of the art of chiromancy'.

Assuming that Hartlieb did know something of the art — and it has been suggested by certain authorities that he merely translated the book — it is easy to argue that the printed version is little more than a series of notes lifted unintelligently from some manuscript book which has since been lost. That the frontispiece depicts Hartlieb holding a thick manuscript book on palmistry lends weight to such a theory.

Scarcely had printing with movable type been invented than books on palmistry began to pour out in a steady stream which was eventually to turn into a flood. Michael Scott's *De Phisiognomia*, printed in 1477, is probably the first printed work to deal with the chirognomy of the hand, but his chapter on the physiognomy of the hand and the description of nails are, of course, included in the book only as part of the more general study of the human body.

By 1480, a collected edition of palmistry, *Ex*

divina philosophia academi collecta, containing many illustrations, had been published at Venice in Latin and Italian, and was in the following years to run into several reprints. It took its form from that of earlier manuscripts which were then presumably in wide circulation, consisting of an introductory apologia followed by a series of full-page woodcuts dealing with special signs and accompanied by only one or two lines of text. The illustrated section was rounded off with a long treatment of the art, touching on mounts, principal lines and special markings, predominance being given to planetary signs and markings. This form was to be the prototype of palmistry books for many years to come.

In between this last publication and the anonymous *Cyromantia Aristotelis cum Figuris*, already discussed, we find a most remarkable treatise which has often been mistaken for a book on palmistry — a confusion particularly noticeable in Heron-Allen. The book, *Compotus Manualis*, written by Magister Anianus, and published on the 14th November, 1488, has nothing whatsoever to do with palmistry, but because it contains several woodcuts of hands, somewhat in the palmistic tradition, several writers have taken it as a work on chiromancy. Anianus died long before the work was published in Strasbourg, for research shows that he lived from about 1350 to 1400 and that he was in all probability a French monk, perhaps from the monastery at Aniane. His main interests appear to have been astronomy and mathematics and these, allied to his penchant for Leonidian hexameter, resulted in his *Compotus*, which is centred around calculating the dates of Feast days by using the parts of the hand as a mnemonic.

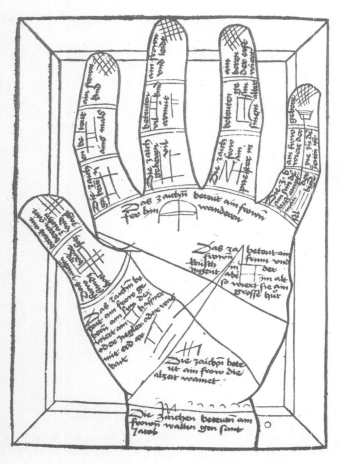

192 *A page from* Die Kunst Ciromantia

THE SIXTEENTH CENTURY

At the beginning of the sixteenth century the history of palmistry ceases to read like an extended and incomplete bibliography. The spirit of individuality which was already permitting autobiography in literature and portraiture in painting has preserved one or two anecdotes relating to the lives of individual palmists which, for the first time, present the history of palmistry in human terms. A strange medley of chiromancers parade through the sixteenth and seventeenth centuries — strange for other reasons than that they studied and practised this art. Most of them were what we might be tempted to call *typical* early Renaissance scholars: brilliant in many subjects, universal in comprehension, and above all filled with the spirit of enquiry and research which then pervaded the Italian, Germanic and French atmospheres, and which was gradually to drift over to England — as usual over fifty years later. But perhaps the word typical is not the right word to describe men so strangely individual, so devoted to their search as Cocles, Achillinus, Indagine, Tibertus Antiochus, Paracelsus, Goclenius and Robert Fludd, to name only a few of the outstanding students of chiromancy.

It is true that none of the palmistic writings of these men contributed much of scientific interest to the subject, but scientific accuracy was not at any time their aim. Their main contribution to the art was that they gave it the grace of scholarship, refined the earlier teachings with sound argument, and deepened the interpretative content of special signs and symbols. Most of these writings came from the pens of great scholars and widely informed men of the world, many of whom were professors at the universities, and all of whom were interested in the pursuit of knowledge, even of 'scientific' knowledge in its pioneer forms. The growth of a desire for empiricism and rationalism was slow, but it had its roots in the rich soil of which the early forms of chiromancy were a substantial ingredient. When the mechanistic physics of the early eighteenth century met up with alchemy, astrology and chiromancy, they were all, with the strange exception of the latter, turned into 'a veritable cat's cradle of inquiries'. It seems to be merely some strange accident of fate that when alchemy gradually changed into chemistry, and astrology into astronomy, palmistry was ignored as a potential science and had to wait until our own century for due recognition as a legitimate science.

Andreas Corvus, sometimes called Barthélmy Cocles, had a tremendous reputation for practical palmistry during his lifetime, a reputation which lasted for many years after his death. He was born at Bologna, on the 9th March, 1467, and was at various times a student of grammar, mathematics, surgery, medicine, astrology and palmistry before being inevitably caught up in the subtleties of hermetic thought. An abridged copy of his *Ciromantia, opus rarissimus de eadem chiromantiae*, was published in 1497, and reprinted many times during the following century, being translated into several languages, and having such repercussions that scarcely any book of the next century failed to credit his ability and ideas. However, the book is now sought only by collectors of historical curiosities for, chiromantically speaking, it is not of very great interest. Its text deals less with special signs than its predecessors, and involves itself with interpreting the mystery of the hand in terms of the relationships between the four main lines, but it is not a comprehensive book, nor is it systematic or accurate in its analysis. One very interesting point about it, however, is that the advertisement claims it as being useful and even necessary for all those who wish to practise the art of surgery or medicine,

193 This table of 'special signs' is representative of the less sophisticated kind of early palmistry, which has survived to some extent in certain types of modern palmistry. Each of these hand patterns carries some interpretation of past or future life.

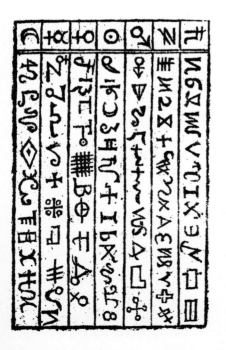

suggesting a relationship between medicine and palmistry such as is slowly being established today.

Several legends concerning the life of Barthélmy Cocles have found their way into palmistic tradition, the most interesting being an account of the prediction which ultimately involved his own death. The various stories are contradictory in detail, but it would seem that Cocles had warned a constable of Hermes Bentivoglio (the son of John II, the tyrant of Bologna) that he would commit a 'detestable murder' on the 24th September, 1504. It was on this very day that Cocles himself was killed by a blow upon the head, dealt by this same constable. Several of the stories claim that Cocles knew that he was going to die on that day and in that manner.

Guichard records an alternative version of the story, apparently entirely ignorant of the fact that Barthelemy della Rocca was one of the many pseudonyms used by Cocles.

In this version, Cocles had foretold that on the 24th September, 1504, Barthelmi della Rocca would fall by the sword of a constable of Hermes Bentivoglio. It is said that Cocles foresaw the tragic end of Barthelmi and that he, having foretold the constable some days before that he (the constable) was on the eve of committing a murder, at the same time warned Barthelmi to arm himself with sword and helmet on leaving the house. One of the most instructive points which emerges from this story is that Cocles did not always base his predictions on hand markings alone. No palmist, however excellent, could predict the name of a murderer and the exact date of his crime by examination of the potential victim's hand, or even from that of the murderer. Either Cocles had some inside information concerning an intrigue against his life (one version of the story insists that Cocles was murdered because he had predicted the untimely death of Bentivoglio) or he was at times a seer, a fortune-teller pure and simple, using hands as a springboard for his own brilliant intuitive process. That Cocles, like many other palmists, could foretell a person's death is evident from the numerous stories about him; for instance, he told Lac Gauric (the famous astrologer who had predicted the death of Henry II 'by a wound in the eye') that he would die 'a most cruel and unjust death' several years before the unfortunate man was tortured to death on the rack. Cardan, the sixteenth century astrologer who is

supposed to have committed suicide to keep to his predicted date of death, records that of the forty-five people to whom Cocles had predicted a sudden death, only two failed to fulfil his prediction. But to predict with absolute precision of date and circumstance is only possible with some sort of extrasensory perception, which would carry the prediction well out of the bounds of palmistry proper.

The writings which Cocles has left to the world confirm this conclusion, for it is apparent that, going by the system of interpretation advocated in his books, little of accuracy could be told about the character of a person, let alone his past, present and future. Cocles' reputation as a palmist is ill-founded if his written palmistry is any guide, and the only conclusion to be drawn is that he was a brilliant prophet who hid his abilities behind the external form of chiromancy. By all accounts, the predictions of the great seer Nostradamus were based on even more slender externals than the hand, for his visions came to him directly from the stars.

Tibertus Antiochus was at least as famous as Cocles for his palmistic ability. Though born in Italy, he passed all his early years in Paris where, as he studied, he became more and more preoccupied with natural magic — with chiromancy, astrology and the various occult sciences. In order to give his natural bent for prediction a good foundation of logic, he set himself the task of becoming learned in as many different fields as possible. He became accomplished in literature, physics, medicine and mathematics, and more than proficient in the occult sciences which were then so popular. When he at last considered himself to be sufficiently erudite he returned to his native Italy and very quickly became famous for his ability, 'consulted as if an oracle by people of all estates and conditions'. His reputation was so great that his rooms were always filled with important visitors. Notwithstanding all his advantages and the great riches which his ability brought him, he led a miserable life, and ended on the scaffold.

Pandolph IV, the Malatesta, who sold Rimini to the Venetians in 1503, was impressed by Tibertus Antiochus' reputation and consulted him on certain matters of state.

Tibertus complied, and told his patron, at that time one of the most flourishing and powerful princes of Italy, that he should suffer great want, and die at last

194 *Woodcut from Cocles'* Ciromantia *published at the beginning of the 16th century*

When this line is reflected towards the fingers, it signifies a depraved and ignorant kind of person. Should the line actually touch the finger it signifies a man of unbalanced mind, though courageous and magnanimous, towards friends in truth covetous rather than generous

like a beggar in the common hospital of Bologna. Pandolph's best friend and military adviser, Guerra, also consulted Antiochus, and was calmly informed that he would be murdered by his friend and leader. Guerra was suitably impressed but a little doubtful, and asked the chiromancer if he knew when he himself would die. Antiochus replied that 'it was decreed from all eternity that he should end his days on the scaffold'. Oddly enough, the three separate predictions intertwined and created a little tragedy more suitable for an opera by Verdi than for a history. As might be expected, it was Pandolph himself who stabbed Guerra to death on a false suspicion of treason. For some obscure reason the tyrant suspected Antiochus of complicity in the imagined treachery, and had him incarcerated in one of the Rimini towers. However, with the aid of the gaoler's daughter the innocent chiromancer tried to escape, but was surprised by a sentinel whilst lowering himself by a rope into the moat. He was taken before Pandolph, who immediately condemned him and the gaoler's daughter to death. The fate of Malatesta followed the precise direction that Antiochus had predicted. When Count de Valentinois seized Rimini, the tyrant barely escaped with his life. He was pursued from place to place by his enemies, abandoned by all his former friends, and finally by his own children. He at last fell ill of some languishing disease at Bologna, and, having no other place to rest his head, was taken to the local hospital, where he died.

Antiochus wrote several curious books on physiognomy and pyromancy, but his only remaining book is a Latin treatise on chiromancy which was published by Benoit Pectoris in Bologna in 1494. A French translation was made by Louis de Corbière, but the manuscript was never printed. It is hard to determine what method Antiochus himself used for prediction, though one account runs that 'he consulted the stars and the lines on the palm'. He appears to have been conversant with all forms of fortune-telling — but his lasting fame as a palmist would suggest that his real metier was chiromancy, perhaps augmented by simple astrology.

Doctor, anatomist, physician, physiognomer, chiromancer, 'the greatest authority on scholastic philosophy of his time', Alexander Achillinus was born in Bologna on the 29th October, 1463, and died there in August, 1512. Besides earning for himself the

Introductiones apotelesmati-

CÆ ELEGANTES, IN CHI-
romantiam, Physionomiam, Astrologiam natu-
ralem, Complexiones hominum, Naturas Planetarum, cum Periaxiomatibus de faciebus Si-
gnorum, & Canonibus de ægritudinibus, nus-
quam ferè simili tractata compendio,

AVTORE

IOAN. INDAGINE.

LVGDVNI,
APVD IOAN. TORNAESIVM,
TYPOGR. REGIVM.

M. D. LXXXII.

195 Title page from Introductiones Apotelesmaticae *of 1582*

title of 'the second Aristotle' he was a great student of Averroes, and it could well be that several of the chiromantic theories which he later propagated came from this Arabic source. He is remembered chiefly for his anatomical research, for he was one of the first to take advantage of Frederic II's edict which permitted the dissection of corpses, and did not delay in putting all his findings into writing. He is particularly notable for his audacious questioning and correcting of Galen, and for his anatomical discoveries. His books on palmistry are strangely traditional coming from a man so conversant with original pragmatic research, but his second book on the art *De subjecto chiromantiae et physiognomiae* had a justifiably high reputation in his day, and was reprinted several times after the first Bolognese edition of 1503.

Patritio Tricasso da Cerasari, commonly known as

Tricasso, has been described as one of the most celebrated chiromants that the world has ever known. He was a Mantuan, a firm disciple of Cocles, and more obsessed by occult studies than even Antiochus. Sadly, little is known about his life, except that he lived during the second half of the fifteenth century and that he wrote many books on chiromancy — always carefully acknowledging his debt to Cocles. His first book, *Esposizicie del libro di Chyromazie da Bert. Cocles*, which was published in Venice around 1531, was written according to his own description *come agitato di furvo divino*, 'as if moved by a divine fervour'. At least two other books on chiromancy were published during his lifetime, and the last, *Epitomia Chyromanci*, illustrated with over seventy figures, was translated into French and published in Paris in 1560. Like Achillinus, Tricasso had come into contact with the Arabic philosophy of his day, and it is fairly certain that at some time he published a book on the interpretation of dreams which, according to some authorities, was a translation of the Arabic work by Achmat, son of Selim, who lived in the ninth century. The Arabic text, which is now lost, was fortunately translated into Greek, and was eventually published in Latin and Greek in 1603 and follows in content the Indian, Persian and Egyptian doctrine contemporaneous with Achmet. Such evidence as this concerning the introduction of Eastern ideas to the West — particularly in so esoteric a subject — is further certain evidence of the way in which Indian palmistry reached the West. As Heron-Allen remarked, 'there is nothing in the West that has not come from the East'.

Tricasso's writings on palmistry emphasise more strongly than any others the contradictions contained in the early forms of palmistry. He takes infinite care in his advice on how best to study the hand; for example, giving lists of factors which have to be taken into account, like the temperature of the room, the extent of lighting and other commonsense measures. On the other hand, however, many of the signs which he describes as being found on the hand have no actual existence. He claims, for instance, that the letters of the alphabet have certain significance when found on certain mounts: a letter A on Venus signifies infidelity; F on Mars is a sign of a stupid man, a babbler and liar; F on the mount of Moon signifies a type of man who will take

176

pleasure in study and speculative thought. Such superstitious nonsense, which is probably derived from secret teaching concerning the properties of the Talmud, appeared alongside passably accurate observations concerning the nature of the hand.

But Tricasso, was by no means the most famous chiromancer of this time. John Indagine, a German Carthusian prior, was even more highly regarded on the continent, and had even greater effects on the development of chiromancy, his name and theories being quoted well into our present century. His famous *Introductiones Apotelesmaticae*, published in 1522, was reprinted often in many languages.

Little is known of Indagine's life before 1522. He was probably a descendant of the family of barons and counts called 'von Hagen' which had extensive powers in the Rhineland, throughout Lower Saxony, and indeed in Germany as a whole. At all

196 Portrait of Paracelsus; an engraving by Hirshvogel made in 1538. The words in Latin above Paracelsus' head are his personal motto: "Let no man who can belong to himself belong to another". By courtesy of the Central Library, Zurich

events, Indagine was educated in the courts of Germany, and eventually became dean of St. Leonard's bishopric in Frankfurt-am-Main, and at the same time priest at Steinhem, where he spent most of his life. He was an extremely learned man in many fields, and at one time acted as an ambassador to the Pope, though it appears that he had many sympathies with the revolutionary theories of the day, and in spite of being a Catholic priest, he showed definite Protestant leanings. He was a close friend of Brunsels, the astrologer, and this friendship combined with his religious attitude caused his *Introductiones* to be placed on the index of forbidden books. His first book was printed, at his own expense, by Johann Schott in Strasbourg in 1522, and was immediately popular and widely read. Indagine has a much more personal approach to the art than any of his predecessors, and, true or false, such anecdotes as these tend to rid palmistry of its obscure mystical flavour and to make it interesting to the common man:

> And often there will be found on the line of life two little circles, or sometimes only one, which signify the loss of both eyes, or one, as the case might be. They are seldom found, though I myself have experienced them, for on the same place of my own hand is the same mark. When I first observed them, I recalled in what danger I was of losing one of my eyes, and, one day whilst sitting by the fire in wintertime, I fell in, and scorched my left eye in the flames and was severely tormented thereby.

When Indagine's books were being published, prophecy, nothing daunted by the failure of the predicted end of the world in 1500, was at its peak on the continent. Nostradamus had written his remarkable *Centuries*, and all forms of predicting the future were practised on every level of society. Brant's *Ship of Fools* had tried already to put the false astrologers in their place as early as 1488, but had done little to stem the flood of sciences which attempted assiduously to reach into the future. In Germany, both the study and the hatred of occult sciences, which some saw as legitimate studies and others saw as tinged with witchcraft and pacts with the devil, had almost reached the point of madness. Men took sides for and against such sciences with bitter argument. Lorenz Fries, a contemporary of Indagine, and possibly one of his friends, had published a defence of astrology as a retaliation to

Luther's own outspoken comments about the 'false art'. One German bibliography mentions a Johannes Hasius who advertised on a church door in 1516 that he was prepared to practise and teach the art of palmistry to all comers, and this was immediately forbidden by the medical faculty. The various contradictory official attitudes to palmistry and astrology, which in those days were regarded as being different aspects of the same study, were as varied and opposed as the teachings of these arts themselves.

After the publication of Hartlieb's book in 1475, there was a gap of nearly fifty odd years before another treatise appeared in German. This book was the supposedly anonymous *Die Kunst der Chiromantzey usz Besehung der Hand*, of 1523, which was quite clearly a translation of Indagine's Latin version that had been published a year earlier in Strasbourg. The text sticks fairly closely to Indagine's and it may well be that this was thinly disguised plagiarism: at all events, in view of the widespread fame of Indagine, it is strange that his name should not be connected with the book until the last century. Of course, in the intervening period between Hartlieb and this Indagine edition, palmistry

197 Title page to Rothmann's Chiromantiae, *1595*

books had continued to appear in Germany written in Latin, but on the whole they were uninspired books, and in most cases little is known about their authors. For example, Johannes Hasius or Hase published his *Prefatio Laudatoria in Artem Chiromanticam* in 1519, but not only is the book so rare as to be almost unobtainable, but there is little information about the author or his life.

We are on better ground with the next important German chiromancer, Paracelsus, for his many biographers have sketched his career in details both factual and fanciful, to such a degree that it is almost impossible to think of the early sixteenth century in Germany without immediately conjuring up his Faustian image. 'Everything that is within can be known from what is without' is a healthy soil for the growth of chiromancy, and the accuracy of Paracelsus' vision is all the more remarkable when we recall that he believed firmly in the tradition that the art had been introduced to the West by the Magi. These two beliefs, so opposed, together represent the whole of Paracelsus astride the gulf which separates the platonic mysticism that gave birth to modern science, and the magnificent mediaeval disregard for historical accuracy.

Paracelsus left only one very short treatise on palmistry but from his frequent reference to the art, and from his legendary and professed ability, we can be certain that he was one of its finest students. As in so many things, Paracelsus treated palmistry with a vision and understanding way beyond that of his age — in a manner which recalls the Indian and Chinese attitudes. In his estimation, chiromancy was of value for two reasons: first as a means to knowledge, 'for not without good reason was chiromancy so highly honoured by the ancients: we use it only for soothsaying, but they used it as a means of learning the arts'. Secondly, palmistry was of value for diagnostic purposes. Like his predecessors, he looked into the skies for the future of man's life, but unlike his contemporaries, he looked into a man's hand for signs of his diseases. In this respect he was the first modern palmist: his detailed examination of his patients is all the more surprising in a time when learned doctors were not expected to even visit their patients but relied for diagnosis on oral or written descriptions of the illness. His attitude to palmistry is merely a by-product of his own Celsian philosophy, for he argued that since nature is the great healer, then it is to be expected that nature will manifest her own disposition towards physical or mental disintegration.

Paracelsus was born in Switzerland in 1492, the son of a physician, and is reputed to have learned all the occult arts, including palmistry, from a wandering gypsy tribe with whom he spent many of his early years. It is almost certain that his wanderings took him as far as the Italian universities, where he can hardly have failed to meet the great chiromancers of his day. One modern scholar, J. B. Craven, thinks that Paracelsus, 'during his long travels in the East, had evidently become acquainted with the Indian secret doctrine'. He died at Salzburg in 1541.

The link between chiromancy and astrology was not broken until well into the nineteenth century — and even then not with finality — but the two arts had tended to develop along different lines. Joannes Rothmann's *Chiromantiae Theorica Practica*, which appeared in 1595, attempted to bring the two arts together, and to strengthen each with the other's virtues. The highly abstruse and theoretical astrology would benefit by being tied down to so worldly a thing as flesh and blood, while palmistry, already struggling in a tightly fixed symbolism, would be given more freedom by its association with an art which allowed a prolix individual reading for any one symbol. Rothmann's book was described by a nineteenth century palmist, Katherine Saint-Hill, without much apparent reason, as 'a matchless piece of writing'; but it certainly was a fascinating book seen against the background of its age. Its argument is directed towards showing that the casting of a nativity by astrological means, and the reading of the hand, always result in two forecasts which agree in the chief events of that person's life. Rothmann's attempt to create a new type of palmistry was unsuccessful, but the book itself was very popular, attaining the questionable virtue of being the only German treatise on the art translated into English until our present century. This translation was made by George Wharton, just over fifty years after it had first been published. Absolutely nothing is known of Rothmann himself.

Besides numerous translations and Latin editions of the accepted chiromancers' books, new writings came in thick and fast towards the end of the sixteenth century. Rudolph Goclenius published his *Aphorisma Chiromantica* at Nuremberg in 1592, and

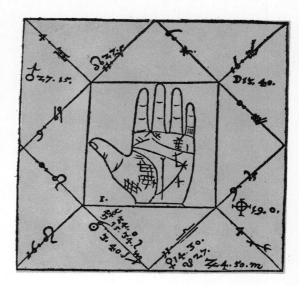

198 A drawing from Rothmann's Chiromantiae. *The Latin description of this hand reads:*

One born at Uratislavia in the Year of Christ 1567, Aug. 17. Hour 12. 10. in the Afternoon. He is promised long life and will seldom be troubled by disease: his complexion will be for the most part phlegmatic. The angular position of Mercury in this particular house indicates ingenuity. The mid-heaven, irradiated by the trine of Jupiter signifies an affluence of joyful and early-attained honours without impediments. (The astrological reading continues in this vein until the horoscope is compared with the hands.) Now if we trace these things by the lineaments of the hands we shall find the following agreement:

1 In the first place the mount of Venus being particularly furrowed shows that Venus has the best position in the genture.
2 There are three clear lines in the first joint of the little finger which tell of the dominion of Mercury, whereat we assume an excellent wit and commendable behaviour.
3 The sun's place (Apollo) has its lines well positioned which is a sign of honours, and the same significance is seen in the partile sextile of Jupiter and the Sun who is angular in the genture

the early part of the next century is scattered with his new books and reprints. Goclenius was more socially acceptable than Paracelsus, who had been hounded out of many places for manifesting too much ability and for practising necromancy. His medical, philosophical and astrological talents gave him a lectureship at Wittenberg University and later at Marburg, which enabled him to do research into occult subjects with considerably more comfort, if with less intensity, than was afforded Paracelsus.

199 Frontispiece from Ludicrum Chiromanticum, *published at Jena in 1661*

THE SEVENTEENTH CENTURY

Rupolph Goclenius was born in Wittenberg in 1572, and died there in 1621. He wrote at least two books on palmistry, one of which he published when he was only twenty years old, which is reason enough for supposing that the ideas therein were based largely on the teaching of Paracelsus. Goclenius was indebted to the Swiss for many of his ideas, both sound and unsound, and it would be the sort of irony that would have delighted Paracelsus to have his teaching systematised and recorded by a scholarly 'authority' such as Goclenius, who represented the sort of figure against whom his invective had been directed throughout his life. A new edition of *Uranoscopae, Chiroscopae, Metoposcopiae* appeared in Frankfurt in 1618; three years later *Physiognomia et Chiromancia Specialia nunc primum in lucem emissa* came from the presses of Marpurgi and Cattorum, and, in the middle of the century, of Halle. *Chiromantische Anmerkungen* appeared in Hamburg in 1692, but this, like many of the others, is merely the earliest known edition and the dates of the first printings are not recorded.

One presumes that Ludwig Heindrich Lutz was German, but the earliest edition of his work was actually in French, and was quite possibly a translation. It was entitled *La Chiromancie Médicinale*, and appears to have followed a type of Paracelsian diagnostic palmistry. A later book appeared in German, printed at Nuremberg in 1672 with the Latin title *Cheirosophia Concentrata*.

Perhaps the most remarkable chiromantical work of the seventeenth century was the one edited by Joannes Praetorius of Zeitlingen and published at Jena in 1661. This was *Ludicrum Chiromanticum*, which consisted of an edited collection of palmistic writings taken mainly from that century. More than ten complete texts have been preserved in this book, the most interesting being by Pompeius, Fludd and Goclenius. The *Delivis Chirosophiae* of Pompeius was an earlier, less complex, though altogether cruder version of the 1682 edition of *Praecepta Chiromantica*, published in Hamburg. This is one of the most interesting palmistries of its time: it deals at length with all aspects of chiromancy and makes special mention of planetary types. Unfortunately, there are no illustrations in this early edition of the work, but the later edition has a special section of over fifty woodcuts illustrating the points raised in the text. The treatise by Robert Fludd, the English mystic,

who had died some thirty years before, follows the usual pattern, but devotes more space to special signs and symbols. The text and illustrations are lifted piecemeal from his *Utriusque cosmi historia*, which must have been avidly read at Jena and Wittenberg.

The treatise by Goclenius is merely a reprint of his *Aphorisma Chiromantica*, originally published in 1592. Another very valuable inclusion in the book is an anonymous treatise of the *Summa Chiromantica* type, which runs only to sixteen pages and is not illustrated.

The remaining collection of treatises in the volume are not without interest, but all knowledge has been lost concerning the authors, and it would be tiresome to repeat all the names. At page 489 of *Ludicrum Chiromanticum* there is a bibliography of over 70 chiromantical books or documents, and on page 495 a list of all known references to the art made by well-known people. The most interesting name which appears in this list is that of Philip Melanchthon, the palmist who had in 1550 accurately predicted that one Catherine Lamschucken, the wife of a doctor Pedingerus, would die before she was thirty.

As a whole, *Ludicrum Chiromanticum* is invaluable to the study of early palmistry; little of the material is new, but the assembled texts represent almost all shades of teaching on chiromancy, and between them they are a fairly complete commentary on the art as it was practised up till that time. The editor of this remarkable collection of teachings and superstitions, Joannes Praetorius, was born in 1630 and died at the age of fifty. He was at one time Professor of Philosophy at Leipzig University, where chiromancy was included on the official curriculum, and his many books, mainly devoted to astronomy, astrology and chiromancy, earned for him a reputation for scope of occult learning and for a certain literary humour. His other books on palmistry were *Cheiroscopia et Metoposcopia*, printed at Jena in 1659; *Philologemata Abstrusa de Pollice*, published in his university town towards the end of his life, in 1677; and *Collegium Curiosum*, printed in German, in 1704, after his death.

A great deal of the character and popularity of palmistry in that century can be gleaned from *Ludicrum Chiromanticum*. Praetorius' erudite listing of the many treatises on the art suggests something of

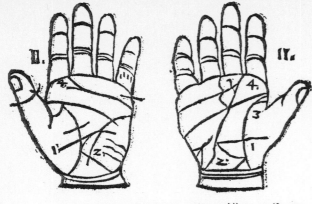

Spectant hæ palmæ mulierem: quæ infanticidium commiserat & Schüdizii ideò die 1. Maji, anni, 1650. suffocata est: Ipsiæ autem statim anatomiæ subjecta: ubi ego lineamenta manuum scrutatus, seqq. mortis violentæ, & quidem submersionis animadverti indicia. 1. Linea vitalis justè intersecta erat ad annum ætatis 21. præterpropter: quòd etiam in muliere, ut asserebant, correspondentiam habuit: 1. rupturam verò vitæ in aquis fieri debuisse, monstrabat locus Lunæ. 3. parricidium verò innebsant.

200 *Page from* Ludicrum Chiromanticum

201 *Title page from* The Book of Palmestry *published in English by Fabian Withers, after Indagine, 1651*

how popular the art was. Indeed, so many writers on palmistry begin to crowd into the publishing lists of this period that it is difficult, if not impossible, to keep track of them all. In many cases it is quite impossible as all relevant information has been lost. The writings which are particularly worthy of note, however, are *Chiromantia Harmonica* by Hoeping, published in 1681; the anonymous *Klee-Blat* of 1695, and Ingeber's *Chiromantia* of 1698. In this same year, there was published a reprint of Nicholas Pompeius' *Praecepta Chiromantica*, this time with over eighty small woodcut diagrams to illustrate the text which had appeared in a much cruder form in *Ludicrum Chiromanticum*.

The first definite and reliable account of Far Eastern palmistry crops up in the writings of this period. Baldaeus, in his description of the East

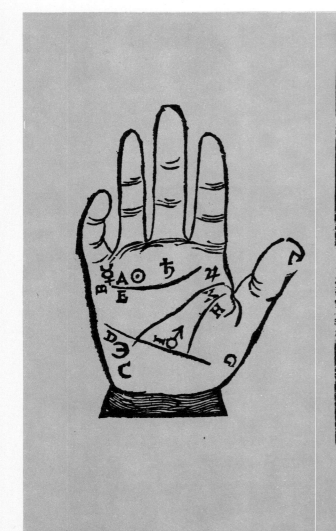

The Book of PALMESTRY And PHYSIOGNOMY.

BEING

Brief *Introductions*, both Natural, Pleasant, and Delectable, unto the Art of *Chiromancy*, or *Manual Divination*, and *Physiognomy* : with circumstances upon the Faces of the SIGNES.

Also, Canons or Rules upon *Diseases* or *Sicknesses*.

Whereunto is also annexed, As well the Artificial as Natural *ASTROLOGIE*, With the nature of the PLANETS.

Written in Latine, by John Indagine *Priest* ; *and translated into English by* Fabian Withers.

LONDON,
Printed by *J. Cottrel*, for *Edw. Blackmore*,
at the Angel in *Paul*'s Church-yard. 1651.

Indian coast of Malabar of 1672, records that an eminent Raja insisted that a Brahman should read his daughter's hand, 'a custom very popular amongst the heathens'. The Raja was probably quite startled to learn that his daughter would have 'seven children, six sons and one daughter, and of these the last son will rob you not merely of your crown so far as your kingdom is concerned, but also of your head so far as your own life is concerned, and will then occupy your throne'.

By now the earlier forms of palmistry had been both refined and rendered more obscure. There had been a tendency to relegate special individual signs to the background, and to give more importance to interpretations by combinations of lines and physiological features. For example, instead of one single line, like the Life line, having significance in itself,

202 *Two pages from* The Book of Palmestry

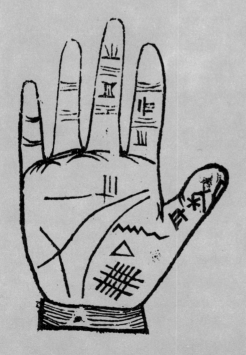
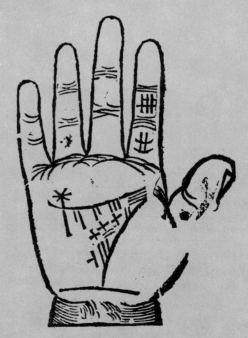

with special readings for breaks, circles and other such markings, a more 'organic' reading was attempted, where each marking on the line was related to the qualities ascribed to that line. In addition the point of origin, its quality, strength and colour, its point of insertion and course, began to take on great importance. By the early part of the seventeenth century the minor differences in nomenclature had been straightened out, and a system of names had been established which is still in use today. However, not all rigid symbol-interpretations, advocated by chiromants like Tricasso, were discarded by all writers; in many cases they were copied piecemeal from earlier books, with no attempt to check their validity. It appears that many chiromants

203 Title page of Wharton's translation of Rothmann's Chiromantiae

KEIPOMANTIA: 57

OR,

THE ART OF DIVINING

BY

The *LINES* and *SIGNATURES* Engraven in the *HAND* of *MAN*, By the *HAND* of *NATURE*,

Theorically,
Practically.

Wherein you have the Secret *Concordance*, and *Harmony* betwixt *It*, and *Astrology*, made evident in 19. GENITURES.

Together with

A Learned *Philosophicall* Discourse of the *Soule* of the *World*, and the *Universall Spirit* thereof.

A Matchlesse Piece.

Written originally in *Latine* by *Io: Rothmanne*, *D.* in *Phisique*, and now Faithfully Englished, By GEO: WHARTON *Esq.*

Manus membrum Hominis loquacissimum.

LONDON, *Febr.* 20.

Printed by *J. G.* For NATHANIEL BROOKE, at the Angell in *Corne-Hill*, 1657. 1651.

demanded only some abstractly formulated system of knowledge, and in fact relied on their own intuitive processes in practice.

In England, palmistry does not appear to have been pursued with the same intensity as on the continent. This was probably a result of two factors: the lack of official encouragement, and the gradual association of chiromancy with the gypsies. Thus both social stratas were affected. The higher class, which usually studied palmistry through the writing and instruction of scholars, slowly became uninterested in the art, for there was no official encouragement towards its study in the universities, as there was on the continent. The lower social strata was also affected. On this level the palmistic tradition was kept alive by a procession of itinerant quacks, who, with their pretended knowledge of the art, fed the human craving to know about the future. Even this oral tradition ceased to be practised openly for fear of persecution.

The gypsies had appeared as if from nowhere. Some scholars support the traditional theory that they came from Egypt, fleeing from the conquests of Subain Selim during the early part of the sixteenth century, but on chronology alone this is hardly likely. Others maintain, possibly with more reason, that the gypsies came from the Pirahs of India, following the incredible devastation and persecutions of Timur-Beg in 1398. Whatever their place of origin, however, the gypsies were widely distributed over England and the continent by the 'fifties. A statute of Henry VIII, of 1530, describes them as:

> an outlandish people calling themselves Egyptians, using no craft nor feat of merchancy, who have come into this realm, and gone from shire to shire in great companies, and used great subtle and crafty means to deceive people, bearing them in hand that they, by palmistry, could tell men's and women's fortune, and so many times, by craft and subtlety, have deceived the people of their money and have also committed many heinous felonies and robberies.

To be a gypsy from then on merited death, a state of affairs which would hardly encourage the open practice of palmistry in the lower classes, for a practitioner would be suspected of being either a gypsy or a witch. The law was not repealed in England until the reign of George III.

Henry's statute is interesting for many reasons. It clearly shows that the gypsies did not come from

204 *A 16th century gypsy chiromancer telling the fortune of a young Italian gentleman; the couple appear to be more interested in each other than in palmistry. From an engraving* *by Bénoit Audran after Caravaggio's* The Gipsy Fortune-Teller *in the Louvre*

Egypt, for they were obviously well versed in at least the outward forms of palmistry, and any practice of the art in Egypt had died away long ago, whilst in India it was popular and respected, even in the highest social circles. The document also reveals the official attitude to palmistry, which is regarded merely as 'a crafty means to deceive people'. Such an attitude is not found on the continent, except in isolated individuals with no official power. Further, for the first time perhaps, we see doubts as to the validity of palmistry as an art. Hitherto, any written documents on palmistry have never questioned its validity, but have merely demanded whether it is 'pleasing to God' that man should seek to know the future. True, certain individuals like Fulke and John Gaule castigated all such arts, but they appear to have been in the minority.

The widespread belief that palmistry was introduced to England by the gypsies is obviously without any foundation, for there was already a written chiromantic tradition in England two hundred years before the gypsies appeared. If anything, the reputation which the gypsies grafted onto the art caused it to degenerate and almost die out for want

of honest practice. There are many references to the difficulties experienced by serious palmists.

. . . let me warn my Reader of those Sycophants, and Delusive Ignorants, through whose Sides this pretious Science is dayly wounded, such spawn of shame, that impudently make profession of Art, not onely in several Countryes, but lurke in Obscure corners, in and about this famous city, many illiterated pieces of Non-sense and impudence, of the famale kind, whose Ignorance transcends the Vulgar Gypsies, and Impudence sufficient to out face a whippingpost.

This invective was written by Saunders in 1664, by which time palmistry was once more becoming acceptable to the general public. In an earlier book, the same author complains:

I know full well that thus so profitable a Science, hath been latterly so improperly and perversely handled, that it hath rather merited the name of old wives fables than a useful science; and of all, our English have merited the least honour, there being not any that heretofore have taken pains to the least credit of the Art, till our laborious countryman Capt. George Wharton, who (to his commendation) hath lately made Rothmann most accurately speak English.

185

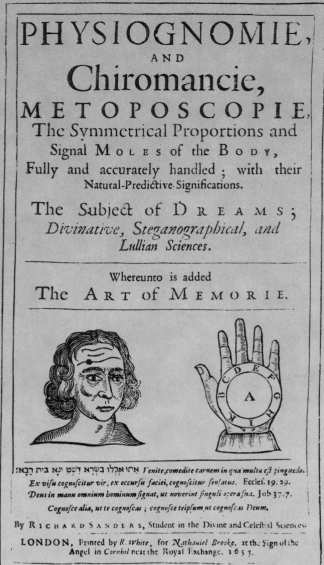

205 *Title page, frontispiece and (far right) sample page from Saunders' famous book on palmistry, 1653*

But if Saunders' complaints are on good ground, his sense of history is not, for Wharton's translation of Rothmann was not the first attempt to regenerate the art in England. The first book to be actually written in English was a somewhat dry translation of Indagine's *Introductiones Apotelesmaticae*, made by one Fabian Withers in 1558.

Several years before Fabian Withers' book appeared, Thomas Hyll had promised his eager public a book on palmistry, 'that thou thereby mayst infalibly judge the state and condition of any manne'. But Hyll's public had a long time to wait before the book appeared, for it was not published until 1613, several years after Hyll's death. Hyll flourished between 1550 and 1599, earning his bread as a miscellaneous writer, working mainly on compilations and translations for publishers. He appears,

however, to have been a very enlightened 'hack', for a keen interest in physiognomy, astrology and palmistry shows clearly through his writings. Even nowadays Hyll's books make very interesting reading — as indeed they were intended to: *A Brief and most Pleasant Epitomye of the Whole Art of Physiognomie, gathered out of Aristotle, Rasis and others many more, by that learned Chyrugian Cocles and englished by T. Hyll, Londoner, 1556*. Hyll's mind ranged widely, for besides a much reprinted book on gardening and *A Contemplation of Mysteries, containing the rare effects and significancies of certain comets*, we have, in 1576, *The Pleasante Arte of the Interpretation of Dreams*. He must have been well known in his day for astrology and palmistry, for he was included in the *Anti-Prognostication* issued by Fulke in 1560, long before the majority of his books had been published.

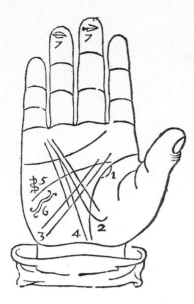

Aphorisms explaining the 47. Figure.

1. SUch a sign in the beginning of the Line of life in children, if it be perfectly seen, signifies the childe shall be choaked, or killed with worms; but if it be imperfect, it implyes extream danger of death from the Maw-worms, according to the proportionable time of age.

2. In these lines it is diligently to be noted, whether they be such really as we declare them to be; for they may often deceive and seem such when they are not; also the fraction, and discontinuance is to be noted.

3. In these lines it is to be observed whether they go by the mount or brawn of the hand from the wrist, or otherways; for those signifie the accidental goods of Fortune, but these denote the gifts of Nature, Natural good.

4. Between these lines there is also difference; the Scheams of the hand are in the 39 and 13 Figures of one manner, in the 32 and 12 Figures of another; also there are other lines placed in the place of the Liver line, but broken and discontinued, and that not rightly; so as the Line of the Liver often seems to be wanting; but we may not so pronounce as if it were indeed wanting, but Testimonies ought to be gathered from all other observations.

5. Such a character in the quadrangle neer the end of the Natural line, denotes an ambitious, proud, self-conceited, evil person.

6. Such a sign in the mount of the hand, denotes drowning.

7. If such a character turn about the end of the finger towards the nail, y of the fingers, it signifies hanging, strangling, or the man to be a leaper, odious thief, and an adulterer.

Aphorisms

After the efforts of Fabian Withers and Thomas Hyll, new books on palmistry rarely appeared in England. Almost half a century elapsed before another book was written on the subject — the translation of Rothmann made by George Wharton in 1652. Wharton led a very strange and full life. He was born near Kendal in 1617, five years after Mason had ridiculed palmistry 'where men's fortunes are told by looking on the palmes of the hand', and was destined to become one of the group of Englishmen who were to give a new impetus to occult studies. At Oxford, Wharton befriended Elias Ashmole and introduced him to alchemy and astrology, which he himself was studying. When civil war broke out he took the Royalist side, for which action he was created a baronet after the Restoration. The years between the wars and his reward were spent

in studying the occult sciences, in denouncing Lilly, the astrologer who in 1661 predicted the great plague and the fire, and in lampooning Parliamentary proceedings. Wharton's bitter satire sent him to prison in 1648, but he contrived to escape, only to be caught a few months later. Through Ashmole he learned that the Council of State fully intended to hang him for sedition, and it was only the well-directed influence of Ashmole and his old enemy Lilly which procured his freedom. On his release he had no means of earning a living, and was on the verge of starvation when Ashmole once more came to the rescue and gave him a sinecure on his estate; and in the comparative seclusion of the country, Wharton translated Rothmann into *The Art of Divining, by the Lines and Signature ingraven on the Hand of Man*, published in 1652. He was particularly famous during his day for *Almanacs*, and was one of the leaders of the small group of friends headed by Saunders and Lilly, who studied the prognostic arts in that period which has been described as 'the golden age of the pseudo-sciences in England'. Wharton died at Enfield in 1681.

It is very probable that Charles II studied Wharton's book, for he was himself, like Wharton and Ashmole, fascinated by alchemical research, and even had a secret laboratory under his bedchamber. There can be little doubt that when the baronet met the king there must have been much talk of the subject. By the 'fifties all the books published in

206 Portrait of Jean Belot, the French chiromancer

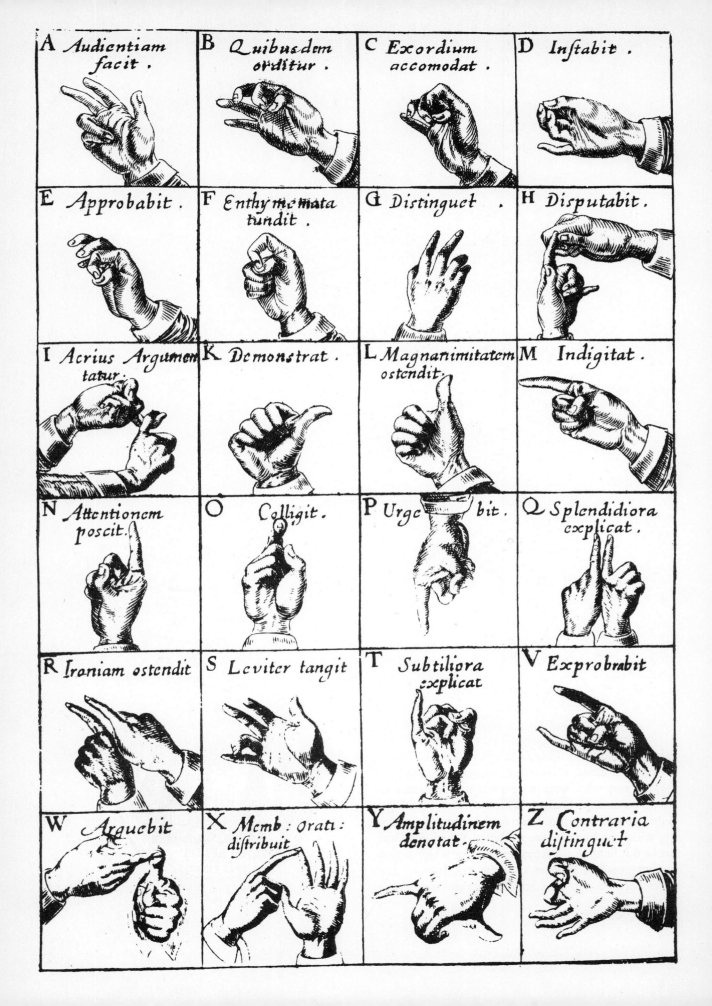

England had been merely translations of continental palmists, like Indagine, Cocles or Rothmann, and nothing which could be described as indigenous had been written. However, this was soon to change, for only a year after the appearance of Wharton's translation, Richard Saunders presented England with his own fascinating book, entitled *Physiognomie and Chiromancie, Metoposcopie*, 1653. It was a book which dealt in a most thorough manner with all aspects of chiromancy and the many allied sciences such as Metoposcopy, the science of divining by the frontal lines. Although containing a certain amount of original material, Saunders' book ranged widely over all the major teachings of his day: very many passages were lifted piecemeal from the French of Jean Belot, whose collected writings had first been published in Rouen in 1647. Saunders is more honest and makes open acknowledgment of his debt:

> ... I have oft filled my buckets in the building of this fabrick, obeying the Oracle of Apollo, who when Aesymus demanded by what means the Megareans might order their Common-Wealth best, answered, if they took council of many.

Saunders' books on palmistry are eminently readable, and they formed part of the solid, though unrealistic, structure around which the *New Chirology* was built at the beginning of this century. They are permeated throughout with a love for strange anecdotes and for the more obscure forms of occult science, like *Onychomancy*, divination by means of nails reflecting the sun's rays, *Oinomancy*, by means of wine, and *Orniscopy*, the ancient science of divination by the flight of birds. The type of palmistry he advocated, and presumably practised, was based exclusively on the interpretation of special signs saturated with alchemical and astrological reference:

> If on the mount of Moon there appear a star, whereof the rays reach towards Capricorn, beware in that month a violent disease, and some danger of death: if they reach towards Sagittarius, which is October, take heed of some madness; if towards Aquarius, which is January, beware a Melancholy not much distant from madness.

In recommending this book to his 'unthankful age', William Lilly makes a neat précis of the chiromancy of the previous century, adulating Saunders' supremacy over the 'long-winded genius of Cocles, infinite contradictory aphorism of Taisnier; abrupt and rustick considerations of Indagines, or too much

208 Portrait of Robert Fludd, from Utriusque cosmi historia

209 Title page to Saunders' Palmistry: The Secrets thereof Disclosed, *1664*

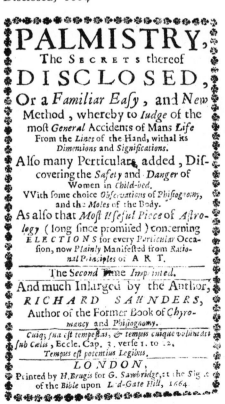

LA CHYROMANTIE NATVRELLE DE RONPHILE.

QVOD TIBI FIERI NON VIS ALTERI NE FECERIS

A LYON,
Chez ANTOINE IVLLIERON,
Imprimeur & Marchand Libraire, de-
meurant en ruë Raifin.

M. DC. LIII.

Auec Approbation & Permiſſion.

210 Title page from Ronphile's Chiromantie Naturelle, *1653*

brevity of Goclenius: not a man of all Europe comes near him (Tricassus excepted) yet is he more copious and significant even than that sharp Italian'. Lilly's observations are excellent, for Saunders' book is an amalgam of all the more acceptable teachings prior to his age, yet it is curious that the astrologer does not include Belot in his list of 'sources' — it leads one to suspect that Saunders was trying to pass off as original much of this borrowed material. The elementary chirognomy, particularly the sections on nails and fingers, is remarkably accurate, whilst the other extreme of special signs, which Saunders took without question from Tricasso, shows the art at its lowest ebb of superstition. Again we observe the strange, almost mediaeval, mixture of fact and fantasy so predominant in the early books. This time, however, the text is enlivened by many piquant anecdotes and illustrations — most of them, one suspects, of dubious authenticity.

Saunders was born in Warwickshire in 1613 and died in London about seventy years later. His main preoccupation was astrology — this no doubt accounting for his friendship with Lilly — whilst the study of palmistry was his second great love. He seems to have been a great character in his day, numbering among the friends of Ashmole and Fludd, and in spite of having passed most of his life in London, he managed to wriggle into a page of Coleville's *Warwickshire Worthies*. The many dedicatory poems (one by his friend Wharton) and the several acrostic verses, bear witness to the high regard in which he was held as a palmist. His first book, which was reprinted many times, was eagerly accepted, and was followed, in 1664, with *Palmistry: the Secrets thereof Disclosed,* a less scholarly book, perhaps a pot-boiler, and certainly aimed at a less discerning public. It is merely a crude summary of the first book, though Saunders claimed it to be a new method of divination, and it places much more insistence on special signs.

John Bulwer, who lived in London round about this time, earned for himself the pseudonym of 'The Chirosopher', and appears to have had some sort of reputation as a palmist in his day. He was a physician, the son of a physician, and dedicated his life to the discovery of a method of communicating knowledge to the deaf and dumb. He was the first Englishman to actually use the hand as a means of speaking to deaf people, and the ideas presented in

190

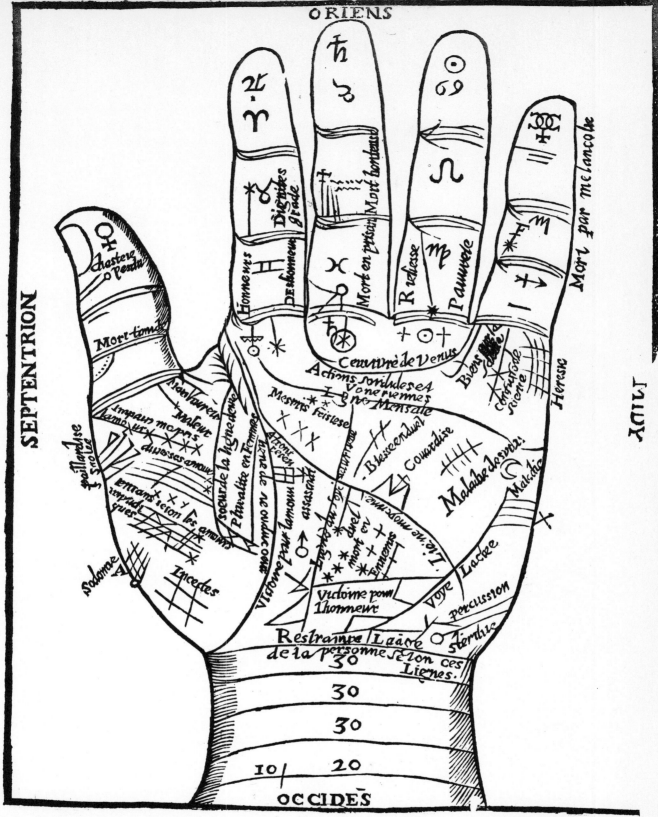

211 *Position of the zodiac signs in the hand. From Jean Baptiste Belot's Oeuvres, 1647. Each of the phalanges is ascribed a zodiacal significance which augments the specific meaning of the particular finger. The arrangement leads to some very interesting relationships: the finger of Jupiter, for example, is said to house the Ram, the Bull and the Twins.*

The Ram is generally described as a leader and of persistent energy; the Bull is usually a reliable and hospitable type, possessive by nature and inclined to be of fixed opinions, whilst the Twins type is active, expansive and of wide though changeable interests

1 *Pallidam lineam à radice indicis versus pollicem, suffocationem genuti filij dicunt significare:hoc affirmat Antiochus.* **2** *Lineam vitæ inter indicem & pollicem tumentem, suffocationem partus, seu alterius infantis dicunt significare.* **3** *Mensalis in superiori parte bifurcata, & pallore suffusa, infantis mortem significat causa genitricis seu nutricis.*

DE DIVERSIS MORBIS ET AEGRI-
tudinibus, Caput XXII.

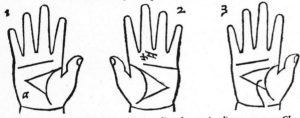

1 *Litera A in monte manus, varias ac diuersas ægritudines notat.* **2** *Chara Eteres Saturni in monte medij, ægritudinum multitudinem denunciant.*
3 *Linea à concauo extendens ramum ad brachium similem radio, ægritudinem intra sex annos, eiusdem lineæ partes si sint grossiores versus côcauum, quàm sunt circa brachium, infra duos annos denotat.*

4 *Lineæ paruæ iuxta radicem mensalis, ægritudines in prima ætate demonstrant, iuxta medium, in media ætate, iuxta finem, in vltima.* **5** *Linearu*

212 *A sample page from Taisnier's* Opus Mathematicus, *1632. The top row of hands deal with the various signs which indicate death by suffocation, while the lower six relate to different diseases and illnesses. There are over 1,200 such drawings in this remarkable book*

his *Philocophus, or the Deafe and Dumbe Man's Friend*, the first book on Chirology, were largely derived from the works of two Spanish monks who were working on the same problem of communication. It was Bulwer, and not Doctor Wallis, as history would have it, who first invented a deaf and dumb language. Although Bulwer left no book on the subject of palmistry, his research into chirology is interesting in the light of modern discoveries concerning the significance of hand posture and movement.

It is difficult to think of Robert Fludd as an Englishman. He had a particular brilliance and individuality scarcely English in character. His natural bent towards mysticism was only a little tempered by his training at Oxford, and his later studies abroad placed him in a milieu more suited to his temperament. An early meeting with Rosicrucianist thought, and with the occult writings of Paracelsus, had an absolute effect on the whole of his life: Paracelsus had an influence similar to that of Boehme on Blake a century later, for it did not overshadow his own individuality, but rather gave it the focus of a sense of purpose. From Paracelsus he inherited a fascination for hermetic thought, for astrology, palmistry and physiognomy, all of which he practised assiduously, and, to judge from the records, to the detriment of his medical career. On his return to England, in 1605, he was made a fellow of the College of Physicians but, like his master, he was never quite accepted by the established medical fraternity. He engaged himself in alchemical and astrological research and entered, as a sideline so to speak, in controversy with men of such stature as Gassendi, Kepler and Mersenne. He published his remarkable *Utriusque cosmi historia*, 'a very little known work . . . far more audacious than any of the hazy theories advanced by Fathers of the Church or mediaeval schoolmen', in Oppenheim, 1619. Unfortunately the section on palmistry in this book reveals nothing new, and is probably included only as further evidence of the significant complexity of the *microcosm*. Craven remarks that the palmistic terms employed in the work are 'illustrated by diagrams which may be seen in any modern book on chiromancy'; not only the illustrations are 'modern' but virtually the whole text also. The text and illustrations from *Utriusque cosmi historia* were reprinted in *Ludicrum Chyromanticum*, 1661. In a sense, this palmistry might well be described as the first English palmistry, for although it was printed in Latin, and in Germany, Fludd was English.

In France, although the gypsies were officially expelled in 1560, their practices appear to have affected the chiromancy of the day even more seriously than in England. Over sixty years after their expulsion Jacques Ferrand reports that:

This art of Chiromancy hath been so strangely infected with superstition, deceit, cheating, and (if I durst say so) with magic also, that the Canonists, and of late years Pope Sixtus Quintus, have been constrained utterly to condemn it; so that now no man professeth publicly this cheating art, but theeves, rogues, and beggarly rascals, which are now everywhere knowne by the name of Bohemians, Egyptians, and Caramaras, who have arrived in Europe since the year 1417.

It is hardly surprising in the face of such circumstances that the first book on palmistry to be written by a Frenchman was published in Italy and in the Latin tongue. This was the magnificent *Opus Mathematicus* by Joannes Taisnier, which was published at Cologne in 1562, and which presents in a systematic and didactic manner a most thorough teaching of the art of chiromancy. The book in question is one of the most detailed ever published on the art: it contains well over 1,300 woodcuts of hands, and deals, still in terms of special signs and combinations of signs, with all the aspects of palmistry. Taisnier is supposed to have borrowed widely from Cocles for his teachings but although it is certain that he was familiar with the Italian's books, it is equally certain that he contributed many new ideas, for one of Cocles' books had the same breadth or scope of treatment as *Opus Mathematicus*.

At all events Taisnier is often cited as an authority in his own right during the following centuries, whilst his book was freely epitomised, quoted and translated by many later authors. Lilly's summary of his teaching as the 'infinite contradictory aphorism' is not quite fair, for Taisnier is on the whole more 'long-winded' than Cocles, certainly more detailed, and no less contradictory than any of his contemporaries. We must not forget that Lilly's pronouncement was meant to be something equivalent to a modern publisher's blurb. According to one biographer, Taisnier gained quite a reputation for stealing the works of other authors, and in exploiting the credulity of his contemporaries. However, his ideas appear to be slightly more original than those of his predecessors, and it is difficult to understand exactly where he 'stole' them from. He was evidently very familiar with the authoritative books on the art and these, allied to his own experience and imagination — particularly his imagination — would suffice to produce the book which can hardly be described as plagiaristic.

Johannes Taisnier was born in Belgium in the year 1509. He studied both the arts and sciences, and eventually turned towards the church. He was made tutor to the pages of Charles V, whom he accompanied to Tunis in the expedition of 1535, and later to Italy. Taisnier's life in Italy was considerably more comfortable than Charles'; he had ample opportunity to study and teach at the academies of Rome, Ferrara, Bologna, Padua and Palma, where he must certainly have collected together all the different Italian chiromantical teachings which he later incorporated in his book. When the king died in 1558, he retired to Cologne in some ecclesiastical capacity, and after the publication of *Opus Mathematicus* in 1562, nothing more was heard of him. There is a seventeenth century abridged manuscript copy of Taisnier's book in the Bibliothèque Nationale in Paris.

The first half of the sixteenth century in France was so filled with the prodigious and startling figure of Nostradamus that it is a wonder that there is any room even for the few chiromancers whose names have come down to us from that time. The inevitable translations of Indagine and Cocles were the first books to be published in France and in French. Antoine du Moulin, did several translations of Indagine, printed in his favourite city of Lyons, where he worked as a publisher for some time. *La Chiromancie et Physiognomie Naturelle* was the first to appear in 1556, and *La Chiromancie Vraye et Parfaite* did not appear until exactly one hundred years after his birth. In 1657, Sieur de Peruchio published *La Chiromance*, a translation of Tricasso, and several other translations of the 'classic' author followed.

Marin Cureau de la Chambre was one of the most famous French palmists of the seventeenth century. So persuaded of his talents was Louis XIV that he relied almost entirely on his judgments in the choice of minions and agents in his political intrigues. De la Chambre had a secret correspondence with Louis in his capacity of private oracle, but his

Signes and Marks that signify Violent
Deaths.

213   *Pages from Saunders'* Palmistry: The Secrets thereof Disclosed

Ill Natures, and Violent Deaths.

1. THe *Letter* D. or the Character of ♋ thus in the Triangle of the Hand, denote a man to be a *Parricide* and morose conditions, yet fortunate in the world, as to Riches.

2. *Lines* uneven, and obscurely appearing on the Root of the little Finger, signifie a man an insidiator, a Thief, given to all manner of mischief.

3. Certain *Lines* upon the *Vital* line, towards the Inferiour part of the mount of the thumb, as falling therefrom, shew a man to be Practical, and experienced in evil.

4. The *Natural* line extending it self no farther then the midst of the Mount of the Little Finger, denote the person to be of an ill depraved life, and consequently in danger of Violent death.

5. The *Natural* line in the *end* thereof a little crooked, and verging towards the fingers, denotes the *person Impudent* and *Wicked*, and if it bend

worldly and official position was merely 'doctor to the King'. Richelieu was also impressed by his abilities, and singled him out to be one of the first members of the French Academy, which was founded in 1666; a sure sign of how highly estimated was de la Chambre's reputation for a great diversity of knowledge, both sacred and profane. Cureau de la Chambre was born at Mans in 1594, and died in Paris on 29th November, 1669, ten years after having completed only three parts of his encyclopaedic work *L'Art de connaître les Hommes*. He had, fortunately for us, included his treatises on palmistry, which had already appeared separately in 1653, in his completed work. Despite his very high reputation as a chiromancer and physiognomist, he contributed nothing very new to the art in his writings.

Jean Belot was another Frenchman with a justifiably high reputation as a chiromancer. He was born at about the same time as de la Chambre, but instead of entering into court life he became a curé. From his early youth he was obsessed with the study of the occult sciences, and naturally enough soon fell in with the teachings of Raymond Lully, the fourteenth century *docteur illuminé* who had tried to put astrology on a new footing by returning to the Arabic sources, and Corneille Agrippa, the

physician of Emperor Maximilian I. Both these excellent astrologers 'filled his head with all sorts of chimerical ideas', one of which, however, resulted in his very entertaining *Instructions pour Apprendre les Sciences de Chiromancie et Physiognomie*, which were eventually collected together under the general heading of his 'works', published in Rouen in 1647. This long treatise was freely quoted, often without credit to the Frenchman, in Saunders' book of 1653, whilst several of the woodblocks were also 'borrowed' for this edition. Although much of the actual chiromantical teaching is obviously inaccurate and not based on pragmatic rationalisations, many of Belot's anecdotes are fresh and lively, and the style of the book breathes a more popular approach than any of its predecessors. The most interesting inclusions in *Les Oeuvres* are the attempts to tie the usual chiromantical symbols with the astrological *glyphs* and to deepen thereby the significance of the different parts of the hand. This book is perhaps the first one in chiromantical history which is aimed at the general public in style and content.

This spirit is entirely lost on Rampalle, the Provençal writer, whose unoriginal translation *La Chiromantie Naturelle* first appeared in 1653, supposedly from the Latin of an untraceable author — Ronphile.

The various anecdotes and theories contained in Adrien Sicler's *La Chiromancie Royale et Nouvelle* are constantly quoted and referred to in the seventeenth century. It is strange that a chiromancer who was evidently so respected in his day, and who had such an influence on his followers, should have been almost completely forgotten. The sole evidence of his existence is *La Chiromancie Royale*, a copy of which is preserved in the Bibliothèque Nationale. Nothing is known of Sicler or his life save what can be found in this book, for none of the national biographies makes any reference to his name.

Sicler's book is dedicated to Camille de Neuf-Ville, Archbishop of Lyons and Primate of France, and is certified by Alexander Richard, Doctor of the Faculty of Paris as being (in direct contradiction of its title) 'an abridged form in good order of all that the most excellent authors have written on the subject'.

The observations which Sicler has to make on palmistry being essentially an art of combination is frequently contradicted by his own palmistic anecdotes. In the introduction to his book he compares the art of chiromancy to the art of painting, arguing that any artist who would draw a face composed of different elements taken from different faces, 'an ear from one head, from another a nose, from yet another an eye' would only end up with the picture of a monster. He argues that the analogy holds good for palmistry which 'desires the union and not separation of its parts and each individual item should be judged together as a whole'. His own account of his experiences denies this theory of 'organic palmistry', for he appears to work along the old lines of 'pure symbols'. He tells, for example, how a man he met at Nîmes had a certain marking upon his thumb, and this mark was interpreted duly as being an indication of death on the wheel. Sicler reports that his prediction came true when the man died in 1659.

Towards the end of the seventeenth century a new spirit began to pervade the search for knowledge and understanding. There was a reaction against obscurity, against undirected dabbling in the various fields of research; and a need for a systematic approach to the problems of investigating nature began to make itself felt. It was the first stirring of the now established need for accuracy of description which became the chief aim of science. Boyle's words, in his *Skeptical Chymist*, published in 1661, were directed not merely towards physicists and chemists, but towards all faithful investigators of nature:

> *If judicious men, skilled in chymical affairs, shall once agree to write clearly and plainly of them, and thereby keep men from being stunned, as it were, or imposed upon by dark and empty words; it is to be hoped that these (other) men finding that they can no longer write impertinently and absurdly without being laughed at for doing so, will be reduced either to writing nothing, or books that teach us something, and not rob men, as formerly, of invaluable time; and so ceasing to trouble the world with riddles or impertinences, we shall either by their books receive an advantage, or by their silence escape an inconvenience.*

Such words sounded the death knell for the type of palmistry which had been practised up to this time. Boyle's plea was heard, for *Ludicrum Chiromanticum* was the last chiromantic document not written 'clearly and plainly'.

Unfortunately, the new spirit of research did not take a great deal of interest in palmistry; the unpleasant gypsy reputation and the obscure treatises of the past were probably too prohibitive for chiromancy to interest honest investigators at this time. Torreblanca, writing shortly after the time of Boyle, sums up the case against palmistry with some emotional fervour:

> *As for . . . [palmistry] by which people pretend to divine concerning the affairs of life, either past or to come — dignities, fortunes, children, events, chances, dangers, etc. — such chiromancy is not only reprobated by theologians, but by men of law and physics as a foolish, false, vain, scandalous, futile, superstitious practice, smelling much of divinery and pact with the devil.*

It is the spirit revealed by this sort of invective which changed the history of palmistry; for under its sting chiromancy withered and almost died. Alchemy gradually evolved into chemistry, astrology into astronomy — and as early as 1652 John Gaule was careful to distinguish between astrologers and astronomers, the former 'of whose Astrall considerations is so pure and moderate, as that it abhors to enter upon anything that is Magical; or to end with anything that is Mantical'. But chiromancy was relegated by fear and superstition into the background, and did not find its modern equivalent until the nineteenth century.

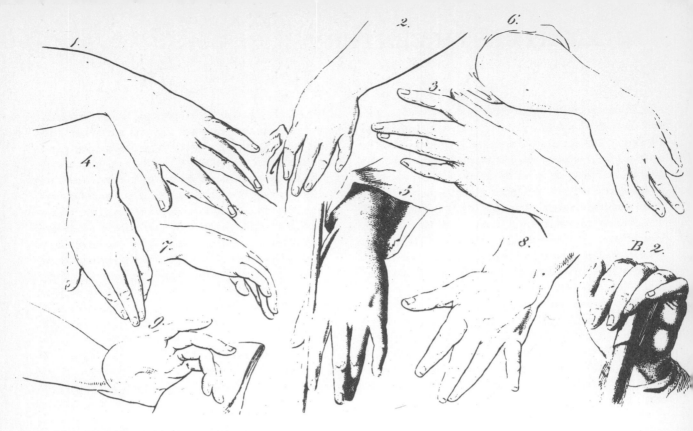

214 *A plate from the French translation of Lavater's* Physiognomische Fragmente, *published as a centenary edition. Lavater's comments on these particular hands run as follows:*

One and three contend with five for the finest expression of pure and noble heart. Two appears more feminine than one or three, however it does not seem to indicate to quite the same degree as the others the particular ability for woman's work. Four shows more delicacy even, but less ability. I would wager that five is the hand of a drawer of extreme clearness, full of good taste, of elegance and distinction, but lacking in genius. Six contains no mark of grandeur, nor also of pettiness, but it shows nobility of spirit

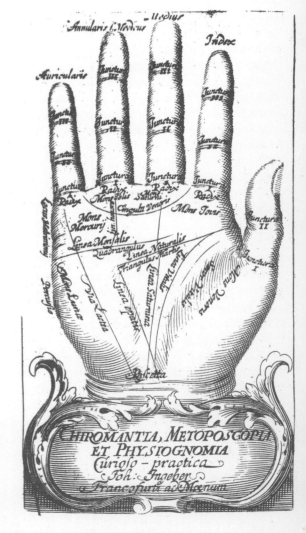

215 *Frontispiece to Ingeber's* Chiromantia, Metoposcopia et Physiognomia. *Metoposcopy is the art of interpreting the lines of the forehead*

196

THE EIGHTEENTH CENTURY

The older form of chiromancy died slowly. The first half of the century saw it lingering on in the form of translations and reprints. Germany was the only country to produce new writers on the art, but even there it was a sign of the times that the majority of these books were published anonymously. Praetorius, who had died twenty years earlier, was honoured with the appearance of his *Collegium Curiosum* at Frankfurt in 1704; Mayer's *Chiromantia et Physiognomia Medica* was reprinted in Dresden in 1712. Johann Albert Fabricius published his *Gedanken von der Erkenntniss der Gemuther etc.* at Jena in 1735, and the early part of the century saw books by Schalitz, Ingeber, Job and Peuschel, none of which added anything of originality or value to the study. Of all these writers, only Peuschel, in his influence on Lavater, made a contribution to the future of palmistry. In its old form, now obscure and repetitive, chiromancy had ceased to interest the scholars of the day: their way of thinking had changed a great deal, whereas chiromancy had changed scarcely at all. The art could simply not be fitted into the new intellectual and emotional need for a 'scientific method'.

The beginning of this scientific method destroyed the old form of chiromancy and did not put anything in its place. Physiognomy did not suffer quite so badly, however, for the older school, represented in Germany by Pernetty and Peuschel, gave birth to a prodigy who regenerated that art, and sowed the seeds of the new chirosophy. His name was Johann Kaspar Lavater.

The scientific spirit began first of all as a new feeling for detached observation. Lavater, the most acute of observers and the most gentle of writers, caused a revolution in physiognomy, and almost caused a revolution in chiromancy, by his feeling for this new spirit. His remarkable *Physiognomische Fragmente*, written between 1775 and 1778, breathed such freshness of vision and such beauty of prose that it was an immediate success, and was translated into several languages within a few years of its completion. 'Suffer not the smallest, the most accidental, apparently insignificant, remark to be lost,' he wrote, 'let each be carefully collected; though, at first, its signification be unknown. They will soon or late be found useful.' It is a pragmatic spirit which would have been quite out of place a few years earlier.

Lavater was born at Zürich on November 15th,

1741, and died in 1801, following a wound received when the French Army entered his home town in 1799. He was distinguished for his religious piety as a Protestant minister, he was a poet, and wrote several books on mysticism, and these spiritual qualities, combined with his sense of methodicity, led to a system of physiognomy which is still highly stimulating intellectually and satisfying emotionally:

Each man is a man of genius in his large or small sphere. He has a certain circle in which he can act with

216 *The hand of Napoleon, after a diagram reproduced by le Norman in* Souvenirs Prophétiques

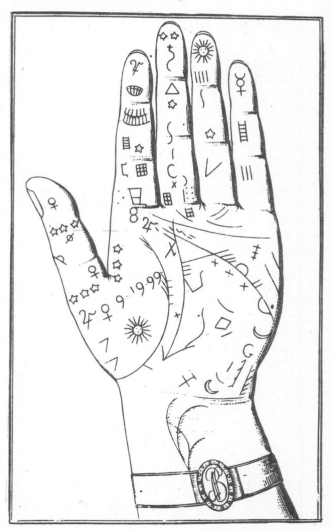

*inconceivable force. The less his kingdom the more con-
centrated is his power; consequently the more ir-
resistible is his form of Government. Thus the bee is
the greatest of mathematicians, as far as its wants
extend. Having discovered the genius of a man, how
inconsiderable soever the circle of his activity may be,
having caught him in the moment when his genius is in
its highest exertion, the characteristic token of that
genius will also be easily discovered.*

Lavater's contribution to palmistry was more in the
nature of suggestions: 'the hands of man are equally
diverse and dissimilar as their faces ... just as it is
impossible to find two faces perfectly alike, so it is
impossible to find two people whose hands resemble
each other perfectly,' and in addition, 'the hand cannot dissemble' like the face. He was discovering
what Aristotle discovered over two thousand years
ago.

In *Physiognomische Fragmente*, Lavater included two
plates of hands taken from an artist's drawing, and
gives a sketchy but very accurate analysis of their
hand types. His suggestions, hints and methods
were not taken up by a palmist for over fifty years,
until D'Arpentigny first became interested in the
hand.

Except for the occasional reprints of the accepted
'classics', the eighteenth century saw no new books
on the subject of palmistry in Italy, France or
England. In these European countries at least the
century might well be described as the 'Age of
Reason', for in many fields of study it marked the
end of wild fantasy and initiated a systematic method
of investigation. When the art of chiromancy was
revived in the next century it appeared in two separate streams of thought; the one representing the
old traditional system of interpretation of fixed
signs, the other representing the beginning of an
entirely new approach to the hand — an approach
which was fondly, if inaccurately, called 'scientific'.
Both these forms of palmistry persist today, but
with few exceptions we shall be concerned only with
the rise and development of the second form, which
was a pragmatic attempt to reconstruct palmistry
on a systematic basis. The earlier form has had very
little added to it since the days of Belot or Saunders,
but it is still popular with those minds who are
anxious to by-pass active thought and methodical
analysis in favour of an easy but ineffectual system
of special signs.

*217   A portrait of Adèle Moreau, from the frontispiece to her
book on palmistry*

THE NINETEENTH CENTURY

Although there were no lively and original books on palmistry during the eighteenth century, one must not conclude that there was no practice of the art. There seem to have been a fair quota of rogues, vagabonds and charlatans (in 1711 Addison could write 'he found his pocket was picked: that being a kind of palmistry at which this race of vermin [gypsies] are very dextrous') but it was completely lacking in original minds, and there was no central figure, no great practitioner of the art, to add to the body of palmistry and to keep the tradition alive by changing it.

Of the charlatans, the most famous was a Frenchwoman, Marie-Anne le Normand, who was born at Alençon on 16th September, 1768. Most details of her life have been preserved in her *Souvenirs Prophétiques*, but since there is no doubt that her imagination was infinitely stronger than her sense of reality, it is likely that few of the things she relates are based on truth. Had she not had the good fortune to become a cartomancer to Josephine de Beauharnais, the fashionable young widow, she would probably never have been heard of at all. When her mistress married Napoleon, le Normand quite naturally became the most important fortune-teller in the Court. Although her greatest strength lay in her ability as a cartomancer she was, by all accounts, a proficient palmist; her sense of drama, and the popular craze for Egyptology, lead her to claim that all her divinatory powers came from the Pharaonic age, and in this respect, quite certainly, she was a charlatan. She was gifted, however, with a certain degree of prophetic power. Her writings are filled with somewhat dubious accounts of her power, and through them we learn much of Napoleon's penchant for astrology and chiromancy, and of le Normand's relationship with the Emperor. Although she certainly overstressed her role in the Court, particularly her relationship with the superstitious Napoleon, there can be no doubt that she was consulted by him, and indeed by all the greatest people of her day.

One story, repeated by Neroman in *La Grande Encyclopédie des Sciences Occultes* relates how, after the siege of Toulon, Napoleon went to visit le Normand to enquire into his future. He was, at that time, merely a succesful general, and there was no indication of his impending meteoric rise to fame, but le Normand made the most far-reaching prophecies. After taking some sort of hand impression from ashes, she proceeded as follows:

One can never tell, General, how one's prophetic words will come to fruition . . . I shall, therefore, be most prudent in what I have to say; but this at least I can assure you of: the Command which you desire will be given to you — as a dowry in marriage with a beautiful woman who already has two children. You will go off to make war in Italy, and return in such glory that you will be the most famous of all Frenchmen. I do not wish to say more.

However, she does go on to observe that his hand reveals certain chance markings about which it was best not to speak, and she reminded him of the age-old interdiction against certain kinds of knowledge, about which it was best to pass over in silence. Her last council to him was that he 'should beware of pride, for it can carry you high, and it can also throw you lower down than you were originally'.

The authenticity of this prediction is vouched for by a friend of Napoleon's who was told the story by the Emperor immediately after the interview. De Givry, writing about a much later session between Napoleon and the chiromancer, claims that le Normand:

. . . at once laid bare before his eyes his tastes and inclinations and the most secret details of his character; above all, she announced that famous divorce, which was only a project at the moment, but which was already alarming Josephine. He requested her to compile a complete record of her predictions; this document was deposited at the Prefecture of Police. Napoleon was greatly impressed by what the sibyl had announced to him. Fearing the difficulties which a woman gifted with such acute discernment might create for him if she retained her freedom of speech and action he had her arrested and secretly detained on December 11th, 1809. She remained in detention for twelve days, and was not released until the divorce was accomplished.

In her *Mémoires historiques et secrets de L'Impératrice Josephine*, le Normand reproduces drawings of the left hands of both Napoleon and Josephine, with a long and detailed analysis. In general outline the hands may have been based on actual observation, for in type the drawings correspond to the hands of these great people in their many portraits. Furthermore, Napoleon's finger of Jupiter reveals a strong inferiority complex, and Josephine's finger of Mercury indicates some relationship difficulty, both

"As is the mind, so is the form"

CHEIRO'S
LANGUAGE OF THE HAND

——A——

COMPLETE PRACTICAL WORK ON THE SCIENCES OF CHEIROGNOMY
AND CHEIROMANCY CONTAINING THE SYSTEM, RULES,
AND EXPERIENCE OF

CHEIRO
(COUNT de HAMONG)

*Fifty-five Full-page Illustrations, and over Two Hundred Engravings of Lines,
Mounts, and Marks*

DRAWINGS OF THE SEVEN TYPES BY THEO DORÉ

———

*REPRODUCTIONS OF FAMOUS HANDS, ALSO NORMAL AND ABNORMAL HANDS
TAKEN FROM LIFE, INCLUDING*

The hands of Madame Sarah Bernhardt, Mark Twain, Madame Nordica, Col. R. G. Ingersoll.
Mrs Frank Leslie, Mr. W. T. Stead, The Right Honorable Joseph Chamberlain, M.P.,
Austen Chamberlain, Esq., M.P., Mrs. Annie Besant, Sir Frederick Leighton, P.R.A.,
Sir John Lubbock, M.P., F.R.S., The Countess of Aberdeen, Sir Edwin Arnold, The Lord
Chief Justice of England, The Swami Vivekananda, Rev. C. H. Parkhurst, D.D., Lady
Lindsay, Sir Arthur Sullivan, Lady Henry Somerset, A Prominent Member of the House
of Commons, Madame Melba, Lord Charles Beresford, Mr. William Whiteley, Gen.
Sir Redvers Buller, V.C., K.C.B., Rev. Minot J. Savage, and H. N. Higinbotham, Esq.

TENTH EDITION

Containing Illustrations of the Wonderful Scientific Invention
the Apparatus for

"THOUGHT PHOTOGRAPHY AND REGISTER OF CEREBRAL FORCE"

Publishers:

F. TENNYSON NEELY,
114 Fifth Avenue, New York.

NICHOLS & CO.,
23 Oxford Street, London W.

218 Title page to Cheiro's book on palmistry

historically authenticated facts. However, le Normand's description of special signs is completely fantastic, and the analysis so imaginative as to suggest that she knew nothing of traditional palmistry. She confuses the true positioning of the mounts, believing them to be at the finger-tips, and interprets with naive freedom the special and peculiar signs allegedly found on these hands in terms of a system which must have been esoteric to anyone but le Normand herself:

The two stars at the extreme tip of the finger of Saturn declared that Napoleon would end by putting on the frontlet of kings : that he would be publicly crowned in archepiscopal cathedral built by islanders in France.

The 'analysis' was written several years after Napoleon had died on St. Helena, and only sixteen years before she herself was to die at the age of seventy-four — despite her prediction that she would live to be over a hundred.

One of the pupils and successors of le Normand, Madame Adèle Moreau, appears to have been a little more restrained in her claims of proficiency in the art of palmistry, but none the less successful. Moreau not only used her teacher's name to enhance her own reputation, but even went so far as to practise in the self-same 'cubicle' that le Normand had used before her death. Madame Moreau's book of 1869, entitled *L'Avenir Dévoilé — Chiromancie Nouvelle* was, in many ways, a disappointment, for it revealed neither the future nor any really new system of chiromancy. In other respects, however, it is a fascinating book, for it throws much light on the social and intellectual demands made of an early nineteenth-century palmist in Paris, consisting largely of intimate accounts of her clients, their reactions and needs, and the outcome of her predictions; and the text prefigures the sort of autobiographical palmistry which Cheiro was to pursue so entertainingly in the next century. In style and content, if not in teaching, the book is fresh, lively and full of fascinating details.

One innovation made by Moreau is contained in the advertisement which informs her readers that she 'receives every day except Sunday and Feast Days, between the hours of 9 and 6', and that she is prepared 'to take consultations by post in the form of photographs and prints'. This must surely be the earliest recorded use of photography for chiromantical purposes, and confirms the suspicion that le Normand used hand prints in her readings.

Moreau's intentional attempts to create a new type of palmistry were not as successful as her attempts to be entertaining: her description of planetary types in terms of endocrine theories not only leads to confusion but also tends to obscure the real issue of palmistry, which is, after all, interpretation of the hand. Still, for all her mistakes, as a writer on palmistry she is surprisingly erudite in many ways, and produces a very entertaining book on the subject.

The two great Frenchmen whose efforts completely changed the study of palmistry were born within three years of each other: D'Arpentigny in 1798 and Desbarrolles in 1801. But this proximity in time was perhaps the only thing they had in common; in every other way, in temperament, background and intellect, they were very different individuals.

Casimir Stanislas D'Arpentigny was born on the 13th March, 1798 at Yvetot, and was from his earliest years destined for a military career. He was sent to be educated at St. Cyr, but his malicious humour proved too much for the military college, and a particularly witty lampoon of the Commander-in-Chief led to his expulsion. His keenness to be a soldier was stronger than mere circumstance. He enlisted in the ranks — a courageous act in those days for a man of means — and fought his way towards a commission in three years. He served with distinction, being wounded in one battle and decorated in another, and retired with honour at the early age of forty-eight. From that time on he adopted a literary career, for he was, according to one account, 'equally expert with the pen as with the sword'.

He had long been interested in palmistry. During the Peninsular War in which he served he had met a gypsy girl, a *gitana*, whose fortune-telling from the hand fired off an interest which led eventually to the regeneration of palmistry and the establishing of a new study of the hand. D'Arpentigny was not so much impressed by what the *gitana* said as by the terminology she used, which was to D'Arpentigny's mind an echo of some long-lost system of knowledge. Once he was free of his duties he made a thorough search into the literature of the past; 'he examined the writings of Avicenna and of Fraetichnus, and by their means corroborated the opinions of Antiochus, Tibertus and Taisnier; he dived into Plato and Aristotle, he interrogated

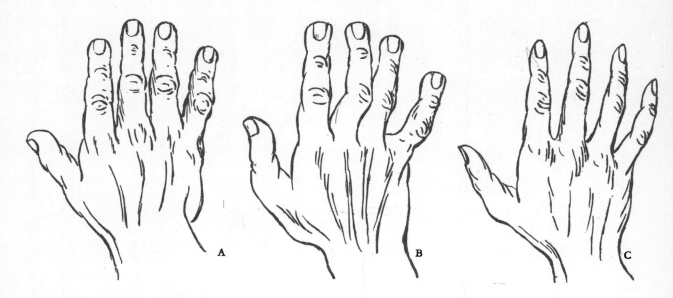

219　The seven hand types of D'Arpentigny
A Elementary. B Spatulate. C Psychic. D Square. E Knotty
or Phylosophic. F Conic. G. Mixed

Ptolemy and sought inspiration from Averroes, in short he mastered the literature of the subject, learnt all that was to be learnt from others, and then, having stored his mind with the observations of his predecessors, he came to the conclusion that nothing but doubt could result from his studies until he had certified his knowledge by actual experience.'

It appears that he was in the habit of attending the soirées of a rich landowner who lived near by, and that this man had a keen interest in scientific and mathematical subjects. The man's wife was quite different in temperament, however, preferring the aesthetic things of life, and keeping herself in the company of artists, philosophers and poets. What might well have turned into the usual domestic incompatability was avoided by the couple arranging

that each should hold separate soirées for each of their separate groups of friends. Captain D'Arpentigny, 'being neither a mechanician nor an artist', was, with surprising good grace, invited to both sorts of reception. His keen interest in the human hand spurred him on to observe that the general hand types at each of the soirées was always different: he noticed that the artistic type of hand was always smooth in character, whereas the scientist's hands were always knotty:

> *Connected with the smooth finger, he observed an impressionability, caprice, spontaneity, and intuition, with a sort of momentary inspiration which took the place of calculation, and a faculty which gave the power of judging at first sight. In this class he placed the artists. The knotty finger, on the contrary, he observed to be connected with reflection and order, aptitude for number, and an appreciation of the exact sciences. In this category he placed mathematicians, agriculturists, architects, engineers, and navigators; all, in short, who were led to the application of acquired knowledge.*

These observations, with the refinement of many years' careful study, were 'simply and neatly expressed' in a book *La Chirognomie*, published in 1839. It was an immediate success, and the word which he had coined to separate his own study of the hand from the earlier, and by then disreputable, chiromancy, came into common parlance.

His research led him to distinguish six basic types of hand. To this classification he added a seventh which was a 'mixed hand', incapable of separate classification, and partaking of certain qualities of

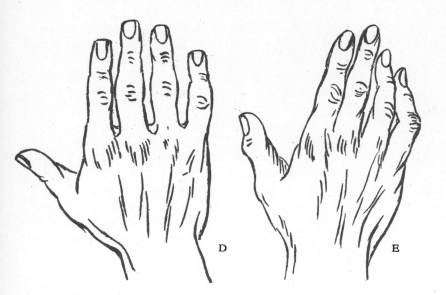

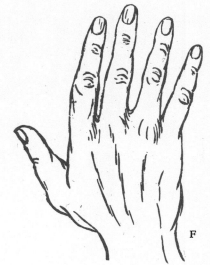

D   E   F

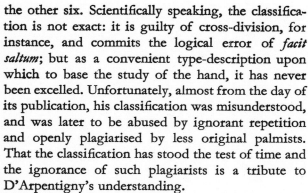

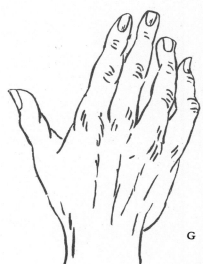

G

the other six. Scientifically speaking, the classification is not exact: it is guilty of cross-division, for instance, and commits the logical error of *facit saltum*; but as a convenient type-description upon which to base the study of the hand, it has never been excelled. Unfortunately, almost from the day of its publication, his classification was misunderstood, and was later to be abused by ignorant repetition and openly plagiarised by less original palmists. That the classification has stood the test of time and the ignorance of such plagiarists is a tribute to D'Arpentigny's understanding.

The main abuse of his system has been the palmist's refusal to move with the times, and to observe that the type of person, and consequently the type of hand, found in a scientific gathering of the early nineteenth century would be very different from that found in a scientific gathering of today. Similarly the type of person which D'Arpentigny described as 'artistic' has changed. It is not so much that D'Arpentigny's classification is wrong as that the meanings behind many of the words he used have changed. This is the real cause of all the ignorance and confusion which has reigned in the many books on chirognomy which have been written since his day.

D'Arpentigny was described by someone who knew him as 'a man of refinement in every sense of the expression; he became, almost subconsciously, a man of science, gifted with an ardent desire for knowledge, and singularly adapted by the nature of his highly impressionable organisation for the

rapid assimilation and comprehension of things'. The chirognomer himself said that his ability to understand the human hand came by 'divine inspiration'; but there are more certain signs that it was in fact his open mind and his ability for painstaking research (which often leads to divine inspiration) that led to his now world-famous theory of types. As an observer and tabulator, D'Arpentigny can be ranked with Lavater; as an original thinker on the significance of form, he can be ranked with the German morphologist Carus.

Adrien Adolphe Desbarrolles was born at Paris on 22nd August, 1801, and died there in February, 1886. He travelled widely on the continent, and finally settled down to do research into chiromancy. Fifteen years continual effort finally produced *Les*

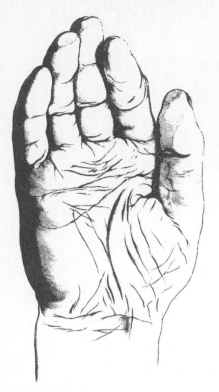

Mystères de la Main in 1859, which ran to over twenty editions during his lifetime. In 1869 his *Journal de Chiromancie* appeared, and ten years later *Révélations Complètes*. He later added to these *Les Mystères de L'Ecriture*, which was for a long time the standard work on Graphology in France. None of these monumental works has yet been translated into English.

Desbarrolles, after having been disappointed with all the theories behind palmistry, decided to work his ideas out in terms of an entirely different system:

> *I studied the system of the Kaballa, which taught of the stellar and planetary influences on the whole of creation, and upon man in particular, and which emphasised the relationship between both instincts and feelings and the corporeal body imposed upon them, for good or for evil by the good or evil influences of the stars of our system at the moment of birth, or at the moment of conception.*

The palmistry system which he evolved from his

220 *Plate from Carus' book showing the right hand of a drunkard and suicide case*

221 *Page from the December 1893 issue of 'The Palmist', text by Katherine St-Hill*

THE STUDY FOR THE MONTH.
DIPHTHERIA.

The hands which we show this month for the contemplation of our students are the hands of three cases of diphtheria taken in a London Hospital. They are all the hands of little children of three to five years of age. There is a little difference already showing in the outline, according to the several dispositions that are beginning to develop. No. 1 has the widest, shortest hands of the three, No. 2 the strongest thumb, and No. 3 the most refined little hand, in spite of the great development of the Jupiter finger, with its wide lower phalanx. They have but few lines in their little hands, poor little things, No. 1 especially few. His parents must have been stronger and of a commoner type than those of No. 3, who has a more nervous outline. We have six sets of hands, and of them we reproduce three single ones, but in every case we have, without exception, we find the same mark, in a more or less degree, on the Life line and Head, where they join under Jupiter. This is, without doubt, the sign of diphtheria in the hand. It comes just where we expected it, as all the throat affections and diseases that we have ever found and investigated have all caused a disturbance of one kind or another on the Head line under Saturn, or at its junction with the Life line under Jupiter. There is also to be noted that each of the hands given has a distinct cross in the quadrangle under Saturn. Whether this presages a fatal end to the illness we cannot say for certain, but among our present six cases there is one that has not got this cross, and another has instead a distinct square. The official account of the cases is as follows:—

No. 1.—Case, Diphtheria (Tracheotomy). Name, C—— B——. Age 4. Family history: Three other healthy children; one girl died at 5 years of age of scarlatina; one brother had the same; previous illness, none; present illness, Laryngeal diptheria; tracheotomy; no paralysis at present; child doing fairly well.

No. 2.—Case, Diphtheria (Tracheotomy). Name, Wm. C——. Age 5¼. Family

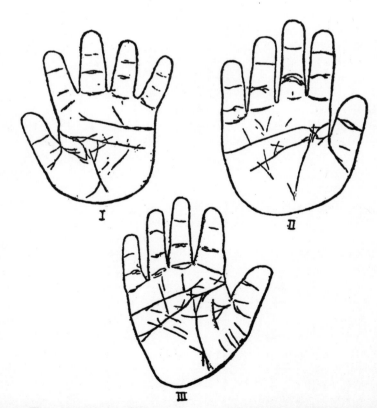

I

II

III

research into the Kaballa and into all the contemporary scientific writings in connection with the nervous system was a curious mixture of theory and practice. He developed on the old theories of Three Worlds, examined afresh the systems of planetary types, and gave a description of each type which eventually led to the detailed 'planetary types' of Benham at the end of the century. To a certain extent his findings corroborated those of D'Arpentigny in the field of chirognomy, but his penchant for occultism tended to tie down his direct observations into too tight a theoretical explanation. In his chirological and chiromantical portraits of 'tendencies' he laid the foundation for all the theories put forward by the English Chirological Society fifty years later, and his detailed, erudite approach to the theories of astral signatures and the working of the astral fluid was to guide the theories and teachings of almost every palmist for the next hundred years. In other words the influence of the Frenchman on the subsequent course of palmistry was absolute. Indeed, except for the notable research done by many modern psychologists on the hand, it would be true to say that almost every teaching during the past hundred years has been but a refinement or simplification of the work of Desbarrolles and D'Arpentigny.

During the early part of the nineteenth century, the spirit of scientific investigation appears to have overcome its repugnance at the gypsy chiromancy connotation, and returned once more to the study of the human hand. The study took on two different aspects — the first related to the medical aspect and the second related to pure palmistry.

It was probably the influence of Lavater that led François Joseph Gall (1758—1828) to evolve his theory of Phrenology, which was based on a systematic description of the influence of the brain on the skull contours. His pupil, Johann Gaspar Spurzheim, did a great deal of original research on human form which was published under the title of *Anatomie et Physiologie du Système Nerveux et du Cerveau en particulier*, in 1810. This work, though not specifically directed towards research on the hand, had a great influence on the Scotsman Sir Charles Bell, an anatomist and Fellow of the College of Surgeons in Edinburgh.

Sir Charles was born in Edinburgh in 1774, two years before Spurzheim, but it was under the latter's influence that he chose as his own contribution to the Bridgewater series *The Hand — its Mechanism and Vital Endowment as Evincing Design*, which was published in 1833. This book was the first of a series written by professional research workers on the hand. Georg von Meissner, working in Leipzig at about the same time, also under the influence of Gall and Spurzheim, was led to do the most detailed research with the microscope. Taking as his subjects 'over sixty corpses of all ages and types', he determined the precise nature of the cutis and papillae on the human hand, and published his findings in *Beiträge zur Anatomie und Physiologie der Hand* in 1853.

None of these scientists and research workers was, of course, specifically interested in palmistry, but their valuable contribution had a great influence on subsequent chiromantical teachings. Their major hypothesis, largely originated by Gall, concerning the intercommunication between the outer world and the brain via nerve structure, and the reciprocal action of the nerve centrum, created a new basis for the theory of palmistry, which was not wholly divorced from the theories being put forward at about the same time by Desbarrolles and D'Arpentigny. Thus Beamish, writing in 1865 about the teachings of the two Frenchmen in *The Psychonomy of the Hand*, finds it necessary to link up the scientific research of Gall, Spurzheim, Meissner and Bell as a prelude to discussing the teachings of the two great French chiromants. He sums up the scientists' findings in terms which savour of a platonism a little out of place in nineteenth-century England:

As water falling drop by drop upon stones, makes, in the course of time, a visible impression — as the strings made to vibrate, influence the sand beneath to receive a certain form, so the mind, acting at every instant of time upon the plastic susceptibility of the hand, leaves ultimately signs which are accepted by the chiromantist as the visible records of the impulses emanating from the great nervous centre.

Fifty years later the theories which they had put forward in the face of so much opposition were, inevitably, accepted as home truths, and we find that Benham's theorising about how the hand might reflect the nature of the brain is merely a simplified version of these earlier hypotheses.

Another scientist, this time with a more specific interest in the human hand, was the German Carl Gustav Carus who, in the early decades of the nineteenth century, was conducting research into the

222 Portrait of Cheiro

223 The hand of a pickpocket, from The Laws of Scientific Hand Reading, *1902, by William G. Benham; by courtesy of G. P. Putnam Limited*

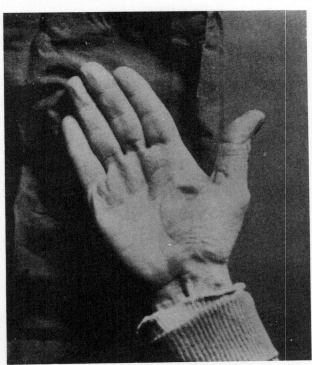

human form in such a way as to influence palmistry right up to the present time. Carus was born in Leipzig on the 3rd January, 1789, and at the early age of twenty-six was made Professor at the Medical Surgical Academy of Dresden, and Director of the Royal Saxon Midwifery Institute. He remained at the Academy until 1827, when he was appointed Royal Physician to the King of Saxony. In addition to his wide research into many aspects of the human form, Carus was a well-known painter in his day. He died on the 28th July, 1869. Among his published works on the psychological significance of the body, his most interesting from a palmistic point of view is *Uber Grund und Bedeutung der Verschiedenen Formen der Hand*, published in 1848, in which he presents a classification of hand types based on physiological characteristics (see page 31). In a sense he was doing precisely what D'Arpentigny was doing in a less systematic way at almost the same time. The major difference between the two classifications springs from the methods employed: Carus took as his basis of division the *function* of the hand, whereas D'Arpentigny classified his types in terms of form and proportion.

Adèle Moreau was about the only palmist in the middle of the century who attempted to present anything new in palmistic teaching. Almost every writer from that time onward until the present day has been preoccupied with adding refinements to the teachings and theories of Desbarrolles and D'Arpentigny. So many books of this kind were published during the nineteenth century that it would be merely tedious to enumerate them all. A. R. Craig's *The Book of the Hand* of 1867 is worth reading for interest's sake, but it adds little to the systems propounded by the two Frenchmen. By far the best book on the subject which deals intelligently with both D'Arpentigny and Desbarrolles, and goes into great detail about the beliefs about the hand throughout the ages, is *A Manual of Cheirosophy*, by Heron-Allen, first published in 1885. Heron-Allen was a Victorian scholar of the best kind; he had done a great deal of research into the history of palmistry, translated D'Arpentigny's *Chirognomie* into English, and had written many books on the subject of chiromancy. His translation of D'Arpentigny, entitled *The Science of the Hand*, published in 1886, contained an excellent bibliography of over 120 books on palmistry ranging from the early incunabula to those published in his own decade. His excellent introduction and text to *A Manual of Cheirosophy* can still be read today, and form an invaluable introduction to the best traditional teachings about the hand.

In London, towards the end of the century, a group of people set out to establish palmistry on an empirical and respectable footing, and were in fact instrumental in mitigating the old and well-established gypsy chiromantical tradition which was still so strongly imbued into the ideas of chiromancy. The three leaders of this movement were Katherine Saint-Hill, Ina Oxenford and Charles F. Rideal, all of whom appeared to have a private income, a more than average interest in palmistry, and an almost grotesque reverence for D'Arpentigny and Desbarrolles. In April 1889 Rideal founded The Chirological Society, with Saint-Hill as president and Oxenford as treasurer, and with the explicit aims of 'firstly, raising the study of the hand to the level of scientific research; secondly, for promoting the study of Palmistry in all its branches; thirdly, as a safeguard to the public against charlatans and impostors'. The tragedy is that none of them had the intellectual ability, integrity and high mentality to achieve any of these aims. Nevertheless, they tried. Meetings were held in members' homes, and attempts were made to formulate some working plan for the society. Gradually an enthusiastic group of people were gathered together who seriously aimed at establishing the valid rules of palmistry. They toured hospitals, mental institutions, and schools in order to examine as many different types of hands as possible; they amassed a considerable collection of hand casts in plaster, and they instituted a system of elementary examinations within the framework of the society. Unfortunately, parallel to their laudable attempts at research work, they offered their services as 'palmists' to garden fêtes and private parties, and in this way did a great deal of damage to any reputation which their more serious pursuits might have brought them. Oddly enough, they never established the practice of taking prints of hands for reference, but for some obscure reason preferred to make a tracing of the hand in question and then to 'fill in the lines of the hand afterwards'; hardly a practice conducive to good palmistry.

By May 1892 the society was large enough to publish its own journal, *The Palmist*, and through its pages we can trace the rise and fall of this group of people who, although claiming to 'refuse to take any theory on trust, from however high an authority', arrived at no new and valid theory of palmistry after the combined efforts of some twenty years or so. The first editions of *The Palmist* contain something of the pioneer spirit which must have characterised the early years of the Society, but gradually the spirit is swallowed up in useless theorising, social activities and a change of interest towards graphology. The journal, and with it the society, closed down in 1898, having completely deviated from its original aims.

Katherine Saint-Hill and Ina Oxenford continued to write books about palmistry and allied arts long after the society had been disbanded, and in the 'twenties Oxenford even goes so far as to claim that

> To Mrs. St-Hill ... *modern Chirology owes its exodus from the mists of superstition. Her discovery that 'one sign can only mean one idea' has simplified the whole matter, and rendered a logical foundation possible.*

Of course, the claim is completely without any basis; not only has palmistry still to emerge from the mists of superstition, but any teaching which relates one idea to one meaning can only make more obscure the hopes of establishing a valid system of thought.

These serious activities to establish a reputable science of palmistry were (and still are), technically speaking, illegal. *The Palmist* continually refers to the intervention of the law. A common practice of the police was to arrest a palmist at a garden fête on the Saturday, and to hold her until the Monday in gaol when she would be fined. The law appears to have persecuted only the lower form of palmist, the old lady or the tented madame in the garden fête, for there are no records of any Bond Street palmist having been arrested.

Nor was the law the only opposition that charlatans and serious research workers alike encountered. There was a large section of the community which was not merely suspicious of palmistry, but even openly hostile, many of them believing it to be contrary to religious belief. Cheiro, who was working in Bond Street at this time, records a couple of significant stories of his experiences:

> I had not been in London one month before a Catholic priest refused to give absolution to an entire family because they had consulted me against his orders. In America, during my first year, I was visited by two

clergymen, with the object of persuading me that my success was due alone to the agency of the devil. One went so far as to tell me that God had sent him to offer me a clerkship — at a small salary, of course, — if I would only give up my relations with the Evil One.

The anomalous thing is that in the very book in which these words appear, Cheiro reproduced the hand print of the Lord Chief Justice of England, several M.P.s and one parson.

The end of the nineteenth century saw the publication in America of two books which between them represented the two extreme types of palmistry being practised and taught in England, America and on the Continent at that time. The first book, which marks the lowest ebb of palmistic teaching, was *The Study of Palmistry for Professional Purposes*, published in Chicago by Comte C. de Saint-Germain, who described himself as being 'President of the American Chirological Society', and of the 'National School of Palmistry'. The second book, which incorporated all that was best in chirological teaching, was by William G. Benham, entitled *The Laws of Scientific Hand Reading*, published in New York and London in 1900.

Saint-Germain's book was first published in 1897 in two volumes, and has persisted in its original form in several editions up to the present day. Almost everything about it is bad. Typographically it is difficult to read, as about one third of the text is underlined in a most unaesthetic manner; the illustrations are crude, consisting of drawings of hands resembling in content, but altogether inferior to, the ones which appear in Taisnier's *Opus Mathematicus* of 1562. This book is advertised as containing an introduction by the late Adolphe Desbarrolles, who had in fact died some thirty years earlier, and the subsequent text is constrained to admit somewhat weakly that Desbarrolles had not in fact written the introduction, but claims that it none the less represents 'his innermost convictions' and is a synthesis of his best thoughts. This must surely be among the most incredible confidence tricks that an author has ever used. The text of the book is based almost exclusively either on the chirological teaching of D'Arpentigny or on a chiromantical teaching which is little advanced on the mediaeval systems of special signs. A typical example of a 'reading' (taken incidentally from Saunders) is the case history of 'A Man Poisoned by His Wife, Who Had Led Him

a Terrible Life', the whole story being revealed by a black dot on the line of Head, under the mount of Saturn! The Palmistic Dictionary which is appended at the back of the book, and which is supposed to contain an alphabetical list of 'All Prominent Chiromants and Defenders of Chiromancy in the Past', and a statement of 'Every Palmistic Discovery and Statement concerning a Human existence from Birth to Dying Day', is the most remarkable conglomeration of inaccuracies and mistakes which have ever been collected together under one title. Even a brief reading of this book reveals Saint-Germain's pretended abilities to be as false as his name (he is no doubt trying to bathe in the reflected glory of the Frenchman whom Voltaire described as 'the one who never dies, and who knows everything') and no great effort is required to trace the source of all his ideas. An earlier book by Saint-Germain, the *Practical Palmistry* of 1897, was based completely on the published works of members of the English Chirological Society, and even goes so far as to copy, piecemeal and without any credit, whole paragraphs from Ina Oxenford's *New Chirology*, which had been published in the previous year. Saint-Germain not only failed to add anything new to the study of the hand, but was largely instrumental in retarding its development in preserving the fragmentary teachings of an outworn tradition as something worthy of serious consideration.

After Saint-Germain's book it is a relief to turn to *The Laws of Scientific Hand Reading*, for Benham's book is a delight for any student of the hand: it is profusely illustrated with a series of well-chosen photographs and drawings of hands; and is, in fact, one of the first books to incorporate photographs for illustrative purposes. Many of the hands used in the book are of Americans, both famous and infamous: Martinus Sieveking, the pianist, Ira Marlatt, the 'Prison Demon' and Henry G. Starr, the outlaw, are among the most interesting preserved, whilst the hands used to illustrate various aspects of chirognomy and chiromancy suggest that Benham's collection of photographs and prints must have been one of the most comprehensive ever formed.

According to his own account, Benham first became interested in palmistry at the age of thirteen when he fell in with an old gypsy who taught him the rudiments of gypsy chiromancy. What she could teach him was little, but the few lessons sufficed,

224 *Cheiro's consulting room*

as in the case of D'Arpentigny and his *gitana*, to give direction to his thoughts.

By any standards, the teaching contained in Benham's book is by far the most comprehensive, accurate and detailed to have appeared in the history of palmistry. Every aspect of good chiromancy and chirognomy is dealt with in terms of a theory which is based on the dualistic concept of body-soul relationship which was expressed by Hawthorne as 'Mankind are earthen jugs with spirits in them'.

According to Benham the life force which animates this spirit enters into the body by way of the finger of Jupiter, and the line markings of the hand form a guide to the way in which the energy is disposed to flow through the body and to affect the different functions which distinguish the character and temperament of an individual. In order to supplement his classification of hand types, which is not merely a repetition of D'Arpentigny's findings, he returns to the old theory of Signatures and gives a very useful guide to the seven pure planetary types, which are supposed in degrees of combination to account for all human types.

The chiromancy which Benham teaches is strictly

'rational' — a deviation in a line is always a sign of a deviation in the qualities represented by that line, whilst no reading can be made by one line or combination of lines without reference to the general formation of the hand. Thus we have firmly established the theory of 'organic palmistry' which is now so much in evidence in modern books on psychological palmistry. Benham's book is one of the first, if not the first, to completely ignore special signs in his teaching, and this, combined with the other exciting new elements in his book, results in a teaching which is based on direct observation, and the most trustworthy aspects of traditional palmistry. His '*Laws*' should be regarded as an essential textbook for all serious students of palmistry.

Count Louis Hamon, better known as Cheiro, is one of the most remarkable figures in the history of chiromancy. His ability as a palmist is legendary and so many people have testified to it that it cannot be doubted.

The difficulty in assessing Chiero is that his theory was unsound, his knowledge of the history of the subject ludicrously inaccurate, his sense of honesty sadly impaired, and his sense of importance

209

verging on megalomania, yet he somehow contrived to be an excellent palmist, and to command the attention and respect of many great people by virtue of his abilities. This is the major paradox in a very paradoxical figure. In fact his many books contribute almost nothing to the theory of palmistry, and like all his contemporaries he based them purely and simply on the writings of D'Arpentigny and Desbarrolles and managed to imbue them with the usual misunderstandings. His knowledge of the 'history' of palmistry is unusually inaccurate, and in spite of the fact that all the historical points raised in his books were taken largely from Heron-Allen, he somehow contrives to mix up dates and names in the most incredible way. He quotes Carus under the name of Dr. Cairn, he quotes the usual Chaldean, Egyptian and biblical sources, misdates and mistitles the only two early books on palmistry he refers to, and entirely without evidence devotes a couple of paragraphs to the persecution of chiromants by the Church in the Middle Ages. In more than one place he reveals his dishonesty — he claims, for example, to have read a translation of *Die Kunst Chiromantia* when he was sixteen years old, and not only had it not been translated into English, but it was not possible to obtain the extremely rare book (let alone from a railway bookstall, to read on a train, as he claims to have done). One further instance of his dishonesty will suffice to give a background of the spirit in which he worked. In one book, *Cheiro's Language of the Hand*, 1894, he reproduces a print of the hand of Sarah Bernhardt, the French actress, and it has quite evidently been drawn over with a pencil — presumably to illustrate some point of doctrine that Cheiro was wanting to prove: he has, for example, drawn a square on the mount of Jupiter, which according to his reading 'protects the subject from any excess arising out of ambition'. His megalomanic tendencies are best illustrated by the story told by Nelson in *Out of the Silence*:

> Once, when staying at a country house, a woman said to him: 'You think that because you are a handsome man that you have all the women at your feet. You are an impostor, a charlatan. I suppose you think that you could bring me to your feet.' Cheiro answered, 'Madame, I do not think — I know it.'

They had a long argument and then separated in anger, she refusing to take her words back. As she left the room Cheiro told her to come to him at midnight. Naturally enough she stormed off to bed in a fit of temper. However, promptly on midnight the woman returned to the darkened room, fell at his feet, and then went away again when he told her to go. There were many witnesses of this example of Cheiro's petulant and childish egotism, which was quite clearly too strong to be swayed by either good taste or consideration for another person's dignity. Cheiro seriously believed himself to be a reincarnation of Count Cagliostro, but there appears to be some doubt in Cheiro's mind as to whom Cagliostro really was. Nelson alludes to a mummified hand of the daughter of Pharaoh Akhenaton, given to him in Egypt by a guide. He is supposed to have carried this about with him until one day it started dripping blood, at which point he rather thoughtlessly burnt it.

His memoirs read something like a dramatic screen scenario, and it is significant that he worked in Hollywood as a scenario writer for many years. His adventures make interesting reading, for not only are they entertaining, but they might even be true. One just cannot tell. He is supposed to have saved a young anarchist from the firing squad by arranging for blank cartridges and hypnotising the boy until he was in his coffin at home. It is claimed that he was in fact a secret agent all his life. Another example of an adventure which revolved around his mediumistic ability is told about his experiences in an American park, late one night. He was returning home when he was stopped and held up by a man with a gun. Cheiro put out his right hand on a level with the man's face, and the poor fellow dropped his gun and, catatonic like, kept his hand and arm outstretched. Cheiro picked up the revolver and walked on. The gangster pleaded that he should be released, and Cheiro did so when he had agreed to lead an honest life in the future. When the man agreed, Cheiro released him, took him out for a meal, gave him money and found him a job. Cheiro's memoirs are replete with such strange stories.

In spite of the obvious chicanery, the many doubts and the many improbabilities in Cheiro's life, he was a remarkable man. He was born on the 1st November, 1866, the son of Count William de Hamon and Mademoiselle Dumas, and educated privately. He travelled widely while still quite young, and is supposed on his own account to have studied palmistry in India under the Braham Joshi Cast.

This is very unlikely, for the palmistry he practised and wrote about contains no ideas that cannot be found in D'Arpentigny or Desbarrolles. He published his first book on Palmistry, *Language of the Hand*, when he was only twenty-eight, and so great was his reputation that the book sold five thousand copies in four months. The press and review columns in most of the papers of this day constantly allude to his ability.

Under another name, Cheiro ran a highly successful champagne business in France, and was one of the forces directly connected with forming the Entente Cordiale (he edited the movement's paper). During the Russian wars with China and Japan he acted as a press correspondent, and eventually he went to the United States to live in Hollywood. While in America he was made a founder member of the Pacific Geographic Society, and eventually he was made a Fellow of the Royal Geographic Society. He wrote many books on many subjects, including a novel, a play and film scenarios. His *World Prediction* was a bestseller, but few of the predictions were in fact accurate. Those which were eventually fulfilled could well have been inspired guesses. He seemed to have excelled in the personal type of prediction, however, and in palmistry he had the greatest success. He predicted the date of Queen Victoria's death, the exact year and month when King Edward VII would die, the terrible destiny of the Czar of Russia, the assassination of King Humbert of Italy, the attempt on the Shah of Persia's life in Paris, and the exact date of Lord Kitchener's death, which, it is interesting to note, Cheiro claims to have been murder.

Whilst the work of D'Arpentigny may be compared with the scientific research of Carus, the writings of Desbarrolles may equally well be compared with the scientific research of his countryman Vaschide. Dr. N. Vaschide was an original pioneer who set out to establish the relationship between the lines of the hand, which he called *images motoriques*, and personality traits. He not only studied very closely the traditional forms of palmistry, but even did many experiments with palmists themselves. He died too early to accomplish his aims. It has been commented as an ironical fact of his life that, after working so hard to establish a scientific method of hand-interpretation, he should have his own death precisely foretold by ordinary palmists. In one of the footnotes to his only book, *Essai sur la Psychologie de la Main* (published posthumously in 1909 by his wife Madame Vaschide), describing the abilities of the many palmists which she and her husband had encountered in Europe, he mentioned that 'Mme Fraya had predicted to the author of this work, during the winter of 1904, that he would die at the age of thirty-three years of pneumonia'. The prediction was fulfilled to the detail.

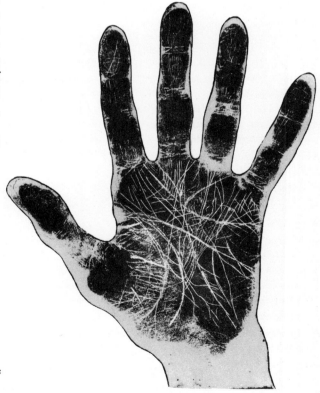

225 *The hand of Gladstone, reproduced from* The Language of the Hand *by Cheiro*

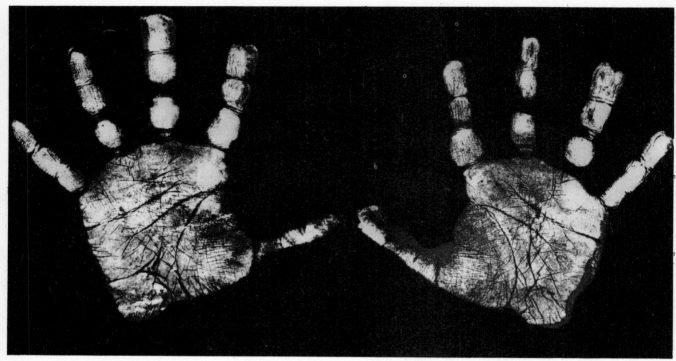

226 *Plate from Spier's* The Hands of Children, *1955. The hands of a boy of six.*

This hand, which has an abundance of lines for a boy of six, shows a very unstable, irritable and highly strung child. The right hand, which also conveys the impression of restlessness because of its too many lines, indicates that the instability is due to heredity. The Head line of the right hand shows a strong inclination to moods of depression. The vivid mount of Venus and the double girdle of Venus of the left hand suggests considerable sensuality and a premature development in this direction. The forking of the end portion of the Head line denotes a critical mind, the prong declining towards the mount of the Moon a tendency to depression, and the little hump in the Head line below the second finger a mendacious disposition. The combination of the critical faculty and the mendaciousness manifests itself as cunning craftiness. The somewhat short Head line proceeding to the mount of Jupiter signifies despotism and self-interest. The feature in the zone of Milieu points to a severe traumatic incident in early childhood; the sudden death of his mother when he was two. Summing up we can say that this boy of six is very unstable, prematurely developed, intelligent, cunning, grasping, somewhat melancholy and extremely sensual. He has hysterical fits of vomiting.

(Text and illustration by courtesy of Routledge and Kegan Paul.)

227 *An example of the sort of photograph which the author uses to augment his collection of prints*

MODERN PALMISTRY

Of the two hundred or so books which have been published in the past twenty years only four or five are worth serious mention. In France, George Muchery is the best representative of the modern school: his two books *Traité Complête de Chiromancie Déductive et Experimentale* and *La Mort, Les Maladies, L'Intelligence and L'Hérédité* (1959) are strongly recommended to the student. In Germany two original workers in the field, Julius Spier and Ursula von Mangoldt, have contributed a great deal of much value to the science. Spier, who was a disciple of Jung, died before he was able to bring out the two sequels to his excellent *Hands of Children* (1944). Levi, who helped in the publication of Spier's book and who contributed two valuable appendices on the hands of the mentally diseased, explains that the reason why we have had only one book from Spier is the scrupulousness with which he approached the subject:

> *The reason for Spier's reluctance in spite of an ever-growing demand, and his own realisation of the pressing need for a comprehensive work on Psycho-Chirology, was his resolve conscientiously and critically to sift his material, and empirically to test his theories exhaustively, before submitting them to the public.*

The work of Mangoldt appears to have been less systematic than that of Spier, but her books — particularly *La Main de votre Enfant* — contain very many valuable observations. In England, the writings of Noêl Jaquin are among the best on the subject. *The Human Hand — The Living Symbol* (1956) is perhaps the most informative, 'the result of forty years of research, experiment and study, involving the examination of hundreds of thousands of imprints of the hands of men, women and children of all nationalities, and from every walk of life'.

In palmistry, as in so many fields of a similar nature, the present is largely a period of assimilation. There is a healthy sign that the two separate streams of thought concerning the nature of the hand, the one medical (nowadays 'psychological') and the other 'neo-traditional', are joining together. It is with great interest that one awaits the establishment, perhaps within the next decade, of a centre for research into palmistry, something on the lines of the existing Faculty of Astrology.

It would be very difficult to make a summary of changes which have taken place in the study of the hand during the past six centuries. In a broad statement, too sweeping a generalisation to be entirely true, I would describe the course of Western palmistry as being from *chiromancy* towards *chirognomy*: that is, from a reliance on the interpretation of line markings towards a general interpretation of the hand form and structure as a whole. This course roughly corresponds with the shift from mediaeval symbology towards modern anthropomorphism. Thus the thought of the late mediaeval period is characterised by an insistence on a fixed hierarchy of symbols manifesting some inner truth, and the palmistry of the day consisted of little more than a series of rigid equations drawn between symbol and reality. Our modern forms of thought are disposed towards picturing every entity as being 'an organic balance' of diverse factors whose individual significance is related solely to the function of participating in this balance. Almost every branch of thought from Aesthetics to Endocrinology teaches this unity of mutual interdependencies. It is not surprising therefore that the modern forms of palmistry should reflect this 'organic balance'. Modern palmistry is disposed to picturing the hand as a unity of which the details can have significance only in relation to the whole. There has been a change in the process of hand reading from simple interpretation within a fixed framework of symbols to a dynamic interpretation of forms in terms of modern psychological ideas.

It is only to be expected that we should observe such a change of attitude to the hand. Each age constructs its own palmistry in strict accord with its own understanding and needs. An orderly hierarchy of God-Angels-Man could not merely tolerate, but even demanded, a reverence for strict symbols. That this lead to a palmistry which was, by our standards, inaccurate, did not greatly trouble the mediaeval mind. Our own rather nebulous conception of a dynamically integrated mind-matter universe leads us to a palmistry which reflects this conception in miniature. The resulting theories of palmistry, a kind of *psycho-chirology* as it has been called, would be as foreign to the mediaeval understanding as symbolic palmistry is to our own. From the point of view of history these two vastly opposed approaches spring from two separate attitudes which reflect some hidden and perhaps constant truth which different people have at different times tried to express in their very different ways.

INDEX

Selected bibliography for further reading:

ALLEN E. H.   A Manual of Cheirosophy (1885)
BEAMISH R.   The Psychonomy of the Hand (1865)
BENHAM W. G.   The Laws of Scientific Hand Reading (1900)
CARUS G. C.   Über Grund und Bedeutung der verschiedenen Formen der Hand in
                 verschiedenen Personen (1846)
CRAIG A. R.   The Book of the Hand (1867)
D'ARPENTIGNY C. S.
                 La Chirognomie, ou l'art de reconnaître les tendances de l'intelligence d'après
                 les Formes de la Main (1843)
                 The Science of the Hand (Excellent translation of preceding book, with
                 copious notes by E. H. Allen) (1886)
DESBARROLLES A.
                 Les Mystères de la Main (1859)
                 Révélations complètes (1879)
JACQUIN N.   The Signature of Time (1940)
                 The Hand Speaks (1942)
MANGOLDT U. V.
                 La Main de votre Enfant
MUCHÈRY G.   Traité Complet de la Chiromancie Déductive et Expérimentale (1958)
SPIER J.   The Hands of Children (1944)
                 (Second Edition of above, with interesting appendix by Levi, 1955)
VASCHIDE   Essai sur la Psychologie de la Main (1909)